John Dryden

John Dryden

A Study of His Poetry

MARK VAN DOREN

INDIANA UNIVERSITY PRESS

BLOOMINGTON & LONDON

CONTENTS

PREFACE TO 1946 EDITION

THIS ESSAY was first published in 1920 by Harcourt, Brace and Howe, New York. Ten years later there was enough desire for it in England, and enough difficulty about securing copies, to justify the second edition which Gordon Fraser published at the Minority Press, Cambridge, in 1931. Now, twenty-five years after its original appearance in America, it is published here again. I am grateful to Harcourt, Brace and Company and to the Minority Press for the freedom I enjoy to present the essay a third time for such use as poets, critics, students, and other readers care to make of it. It is an extended study of one poet's art. It stands or falls by the amount of truth about that poet, or about poetry in general, which it contains.

For this edition I have made a number of minor revisions, but the essay remains substantially unaltered. My original preface prepared the reader for a "more or less enthusiastic" treatment of Dryden. I have kept my enthusiasm. Indeed, the revisions I refer to often consist in efforts to tone up what I once, in an ardor to be judicial, toned down. The essay was a doctoral dissertation at Columbia University, and in writing it I did not take the fullest advantage of a liberty which I still consider myself lucky, not to say unique, for having possessed. This was the liberty to go ahead and say all I could about an important writer, in whatever language seemed suitable to myself and him. The suggestion that I do so came from my brother, Carl Van Doren, and was favorably received by W. P. Trent, the professor whom I would have to please. I would have to please him, that is, with a finished essay; meanwhile the risk was altogether mine. The procedure still seems sensible to me, and I have urged it since on many candidates, but none of them has pursued it. If one ever does, I shall recommend that he avoid the clichés of qualification which I seem to have thought it sounded wise to use. I am happy now to have them out of the way.

Dryden is the kind of great poet it is good to know at any time, for he is a great writer. Of some poets, even though they be very fine, we do not say seriously that they are writers. From the way Dryden wrote there is always something to be learned, and in fact it has been said of this essay, by T. S. Eliot and others, that it shows how the learning may be done. But in twenty-five years I have not seen it being done. I am not saying that it should be done, or that I have succeeded in showing how it could be. I merely observe that contemporary poetry—and criticism—give no evidence of having benefited by the study of Dryden's art.

Clear evidence to the contrary is to be found in the fact that verse is almost everywhere held in contempt. Verse is not everything, but to assume that it is nothing is to ignore a primary source of pleasure and power, and in the end is to emasculate poetry. We have cults of sensibility and sincerity; we are marvelously responsive to ambiguities; we know how to plot the oblique course, to surprise words into revealing three senses when there was none before; we can find politics in metaphor, morality in syntax, and myth in minor parts of speech. But we do not act as if we had ears. Ears are not everything, but the absence of them leaves poetry dangerously dead.

Dryden had a great ear. He attended to the craft of sound, and not vulgarly as Poe and Swinburne did, but with a man's interest in the muscle, the sinew, and the nerve of a poem that must be both heard and understood as saying something. He liked to say things, and in time perfected a verse instrument that could say for him anything he was capable of thinking or feeling. Poetry itself was an instrument upon which he spoke and played. The rhythmical organization of a poem got as much of his attention as the plausibility of its statement. The statement is what interests us, but there is a final pleasure in listening again to the way the lines move. They move in melody, which is everywhere in Dryden, and masculine. This least effeminate of poets was not above admitting that he loved the "sweetness" of good verse. The sweetness he meant was a true sweetness, not incompatible with wit—indeed, in Dryden these are brother virtues which steadily defend and support each other. They are the legs and the head of a body which knows where it wants to go, and how. I am speaking of him, it will be apparent, at his best. On the whole this means his latest, for the poet in him contained a writer who could learn. That is why he deserves an essay; and why poets as different from each other as Pope and Keats have confessed themselves his pupils.

If nothing else, the following pages provide an anthology of Dryden ample enough to exhibit him not only at his best but at his worst. Like most big writers he was capable of bad taste, and my second chapter is an attempt to say something about the ways he went wrong. Those ways are interesting for the very reason that Dryden was big. When he fell, he fell far.

> Behold, where Dryden's less presumptuous car,
> Wide o'er the fields of glory bear
> Two Coursers of ethereal race,
> With necks in thunder clothed, and long-resounding pace.

Gray's famous lines are well glossed by Dr. Johnson, who said that Dryden's horses either galloped or stumbled. But if they stumbled they got up again and raced on. The strength of Dryden is the first and last thing that will strike anyone who reads him through. And it is as admirable now as it ever was. The quality of strength does not always consort with subtlety and grace, but when it is missing from a poet the maximum of no other quality will be a tolerable substitute. I come back to the pleasure there can be in studying Dryden's power. He exer-

cised it in a world where all persons who could read still
thought it necessary and good to read poetry. That world has
been gone a considerable while, but its restoration remains possible. A knowledge of Dryden might help as few things could.

M. V. D.

New York, 1945

NOTE TO MIDLAND BOOK EDITION

I HAVE made no changes in the text of 1946, reprinted here.
During the forty years since I first wrote this book many special
studies of Dryden have been published, and I might have presented their conclusions in modification or support of my own
views. But I prefer to let the essay stand as I last left it; it was
altered very little then from its original form, and I do not wish
at this late date to write what in effect would be another book.
Also, I dislike arguments and discussions in public with other
critics.

If I should ever write another book about Dryden it would
be about his prose, which I more and more admire. I take it to be
the best English prose, unless Shakespeare's is, and it would give
me high pleasure to praise it. But I shall not write such a book,
believing as I do that no need for it exists. All the world agrees
that Dryden was indeed a master of "the other harmony." Not
that this qualifies my admiration for his verse, which I am glad
of the present opportunity to make known once again.

M.V.D.

Cornwall, Connecticut, 1959

John Dryden

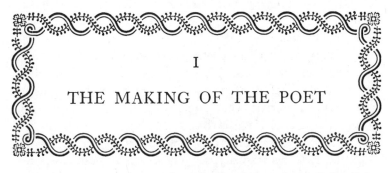

I

THE MAKING OF THE POET

THE WORLD has not been inclined to make way for John Dryden the poet. When he died in 1700, the generalissimo of English verse, it seemed certain to the survivors that the momentum of his name would keep his works forever rolling abreast of the generations. But before a single century had passed, he had begun to live rather in the stiffness than in the strength of his eminence; and another century saw him laid carefully away among the heroes.

Since Dryden was laid away, the world has not been exactly incurious about his tarnished remains. It was the fashion a hundred years ago to classify the poets, and level them into orders; at such times Dryden was likely to be sent with Pope to seek the second level. The nineteenth century, anxious to know what past poets had been great and why, sounded Dryden to the depths for notes which it could recognize; Lowell went eagerly through him, thinking to decide once for all how much of a poet he was, and revising his judgment at every tenth page. Latterly the critics with historical bent and eclectic taste have been busy either at placing Dryden in time or at explaining his imperfections by an appeal to the shortcomings of the audience for which he wrote. This tasting and this research have done much to lay bare huge flaws and inequalities in the surface which Dryden presented to posterity. Little has been done in the way of exploring the large spirit which worked beneath that surface, or in surveying other surfaces less conspicuous. The embattled seventeenth century left a number of bruised and defective monuments, none of which is more engaging than the poetry of John Dryden.

The story of Dryden's poetry is the story of a sinewy mind attacking bulky materials. Since we know next to nothing about Dryden's mind before it ripened, the story naturally begins for us with the materials which are known to have lain at hand during the years of his growth.

The thirty years, from 1631 to 1660, during which Dryden came slowly to his maturity, saw many slender volumes of fine verse published in England, the work of Milton, Herbert, Randolph, Carew, Suckling, Lovelace, Crashaw, Vaughan, and Herrick. Yet after Ben Jonson no one poetic personality was dominant in these years, and there flowed no current powerful enough to draw young writers in. Dryden is temperamentally akin to none of the nine poets who have just been named, and it is unlikely that they impressed him in his youth; although it must be remembered that his first considerable poem, the *Heroic Stanzas* of 1659, contains in the thirty-fifth stanza a faint echo of Milton's *Ode on the Morning of Christ's Nativity:*

> But first, the Ocean, as a tribute, sent
>   That Giant-Prince of all her watery herd;
> And th' isle, when her protecting Genius went,
>   Upon his obsequies loud sighs conferred.

Other poets, past and present, he gradually became acquainted with before 1660. Jonson must always have been to an extent congenial. Chaucer, Spenser, and Shakespeare he was not prepared so early to admire. But by Sylvester he was "rapt into ecstasy"; and Quarles and Wither furnished him thin nourishment. There were hundreds of plays to be read. He was not ignorant of Fairfax's translation of Tasso. Soon or late he came to know Michael Drayton, whose label for Samuel Daniel, "too much historian in verse," Dryden adopted for Lucan in the preface to *Annus Mirabilis;* and whose apostrophe to Daniel,

> And thou, the sweet Musæus of these times,
> Pardon my rugged and unfiléd rhymes,

curiously anticipates Dryden's own verses in honor of John Oldham. We may be certain that he read an abundance of very bad poetry in his green, unknowing youth. Professor Saintsbury has shown that he was acquainted with Edward Benlowes, almost the worst poet England has produced. The poems of William Cartwright which were collected in 1651 include, among some respectable complimentary pieces, two on small-pox which if seen by Dryden before 1649 could have inspired his unhappy effusion on Lord Hastings. The "Clevelandisms" which Lisideius damns in the *Essay of Dramatic Poesy* in 1668 probably were not anathema to Dryden a dozen years before.

Had Dryden never indulged in more than random reading among the poets, it is safe to say that he would never himself have become a poet of dimensions. No one was better aware of what he needed to read than he. "Mere poets," he wrote in the postscript to the *Notes and Observations on the Empress of Morocco* (1674), "are as sottish as mere drunkards are, who live in a continual mist, without seeing or judging anything clearly. A man should be learned in several sciences, and should have a reasonable, philosophical, and in some measure a mathematical head, to be a complete and excellent poet; and besides this, should have experience in all sorts of humours and manners of men. . . . Mr. Settle having never studied any sort of learning but poetry, . . . as you may find by his writings, . . . must make very lame work on 't." Although Dryden was speaking here of dramatic poets, it is fair to accept these sentences as trustworthy guides through the twists and turns of his culture.

"For my own part, who must confess it to my shame, . . . I never read anything but for pleasure," he declared in the *Life of Plutarch* (1683). But pleasure for him meant the satisfying of intellectual curiosity as well as it meant diversion; from the beginning, there can be no doubt, he was pleased to read widely and was avid of information. "He's a man of general learning," sneered Settle. Dryden was not an exact or patient scholar, nor was he obsessed with the pedantry that had produced works like Burton's *Anatomy of Melancholy* earlier in the century. Although he loved learning and argument and could not refrain from literary history and criticism, although he loaded his poems with science and mythology and theology, he was never weighed down with learned lumber. In *The Rehearsal* he is represented with a common-place book in his hand from which he is ever drawing the happiest images and sentences of Persius, Seneca, Horace, Juvenal, Claudian, Pliny, Plutarch, and Montaigne. Though this may not be a true likeness, it brings into relief a bent of Dryden's which must have been apparent early in his career. Congreve records that he had an unfailing memory, and Dr. Johnson was inclined to attribute his large stock of information rather to "accidental intelligence and various conversation" than to diligent and solitary reading. However he may have come by his lore, he came by it eagerly, at a time when the old was mingling with the new, and all the surfaces of knowledge were being broken rapidly into fresh forms.

It is not known exactly when Dryden entered Westminster School,* or in detail what he did there. But a good deal is known, both generally about the character of English schools in those days and particularly about the character of Dryden's master, Busby. The English grammar schools before the Resto-

---

* About 1644, says James M. Osborn in *John Dryden: Some Biographical Facts and Problems,* N. Y., 1940. I am indebted to this excellent work at several points.

ration clung to the old omnibus ideals of education which
stressed the encyclopedic and the sententious. For a century
Latin had led in the school curriculums, supplanting logic.
Wolsey had advised that Virgil be "pronounced with due in-
tonation of voice," out of regard for "the majesty of his verse,"
and during the first half of the seventeenth century the discipline in Latin was especially complete. Exercises in Greek received for the most part only secondary emphasis, although
Westminster School was famous for its Greek studies, three
different headmasters, Grant, Camden, and Busby, having
produced Greek grammars. Charles Hoole, in his *New Dis-
coverie of the Old Art of Keeping Schools*, 1660, furnishes the
best testimony we have upon mid-century curriculums. According to him, boys began very early to translate English verse
into Latin, keeping notebooks by them wherein they entered
choice classical phrases to assist them in avoiding Anglicisms.
The "figura" and "prosodia" of rhetoric were by no means neglected, and for a show of wisdom the pupils were taught to
embellish their themes with apologues, fables, adages, "witty
sentences" ancient or modern, hieroglyphics, emblems, sym-
bols, ancient laws and customs, and biographical illustrations out
of Plutarch. Dr. Richard Busby of Westminster was the most
famous schoolmaster of the century; during his fifty-seven
years of incumbency Westminster produced a remarkable number of notable men. When Dryden published his translation of
Persius in 1693, he dedicated the fifth Satire to Busby, "to
whom I am not only obliged myself for the best part of my
own education, and that of my two sons, but have also received
from him the first and truest taste of Persius"; and before
the third Satire he remarked: "I remember I translated this
Satire, when I was a King's scholar at Westminster School, for
a Thursday night's exercise." Some notion of the school discipline in Dryden's day may be gained from the account left
by another of Dr. Busby's boys. "Betwixt one to three, that
lesson which, out of some author appointed for that day, had

been by the Master expounded into them (out of Cicero, Virgil, Homer, Euripides; Isocrates; Livie, Sallust, etc.) was to be exactlie gone through by construing and other grammatical waies, examining all the rhetorical figures and translating it out of verse into prose, or out of prose into verse; out of Greek into Latin; or out of Latin into Greek. Then they were enjoined to commit that to memorie against the next morning." *

It was Coleridge's belief that the whole tone of Augustan poetry in England was derived from such academic practices as these, which freighted the styles of many generations of schoolboys with conventional imagery and stereotyped epithets. Certainly it was under Busby that Dryden contracted the Latinism of thought and speech which proved later both a blessing and a curse. His Latinism helped him to be clear and strong, as he indicated in his dedication of *Troilus and Cressida:* "I am often put to a stand in considering whether what I write be the idiom of the tongue, or false grammar, and nonsense couched beneath that specious name of Anglicism; and have no other way to clear my doubts, but by translating my English into Latin, and thereby trying what sense the words will bear in a more stable language." But his Latinism also encouraged him to write too much in that diffuse manner which so ludicrously vitiated the verse of the next century. When he was not at his raciest, for instance, he could write lines like these from *Britannia Rediviva:*

> As when a sudden storm of hail and rain
> Beats to the ground the yet unbearded grain,
> Think not the hopes of harvest are destroyed
> On the flat field, and on the naked void;
> The light unloaded stem, from tempest freed,
> Will raise the youthful honours of his head;
> And, soon restored by native vigour, bear
> The timely product of the bounteous year.

* Barker, G. F. R. *Memoir of Richard Busby, D.D. London*, 1895, p. 80.

If Westminster offered a style, Cambridge bestowed the broader gifts of taste and thought. Dryden entered Trinity College in 1650 and stayed at least four years. It is at this point that Aubrey's note in his *Minutes of Lives*, "John Dreyden, esq., Poet Laureate. He will write it for me himselfe," most tantalizes. From 1654 to the death of Cromwell we know little about Dryden; but we may suppose that somewhere he privately read and wrote to advantage during those years, since the *Heroic Stanzas* reveal a mind already careful and full. Dryden was a student; and it is important to know what he learned.

"I am, ridiculously enough, accused to be a contemner of universities," he told Sir Charles Sedley in the dedication of *The Assignation* in 1673, "that is, . . . an enemy of learning; without the foundation of which, I am sure, no man can pretend to be a poet." Shadwell swore in his *Medal of John Bayes* (1682) that Dryden "came first to Town" when "a raw young fellow of seven and twenty." The Reverend Dr. Crichton, however, a contemporary at Cambridge, was warrant for another story: "he stayed to take his Bachelor's degree, but his head was too roving and active, or what else you'll call it, to confine himself to a college life, and so he left it and went to London into gayer company, and set up for a poet." * Whatever the impatience with which he went to London, he took many an occasion in later years to pay beautiful compliments to the universities. In the *Life of Plutarch* he duly acknowledged his debt to Trinity College. And his prologues and epilogues at Oxford are luxuriant with praise of the place. Mrs. Marshall addressed an audience there in 1674 as follows:

> Oft has the poet wished this happy seat
> Might prove his fading Muse's last retreat:
> I wondered at his wish, but now I find
> He sought for quiet, and content of mind;
> Which noiseful towns and courts can never know,
> And only in the shades, like laurels, grow.

* W. D. Christie. *Selections from Dryden*. 2d ed. Oxford, 1873, p. xvi.

> Youth, ere it sees the world, here studies rest,
> And age, returning thence, concludes it best.

Another university prologue ended with the famous lines:

> Oxford to him a dearer name shall be,
> Than his own mother university.
> Thebes did his green unknowing youth engage;
> He chooses Athens in his riper age.

During Dryden's residence at Cambridge the university was under the thumb of the Puritans, who in 1644 had evicted all Royalist tutors. The old academic peace suffered less disturbance than might have been expected. The discipline even improved, and solid progress continued to be made in philosophy and science. It was here at least that Dryden proceeded to widen his acquaintance with the Latin poets, to store his mind with the old scholastic forms of speculation and discourse, to become aware of new trends and processes, to dabble in natural science, to read Descartes and Hobbes.

The same observer who said he saw Dryden dash off to London to set up for a poet declares that while still at Cambridge "he had to his knowledge read over and very well understood all the Greek and Latin poets." A faith then reigned that the classics were a sufficient and final compendium of wisdom, eloquence, and beauty. Addison was not for fifty years yet, writing home from Virgil's Italy, to found a more or less flushed worship of Greece and Rome. The homage of the mid-seventeenth century was somewhat dry, and paid from a distance. Dryden accepted his Greeks and Romans without question, but also without sentiment.

William Gifford, springing once to the defense of Ben Jonson, asserted that "Dryden had merely the Greek and Latin of a clever schoolboy." Dryden had more than that. He not only knew his poets; he enormously respected them, and he used them. His opinions of them were likely to be the traditional opinions that Scaliger's brilliant criticism had made standard. But he employed them for purposes quite his own. His Greek was not half so good as his Latin. His examples from Greek life are very few; he fell back upon Latin texts of Homer and Theocritus, and he knew Longinus only through the French of Boileau, or perhaps the English of John Hall. He preferred the severer muses of the Romans, he said, to "the looseness of the Grecians." He shared here the bias of his age; the Augustans were Augustans, not Hellenes. His "old master Virgil" was never allowed to go so long as a year without the tribute of praise or imitation. Anyone who reads the prefaces to *Annus Mirabilis* and the folio of 1697 cannot remain in doubt what Latin poet was Dryden's lifelong dictator. From another master, Lucretius, Dryden learned the secret architecture of reasoned verse; learned to run swiftly yet carry heavy weights; learned his favorite images of darkness and light, eclipse and chaos, ordered atoms and whirling worlds. In a third master, Ovid, whom he says he read in Sandys's translation when a boy, he found a sparkling mind inferior to the other two, but one that fascinated him. Ovid, the favorite of Chaucer and Spenser and Shakespeare and Milton, the purveyor of mythological lore to every English poet, the "sweet witty soul" who was at once tender and mocking, at once flexible and hard, at once allusive and brisk, taught Dryden his gait, and showed him how to turn all the sides of his mind to the light. For the first twenty years after the Restoration Dryden's London was to reproduce with a certain amount of accuracy the Rome of Ovid. With civil war just past and a commonwealth overthrown, with court and city beginning to realize their power, with peace prevailing and cynicism in fashionable morals rampant, with a foreign culture seeking the favor of patrons and wits, the new city did for a while bear a strange resemblance to the old Empire; so that the vogue of Ovid in those years is not difficult to understand. Juvenal and Persius lent their larger, angrier tones to Dryden at Cambridge. Nor was Dryden

indifferent to the *curiosa felicitas* of Horace; but he was not
equipped, as Ben Jonson and Herrick were, to achieve anything
like it in practice. He knew Lucan's busy epic and Seneca's
bloody plays, and he was fond in later life of paraphrasing Statius on sleep. The following soliloquy on night, from *The Indian Emperor,* which Wordsworth correctly called "vague,
bombastic, and senseless," has often been quoted by incautious
admirers of Dryden in a misdirected effort to prove that he
could do justice to Nature:

> All things are hushed, as Nature's self lay dead;
> The mountains seem to nod their drowsy head;
> The little birds in dreams their songs repeat,
> And sleeping flowers beneath the night-dew sweat.
> Even lust and envy sleep; yet love denies
> Rest to my soul, and slumber to my eyes.

The lines come straight from Statius's *Sylvae.*

Dryden was rarely successful in his descriptions of Nature
and his accounts of the human passions, as we shall see in another place. What data he did possess upon these subjects he
had borrowed, not very happily, from the classical poets. He
had learned from Sappho, according to Addison, that persons
in love alternately burn and freeze. He had learned from Virgil
that in sudden fright the knees tremble and the breath deserts
the frame. He had learned from Lucretius the terminology of
physical love. He contracted from them all his taste for dealing
in blood and hardness and cruelty. But what more deeply affected him than this was the tradition of Roman virtue, male
virtue, which he found recited so admirably in the ancient his-
tories. "When we hear this author speaking," he says of Polyb-
ius, "we are ready to think ourselves engaged in a conversation
with Cato the Censor, with Lelius, with Massinissa, and with
the two Scipios; that is, with the greatest heroes and most
prudent men of the greatest age in the Roman commonwealth.
This sets me . . . on fire." His dedications are replete with

Roman examples, and tempered with a rare Augustan awe, as here in the dedication of *An Evening's Love* to the Duke of Newcastle:

Thus, my Lord, the morning of your life was clear and calm; and though it was afterwards overcast, yet, in that general storm, you were never without a shelter. And now you are happily arrived to the evening of a day as serene as the dawn of it was glorious; but such an evening as, I hope, and almost prophesy, is far from night. 'Tis the evening of a summer's sun, which keeps the daylight long within the skies. The health of your body is maintained by the vigour of your mind: neither does the one shrink from the fatigue of exercise, nor the other bend under the pains of study. Methinks I behold in you another Caius Marius, who, in the extremity of his age, exercised himself almost every morning in the Campius Martius, amongst the youthful nobility of Rome. And afterwards in your retirements, when you do honour to poetry by employing part of your leisure in it, I regard you as another Silius Italicus, who, having passed over his consulship with applause, dismissed himself from business, and from the gown, and employed his age amongst the shades, in the reading and imitation of Virgil.

It was in these spacious precincts that Dryden's imagination was most at home; in this distant and mellow morality Declarations of Indulgence and Test Acts were intrusive trifles, and the necessity of choosing between a James and a William but a dwarfish dilemma.

"The old and the new philosophy" was a phrase often on the lips of Dryden and his contemporaries. The seventeenth century, from Bacon to Locke, saw many inroads made by the new physics and the new psychology upon established modes of faith and behavior. At no period during the century was the shift being made more rapidly than it was in the sixth decade, when Dryden lived at Cambridge. Dryden, witnessing the unequal conflict between scholasticism and experimental science, between formal logic and common sense, may not have comprehended all that was being done. There is no sign that he had unusual

gifts for recognizing or criticizing ideas; he was not a meta-
physician; yet he must have been aware of being present at a
death. It was the scholastic habit of thinking and discoursing
that was dying; it was the disputation that was going out. As
far back as the days when James I delighted to attend the
disputations at Cambridge, disputations had been archaic. And
Thomas Randolph, who studied at Trinity College thirty years
before Dryden, could only praise the Aristotelianism of his in-
struction as something quaint. The medieval tradition lingered
on, however, and Dryden was still able to look upon the ruins
of those "Vast Bodies of Philosophie" irreverently invoked by
Cowley in his poem *To Mr. Hobbes*. To Dryden the hoary
structures were not without their charm, and he did not pass
them by without making them yield the secret of their form,
however little he cared for the treasure of their content. He re-
tained to the last a touch of the scholastic in his method of
framing thoughts and arriving at distinctions. Upon more than
one occasion he showed himself familiar with the language of
the schools, even the jargon. "He delighted to talk of liberty
and necessity, destiny and contingence," said Dr. Johnson. He
had only the medieval idiom for soul and body at his command.
The famous lines on Shaftesbury's

> . . . fiery soul, which, working out its way,
> Fretted the pigmy body to decay,
> And o'er-informed the tenement of clay,

are tinctured with scholasticism; and Dryden's inveterate attachment to the image of circles, whether in the poem on Lord
Hastings (ll. 27-28), in the *Heroic Stanzas* (ll. 17-20), in
Astraea Redux (l. 299), in *The Hind and the Panther* (III, l.
19), or in *Eleonora* (l. 273), betrays the fascination which
ancient forms exercised over his imagination. Finally, it was
from the schools, from the disputation, that Dryden learned
to love argument and ratiocination. Swift called *The Hind and
the Panther* "a complete abstract of sixteen thousand schoolmen,

from Scotus to Bellarmine." Here again it was form, not content, that Dryden enriched himself with. His arguments often are not without serious flaw; but his manner is impeccable. He discovered which gestures convince; he acquired "the air of proving something." Like Ovid in the rhetorical schools of Rome, learning to ring infinite changes on a theme in *suasoriae* and *controversiae*, Dryden by study and by instinct developed an unexampled power, so far as English poetry goes, of handling and turning over ideas and beating them into shape with the scantlings of logic.

"The new philosophy," meanwhile, with its new outlook brought a new language; and always it was language that interested Dryden. Since Milton's days at Cambridge there had come definite innovations. Ramus and Bacon and Descartes were replacing Aristotle, mathematics and experimental science were in the ascendant. The unwieldy amalgam of sixteenth-century natural history was yielding to the attacks of specialists in physics, chemistry, and anatomy. Harvey, Ent, and Ward were publishing the results of their researches. Definite curiosity about definite problems seemed in the way of being satisfied.

Lowell thought science "the most obstinately prosy material." Yet the new science was far from dull to Dryden and his kind. No laborious terminology chilled their ardor and blunted their curiosity, or forbade them to incorporate the new world into their conversation and their writing. Not that they were the first to make use of the material. Donne had found science a brighter ornament for verse than hackneyed mythology. Milton was already ruminating upon the cosmic bearings of astronomy, geography, and chemistry. But they were the first to play exultantly with both the new spirit and the new language. They were frankly dilettanti. The game was expression, and the chase was for metaphors. When Dryden in *The State of Innocence* has Adam awake from his bed of moss and cry,

> What am I? or from whence? For that I am
> I know, because I think,

he does not convince us that he knows more than three words
of Descartes. His astronomy is confused; he mixes the Roman
poets with the Cambridge cosmologists; he has no system.
There can be no honest doubt that he took a good deal of stock
in astrology; among the papers at Oxford of Elias Ashmole,
the great virtuoso and curioso, are to be found nativities of
Dryden and his eldest son, carefully cast. At the close of his
life he wrote to his sons at Rome: "Towards the latter end of
this month, September, Charles will begin to recover his perfect
health, according to his nativity, which, casting it myself, I am
sure is true; and all things hitherto have happened accordingly
to the very time that I predicted them." He was not a scientist.
Yet he picked up the new language, and adopted the new airs;
he established what Macaulay named "the scientific vocabulary"
in verse. Not too long after he went to London, and before he
had won any notice by his writing at all, in 1662, he was made
a member of the newly chartered Royal Society. The next year
he was laying honest Aristotle by with some verses addressed to
Dr. Charleton, who had written a book on Stonehenge:

> The longest tyranny that ever swayed
> Was that wherein our ancestors betrayed
> Their free-born reason to the Stagirite,
> And made his torch their universal light.

In the same poem he celebrated the innovations of Bacon, Gilbert, Boyle, Harvey, and Ent. Three years later he inserted an
apostrophe to the Royal Society in his *Annus Mirabilis,* and put
into the mouth of Crites in the *Essay of Dramatic Poesy* this
query: "Is it not evident, in these last hundred years, . . . that
almost a new Nature has been revealed to us?—that more errors
of the School have been detected, more useful experiments in
philosophy have been made, more noble secrets in optics,

medicine, anatomy, astronomy, discovered, than in all those credulous and doting ages from Aristotle to us?"

The new mechanical conception of nature bore bitter fruit in the domain of psychology and political science, where the astounding Hobbes held sway. It seemed to Samuel Butler, and to others with less humor, that the Sage of Malmesbury, though he might conquer the Kingdom of Darkness in a way to satisfy himself, would end by extinguishing all the light which the remainder of mankind enjoyed. As Donne had exclaimed in the *Anatomy of the World,*

> [The] new philosophy calls all in doubt;
> The element of fire is quite put out;
> The sun is lost, and th' earth, and no man's wit
> Can well direct him where to look for it.

The deplorable paradoxes about the selfishness of human nature which the tutor of the future Charles II was propounding in the treatise on *Human Nature* and the *Leviathan* during the first two years of Dryden's residence at Cambridge were destined to fascinate many a gilded youth after the Restoration, and even to incline old Bishop Burnet "to be apt to think generally the worst of men and of parties."

In the wake of Hobbes came Lucretius, the favorite of Gassendi and Molière,

> . . . to proclaim in English verse
> No monarch rules the universe,

as Waller politely wrote upon the occasion of Evelyn's translation in 1656. The atoms of Lucretius and Ovid became almost the favorite image of poets throughout the century. "Blind chance," "the confused heap of things," "atoms casually together hurled," were phrases that always passed current. The idea of a world left running by itself was poison to the divines but food for the versifiers.

Dryden announced in the preface to *Religio Laici* that he

was "naturally inclined to scepticism in philosophy." Emphasis needs to be placed on the first word in his phrase; he was by disposition rather than by doctrine a skeptic. He thought Hobbes and Lucretius very much alike in a certain "magisterial authority" of utterance. If he bowed to this authority in his earlier years, when he was at college, he was disposed later on to give it no more than casual, good-natured recognition. He never altogether capitulated to any system of politics or morals or aesthetics. He was born and he died with an Olympian indifference to principles. Yet Hobbes and Lucretius both made powerful, permanent impressions upon his imagination. It was Hobbes who inspired his deep distrust of human beings in the mass and his lifelong intolerance of movements that threatened to disturb the peace. Hobbes gave him "the reason and political ornaments," according to the authors of *The Censure of the Rota,* for *The Conquest of Granada,* as well as language with which to defend the Stuart kings in satire. The *Leviathan* had blazed a sinister trail into the thicket of human nature and had revealed dismaying perspectives in what was taken for human history. Dryden has much to say about the State of Nature. On a few occasions he reverts with a kind of pleasure to a golden age among

> those happy isles
> Where in perpetual spring young Nature smiles; *

or among

> guiltless men, who danced away their time,
> Fresh as their groves, and happy as their clime.†

And he has Almanzor say in *The Conquest of Granada:*

> But know that I alone am king of me.
> I am as free as Nature first made man,
> Ere the base laws of servitude began,
> When wild in woods the noble savage ran.

---

* *To My Lord Chancellor,* ll. 135-6.
† *To Dr. Charleton,* ll. 13-4.

But most often the prehistoric rabble which he invokes is

> Blind as the Cyclops, and as wild as he;
> They owned a lawless savage liberty,
> Like that our painted ancestors so prized
> Ere empire's arts their breasts had civilized.*

And *The State of Innocence* ends upon a note that is cold and ruthless, almost ominous, compared with the undaunted serenity that closes *Paradise Lost*. Says Raphael, ushering Adam and Eve out into the world,

> The rising winds urge the tempestuous air;
> And on their wings deformèd winter bear:
> The beasts already feel the change; and hence
> They fly to deeper coverts, for defense:
> The feebler herd before the stronger run;
> For now the war of nature is begun.

There was also something sinister about the world of Lucretius as Dryden adopted it; for in his imagination he did adopt it. Times without number, in both his prose and his verse, the atoms came crowding upon the page; they were his unfailing conceit. They flung themselves together into a "universal frame," a frame held together not so much by spirit or will (as to be sure Dryden felt bound each time to maintain) as by some godless, grinding power. In his fancy the machine was not to run forever. The pageant was to crumble. Chaos would some day reign again. But eternity promised him few of the comforts that it promised men like Milton. If Dryden ever thought of eternity at all, he thought of it as very great and empty.

When Descartes for his purposes sharpened the distinction between mind and matter he performed a doubtful service to philosophy. An analogous distinction was being labored in aesthetics during the seventeenth century. In poetry, fancy was being set against judgment, and although the two were sup-

* *Astraea Redux*, ll. 45-8.

posed to be mutually enriching, they were more often taken to
destroy each other. This distinction was of doubtful service to
literature. As in philosophy the arid dualism of Descartes
obscured the spirit, so in literature the war between fancy and
judgment hindered the imagination. Not that poetry in England suffered a total eclipse, as is often believed. A great deal
of brains and imagination went into the poetry of the latter
seventeenth and early eighteenth centuries. But certain definite
exclusions were made by all who touched the subject either as
poets or as critics, and certain limitations were freely acknowledged. Dryden grew up at a time when the air was filled with
many diverse strains of verse, and no note was predominant.
Yet as he reached maturity he became aware of something that
might have been called "the new poetry." He came to distinguish four forward-looking poets among the throng: Cowley,
Waller, Denham, and Davenant. And behind those Sons of
Ben he was able to discern the forward-peering countenance of
Hobbes.

The new poetry was to be the work of sober wit, the issue of
the conscious faculties. Wit had danced in with the conceit early
in the century, but it had been tortured then as it was not to
be tortured now. "Doctor Donne," a more fascinating man than
the Augustans ever supposed, had been "the greatest wit," said
Dryden at a later date, but "not the best poet of our nation."
The current of conceits which had swept even Milton in had not
much further to flow. "Ingenious Cowley!" cries Cowper in
The Task,

> I cannot but lament thy splendid wit
> Entangled in the cobwebs of the schools.

Yet even Cowley had his clear, free vein; and the cobwebs
that he spun did not last long past the Restoration. Dryden,
who indeed was never exempt from conceits as long as he lived,
declared against them from the first. If the conceit survived in
Augustan poetry, it survived in the circumlocution, which at

least was civilized. The new poets were to have large audiences, and they needed to be understood when they spoke. As in comedy wit was to take the place of "humour," and pungent criticism of society was to supplant an endless elaboration of fantastic characters, so in all verse there was to be an effort to speak a language

> Consisting less in words and more in things:
> A language not affecting ancient times,
> Nor Latin shreds by which the pedant climbs,

Dryden's Style [handwritten marginal note]

to use some lines written to James I by an excellent poet, Sir John Beaumont, who early anticipated Dryden's style. If the word "wisdom" be taken not too seriously, the following passage from Dryden's prologue to *Oedipus* may serve indirectly to express the new ideal. Says Dryden, speaking of ancient Greece,

> Then Sophocles with Socrates did sit,
> Supreme in wisdom one, and one in wit;
> And wit from wisdom differed not in those,
> But as 't was sung in verse or said in prose.

ibid [handwritten marginal note]

Eugenius, in the *Essay of Dramatic Poesy*, makes a triumphant canvass of Dryden's first teachers in verse. The Greeks and Romans, he says, "can produce nothing . . . so even, sweet, and flowing, as Mr. Waller; nothing so majestic, so correct, as Sir John Denham; nothing so elevated, so copious, and full of spirit, as Mr. Cowley."

"The darling of my youth, the famous Cowley," wrote Dryden in 1693, long after he had outgrown his young enthusiasms. There had been a time, shortly after he left Cambridge, when he had known Cowley's work minutely, and had made good use of it. Cowley was a zealous scientist. He studied medicine, wrote a botanical treatise, proposed a College for the Advancement of Experimental Philosophy, was admitted to the Royal Society, and practiced odes on Dr. Scarborough and Dr. Har-

vey. He was interested in everything. He took a naïve delight
in explication, and loved to give accounts of things in verse. His
mind was agile and airy, and worked with a certain dry animation that captivated the attention. At times he was a facile
metrist, and always his spirit was sweet. It is often said that
Dryden's early poems are bad because they are like Cowley.
It is fair to Cowley to say that if they had been exactly like
him they would not have been so bad. Dryden approximated
the plenty but not the sprightliness of his elder. Even in that
plenty there were signs of strength. Dryden's poem to Dr.
Charleton follows closely after Cowley's to Mr. Hobbes in its
treatment of Aristotle and the schoolmen. The *Heroic Stanzas*
and the verses to Sir Robert Howard contain a generous proportion of scientific figures inserted in the Cowley manner. For
years Dryden spoke always in the warmest accents of his "master," and it was not until his last piece of criticism altogether,
the preface to the *Fables,* that he took pains to expose Cowley's
faults. He seems always to have been thoroughly familiar with
his poems. It has long been known that four lines in *Mac
Flecknoe,*

> Where their vast courts the mother-strumpets keep,
> And undisturbed by watch in silence sleep. . . .
> Where unfledged actors learn to laugh and cry,
> And infant punks their tender voices try,

are a close parody of four in the *Davideis:*

> Where their vast courts the mother-waters keep,
> And undisturbed by moons in silence sleep. . . .
> Beneath the dens where unfledged tempests lie,
> And infant winds their tender voices try;

it has not been observed that the famous portrait of Shadwell
near the beginning of *Mac Flecknoe,*

> Some beams of wit on other souls may fall,
> Strike through and make a lucid interval;

> But Shadwell's genuine night admits no ray;
> His rising fogs prevail upon the day,

is replete with echoes from an adjoining passage in Cowley's epic:

> There is a place deep, wondrous deep below,
> Where *genuine night* and horror does o'erflow; . . .
> Here no dear glimpse of the sun's lovely face,
> *Strikes through the solid darkness* of the place;
> No dawning morn does her kind reds display;
> *One slight weak beam* would here be thought the day.

Cowley was dry, and wrote without passion. Dryden's tutors were all mild and self-contained. Mildest among them came Waller and Denham, the pair whom Dryden began as early as the dedication of *The Rival Ladies* in 1664 to name together, and whose twin fames for a century were the outcome of his persistent praise. The importance of neither can be over-emphasized. Dryden said of Waller, "Unless he had written, none of us could write," and of Denham that his *Cooper's Hill*, "for the majesty of the style, is, and ever will be, the exact standard of good writing."

To begin with Waller. The novelty of his numbers will be considered in another place. It was the novelty of his expression and his processes that charmed the wits who read his first volume in 1645, and who continued for forty-two years to hear occasions graced by his easy voice. He had learned the secret which Augustan poets were to need to know, the secret of writing with ease. His ease was ease of mind as well as of meter. He was cool and gracious at the same time. He was not perturbed by his subjects, which indeed were never great—St. James's Park, the repairing of St. Paul's Cathedral, or Her Majesty's taste for tea; even the wars he sang were petty affairs. He was obvious and pleasant, and could in perfect self-possession build up an idea or a conceit in verse that must charm by its symmetry. Thought in him was often fatuous, but it was never absent; Goldsmith was struck by his "strength of thinking." When Dryden in 1680-1 revised Sir William Soame's translation of Boileau's *Art of Poetry* and substituted English names for the French, he wrote "Waller" for "Malherbe," saying,

> His happy genius did our tongue refine,
> And easy words with pleasing numbers join.

"Easy" and "pleasing" were important terms in Restoration criticism of verse. Waller was not without his conceits; his complimentary effusions are full of absurdities. But he is not shocking; and his good will is irresistible. Dryden has not exaggerated his own debt to Waller. He borrowed many things, both good and bad, from the suave old Parliamentarian. By constitution he was scarcely so agreeable as Waller, but he learned from him the accent and the diction of affability. Waller's favorite and most frequent images, those of the eagle and the halcyon, Dryden calmly appropriated. Whenever Dryden's early panegyrical tone is soft and insinuating, as it is in the poems to Charles II, the Lord Chancellor, Lady Castlemaine, and the Duchess of York, he is speaking with Waller's voice. And anyone who will take the trouble to read three poems by Waller on public occasions, the *Panegyric to My Lord Protector* (1655), *Of a War with Spain, and Fight at Sea* (1656-61), and *Instructions to a Painter, for the Drawing of the Posture and Progress of His Majesty's Forces at Sea* (1666), will no longer be in doubt as to whence Dryden derived certain features of his *Heroic Stanzas* and his *Annus Mirabilis*. The dignity and the beauty of those two poems are his own; the occasional notes of sober fatuity are Waller's.

Denham's *Cooper's Hill* owed its vogue largely to Dryden, who neglected no opportunity to praise it. Two lines in that poem,

> Though deep, yet clear; though gentle, yet not dull;
> Strong without rage; without o'erflowing, full,

modeled by Denham on three lines in Cartwright's verses in memory of Ben Jonson,

> Low without creeping, high without loss of wings;
> Smooth, yet not weak, and by a thorough-care,
> Big without swelling, without painting fair,

became classic through Dryden's analysis of them in his dedication of the *Aeneis*. From Denham Dryden acquired the ratiocinative dignity which is secured by quiet rhetorical questions, restful aphorisms, and meditative *enjambement*.

The volume which contained Sir William Davenant's *Gondibert* (1651) is now interesting chiefly for its introductory matter. The epic which followed is important only because it called out poems by Waller and Cowley, and because it needed the elaborate introduction of essays written in Paris the previous year by Davenant and Hobbes. These four prefixtures are interesting despite their failure to convince the world that *Gondibert* was either new or significant. In themselves they reflected or expressed new doctrines in poetry which were not sterile. They prescribed the materials for the new poetry, and they analyzed the psychological processes by which it would be produced. This volume of 1651 was almost a text-book of the new aesthetics.

Waller and Cowley commended Davenant's preoccupation with the manners of men. Said Waller:

> Now to thy matchless book,
> Wherein those few that can with judgment look,
> May find old love in pure fresh language told,
> Like new-stamped coin made out of angel-gold.
> Such truth in love as th' antique world did know,
> In such a style as courts may boast of now;
> Which no bold tales of gods or monsters swell,
> But human passions such as with us dwell.
> Man is thy theme; his virtue or his rage
> Drawn to the life in each elaborate page.

Cowley proceeded in the same tenor:

> Methinks heroic poesie till now
> Like some fantastic fairy-land did show;
> Gods, devils, nymphs, witches, and giants' race,
> And all but man, in man's best work had place.
> Thou like some worthy knight, with sacred arms,
> Instead of those, dost man and manners plant,
> The things which that rich soil did chiefly want.

All this is simply in recognition of Davenant's own pronouncement that a heroic poem gives us "a familiar and easy view of ourselves," and of Hobbes's stouter declaration that "the subject of a poem is the manners of men." "Of all which," says Dryden in his preface to *Troilus and Cressida*, "whosoever is ignorant does not deserve the name of poet."

The manners of men, then, are the business of a poet. How are his expression and his imagination to compass the manners of men? First for the expression, which must be adequate and no more; whose prime qualities must be "perspicuity, propriety, and decency." Davenant and Hobbes were far from eschewing novelties and rarities, as will be seen in another chapter; but they insisted upon adequacy and propriety. "There be so many words in use at this day in the English tongue," writes Hobbes, "that though of magnifique sound, yet (like the windy blisters of a troubled water) have no sense at all; and so many others that lose their meaning by being ill coupled, so that it is a hard matter to avoid them; for having been obtruded upon youth in the schools by such as make it, I think, their business there (as 'tis exprest by the best poet [Davenant])

> With terms to charm the weak and pose the wise,

they grow up with them, and gaining reputation with the ignorant, are not easily shaken off. To this palpable darkness I may also add the ambitious obscurity of expressing more than is perfectly conceived, or perfect conception in fewer words than it requires, which expressions, though they have had the honour to be called strong lines, are indeed no better than riddles, and, not only to the reader but also after a little time to the writer himself, dark and troublesome." That is, the poet should avoid congested and crabbed utterance, should choose his epithets sanely, and should always be sure that he knows himself what he is saying. Dryden draws the same inferences, in *The State of Innocence*,

> From words and things, ill sorted and misjoined;
> The anarchy of thought, and chaos of the mind.

Hobbes went about in an orderly way to dissect the imagination and ascertain its workings. "Time and Education begets Experience; Experience begets Memory; Memory begets Judgement and Fancy. . . . The Ancients therefore fabled not absurdly, in making Memory the Mother of the Muses." There was no mystery here at all. Imagination is a makeshift. If we could keep the whole world fresh and vivid about us all our days there would be no call for Fancy in the metaphysics of true enjoyment. The life of the imagination is a life of sheer pretense. "Imagination," runs a sentence in Hobbes's *Physics*, "is nothing else but sense decaying, or weakened, by the absence of the object." This refusal to credit the imagination with original power, this insistence upon reducing it to its lowest terms and making of it a mechanical device for reproducing experience as such, is crucial in the history of English poetry. When Bacon had examined the mental processes of the poet in *The Advancement of Learning* he had not, to be sure, come to the conclusion that poets are divine, or mad; but he had assigned to them a function more or less creative, which was "to give some shadow of satisfaction to the mind of man in those points wherein the nature of things doth deny it, the world being in proportion inferior to the soul." Now Hobbes ignored the transforming power in favor of the recording power. "For

Memory is the World (though not really, yet so as in a looking glass) in which the Judgement, the severer Sister, busieth herself in a grave and rigid examination of all the parts of Nature, and in registering by letters their order, causes, uses, differences, and resemblances; whereby the Fancy, when any work of Art is to be performed, finding her materials at hand and prepared for use, needs no more than a swift motion over them, that what she wants, and is there to be had, may not lie too long unespied." Which is to say, what is true yet is not the whole truth, that the best poet is he who has the best memory. Ten years before, Milton, in his *Reason of Church Government*, had confided to "any knowing reader" that the great work which he was setting out to do would be a work not "to be obtained by the invocation of Dame Memory and her Siren daughters, but by devout prayer to that eternal Spirit who can enrich with all utterance and knowledge." And twenty-four years after *Gondibert*, Milton's nephew, Edward Phillips, in the preface to his *Theatrum Poetarum*, was to hold a brief for "true native Poetry" as against mere "wit, ingenuity, and learning in verse." But Hobbesian psychology was as potent as Hobbesian politics, and it was not until a century or more had passed that any really philosophical attack was made upon Dame Memory's position. It was in the wake of such an attack that Blake, in the world of painting, explained all of what he considered had been Sir Joshua Reynolds's critical errors by adducing the one mistaken conception that "originates in the Greeks calling the Muses daughters of Memory." It was in rebuttal of theories like those of Hobbes that Wordsworth wrote: "Imagination has no reference to images that are merely a faithful copy, existing in the mind, of absent external objects; but is a word of higher import, denoting operations of the mind upon those objects, and processes of creation and composition."

All this does not mean that Dryden and others who went to school to Hobbes did not write great, amazing poetry. It only explains why they failed to write poetry of a certain kind. Won-

Hobbesian psych. encouraged them not to write personal poetry

der and brooding were simply not of their world. They transformed nothing; the divine illusion was not for them. They created and composed enduring monuments of art, but not in Wordsworth's way. They were not at all times aware of their limitations. Dryden, as we shall see, struggled a long while to trample them down. He spoke often, in common with his contemporaries, of the *furor poeticus;* he championed poetic license; he tried to write like Shakespeare. But like his contemporaries he was bound by triple steel. He had to learn to be great in his own way.

Taine, having no reason to doubt that Dryden had stayed on three years at Cambridge after taking his Bachelor's degree, proceeds: "Here you see the regular habits of an honorable and well-to-do family, the discipline of a connected and solid education, the taste for classical and exact studies. Such circumstances announce and prepare, not an artist, but a man of letters." If to be an artist is to be devoted to an art, and if to be a true artist is to have that devotion not only continue but increase through each year of a long life, then Dryden was truly an artist, and Taine is unjust. Dryden's devotion cannot be called into question. Whether or not the legend be accurate that he was "too roving and active to confine himself to college life" and that he hastened to set himself up in London, it is plain that he, like Ovid, would sooner or later have found it impossible to keep out of poetry. Whenever his career began, it engrossed him solely and entirely. In later years he liked to review this career; his conception of it was dramatic, if not theatrical. He saw himself on a great stage, prominent, almost alone. He carried with him to London, and always kept by him there, an "adamantine confidence," as Dr. Johnson put it, not simply in himself, for he knew what modesty was, but in the powers which study and practice had convinced him were his. Pride of profession, scorn of competitors, devotion to his trade sustained him. Goldsmith made his way into the mid-eighteenth-century literary world by a good-humored unconventionality that

brought relief to sufferers from the prevailing gentilities and
rotundities. Dryden, also without violence of bluster, forced
himself upon his world through sheer display of confidence and
a large, steady assumption of authority. There was a growing
demand for poetry which could be read and generally discussed.
Dryden believed that he could supply the smoothest and most
powerful variety. He was not long in convincing London that
he was right.

It was brought against Dryden by Shadwell, in *The Medal of
John Bayes*, that he had served as a hack to Herringman the
bookseller during his first few years in London, writing "prefaces to books for meat and drink." It is probable that Shadwell
exaggerated the meanness of the relation, if it existed at all.
Dryden's private income was not large, and he must have
turned at an early stage to writing for money, without, indeed,
the spiritual support of Dr. Johnson's avowal that no man except a blockhead ever wrote for anything else. Any connection
with Herringman in these years of his apprenticeship would
have been valuable in that it could place him in one of the
main currents of poetic production, Herringman being almost
the chief publisher of poems and plays at the Restoration.
Somewhere, at least, Dryden was learning what was being written, and coming to feel at home in society; without which
knowledge and feeling he could scarcely have gone far.

Personally, Dryden seems never to have prepossessed anyone.
His youth had not been precocious, and his maturity found him
more mellow than splendid. He was genial in his old age, without any great allowance of spontaneous humor. His mind
always remained warm and strong. Pope told Spence that he
"was not a very genteel man; he was intimate with none but
poetical men." He pretended to be nothing other than what
above all things he was, a writer. He did not profess to be a
hero; he disliked holding himself rigid. "Stiffness of opinion,"
he wrote in the dedication of *Don Sebastian*, "is the effect of
pride, and not of philosophy. . . . The ruggedness of a stoic

is only a silly affectation of being a god. . . . True philosophy is certainly of a more pliant nature, and more accommodated to human use. . . . A wise man will never attempt an impossibility." Dryden's inconsistencies have generally been deplored. But it is precisely to his unending powers of renewal that we owe that serenity and that freshness in which he never fails us. "As I am a man," he told the Earl of Mulgrave in 1676, in the dedication of *Aureng-Zebe*, "I must be changeable; and sometimes the gravest of us all are so, even upon ridiculous accidents. Our minds are perpetually wrought on by the temperament of our bodies; which makes me suspect they are nearer allied, than either our philosophers or school-divines will allow them to be. . . . An ill dream, or a cloudy day, has power to change this wretched creature, who is so proud of a reasonable soul, and make him think what he thought not yesterday."

II

FALSE LIGHTS

DR. Johnson's brilliant example seems nearly to have established for all time the procedure of persons who would criticize the poetry of Dryden. The procedure consists in moving swiftly through his works, line by line and page by page, noting down what passages are in shocking taste and what passages are unexceptionable, and at the end qualifying on the basis of the first the praise which ought naturally to fall to the second. There has been good reason for this. No critic has felt that he could afford to commend Dryden in general without proving that he had taken into account the worst of him in particular. No critic has been willing to go on record as in any way approving the more flagrant stanzas of the *Annus Mirabilis*, the more impossible speeches of the heroic plays, or the more meretricious portions of the *Virgil* and other journeywork. Such caution has been warranted by the fact that Dryden is as unequal as any English poet who has written voluminously.

But now it seems worth while to proceed a little further and ask whether Dryden held any theories which might have been responsible for the obvious defects in his product. For it is evident that the unhappy passages to which exception has in-

variably been taken are not passages wherein the poet's attention seems to have lagged, or his spirits drooped. They are
rather, in fact, his most careful and ambitious performances;
Dryden seldom dozed. Nor can they be explained as indiscre-
tions of youth. They are found everywhere throughout his
works, from first to last. It is plain that Dryden was following
false lights when he committed his offenses against taste. Either
he was pursuing ends which by nature he was unqualified to
reach, he was attempting the impossible, he was speaking a
language which was not instinctive; or he was reaching ends
which were not worth reaching, he was sedulously perfecting
a language which though native was not sterling.

The bad poetry in Dryden can be explained by simple errors
which he made either in choosing his material or in cultivating
his form. On the one hand, false lights led him to employ two
kinds of materials which in his case were spurious: first, the
materials of the fancy, in works like *Annus Mirabilis;* second,
the materials of the human passions, in works like the heroic
plays and the tragedies. The results were absurdity and bathos.
On the other hand, false lights led him to give excessive attention to the form of his verse at times when the matter was of
little import, as in the *Virgil.* The results were artificiality and
monotony. The purpose of the present chapter is to follow Dryden as he pursues his wandering fires, and to sweep away the
rubbish which he leaves behind him. Only after that is done
can we take up in good conscience his genuine performances
before the true flame.

When Hobbes and Davenant separated Fancy from Judgement and sent it off to play alone, they condemned it to dull
company. Their aesthetics, in setting reason over against imagination, did reason no great service and did imagination serious
harm. Dryden belonged on the side of the so-called reason.
He was not a child of fancy; he never lived what is sometimes
too glibly termed the life of the imagination. His true home
was the house of Judgement, and his true game was the adult

game of common sense. But he was given to experimenting. He was curious, to begin with, to know all that could be known about Fancy, whom Hobbes and Davenant had described as sprightly and fair. "When she seemeth to fly from one Indies to the other," said Hobbes, "and from Heaven to Earth, and to penetrate into the hardest matter and obscurest places, into the future and into herself, and all this in a point of time, the voyage is not very great, herself being all she seeks, and her wonderful celerity consisteth not so much in motion as in copious Imagery discreetly ordered and perfectly registered in the memory." "Wit," said Davenant, meaning Fancy, "is the laborious and the lucky resultances of thought. . . . It is a web consisting of the subtlest threads; and like that of the spider is considerately woven out of our selves. . . . Wit is not only the luck and labour, but also the dexterity of thought, rounding the world, like the Sun, with unimaginable motion, and bringing swiftly home to the memory universal surveys." No description could have been more alluring; it is no wonder that Dryden yielded and followed Fancy for a time. The two preceptors also conveyed hints as to the kind of language which the creature spoke. To write with fancy, said Hobbes, one must "know much." A sign of knowing much "is novelty of expression, and pleaseth by excitation of the mind; for novelty causeth admiration, and admiration curiosity, which is a delightful appetite of knowledge." To write with wit, said Davenant, is to bring truth home "through unfrequented and new ways, and from the most remote shades, by representing Nature, though not in an affected, yet in an unusual dress." That is, conceits were to be abjured, but dullness was to be avoided at every cost.

It seems certain that Dryden was thinking of Davenant's happy phrases when in the preface to *Annus Mirabilis* he wrote: "The composition of all poems is, or ought to be, of wit; and wit in the poet, or wit-writing (if you will give me leave to use a School distinction), is no other than the faculty of imagination in the writer, which, like a nimble spaniel, beats over and ranges through the field of memory, till it springs the quarry it hunted after; or, without metaphor, which searches over all the memory for the species or ideas of those things which it designs to represent." Then, as now, it seems to have been difficult to speak of the faculties in other than figurative terms. Dryden here compares wit to a spaniel; elsewhere he declares that the language of the French "is not strung with sinews like our English; it has the nimbleness of a greyhound, but not the bulk and body of a mastiff." The dog image served Dryden's purpose very well. Dryden confessed himself captivated by Davenant's own wit. "He was a man of quick and piercing imagination," he said in the preface to *The Tempest*, in the writing of which he had been assisted by Davenant the next year after *Annus Mirabilis*. "In the time I writ with him, I had the opportunity to observe somewhat more nearly of him, than I had formerly done. . . . I found him then of so quick a fancy, that nothing was proposed to him, on which he could not suddenly produce a thought extremely pleasant and surprising. . . . And as his fancy was quick, so likewise were the products of it remote and new . . . his imaginations were such as could not easily enter into any other man." The words "quick," "piercing," and "surprising" should be noted, because they were much in the mode whenever the poetic faculties were being analyzed. Shadwell, when he was still friendly, even used them to describe Dryden.

"Quick" was not the word for Dryden's fancy. Davenant's own adjective, "laborious," fits better. In the early occasional poems there is no surprising facility of phrase or illustration. In no piece did Dryden ever display a happy gift for turning up images. He speaks from time to time of difficulties encountered in curbing a luxuriant fancy. But it is plain that the difficulties were never real. There are times when, as Dr. Johnson has it, "he seems to look round him for images which he cannot find." His imagination is not bounding, or fertile; he proceeds painfully to scour the surface of life for allusions. His spaniel does not frisk; it must be beaten and driven. To use his own words in another connection, "The fancy, memory, and judgement are . . . extended (like so many limbs) upon the rack; all of them reaching with their utmost stress at nature." The net result is not a pretty or a pleasantly variegated pattern; " 'tis like an orange stuck with cloves," to fall back again upon Buckingham in *The Rehearsal*.

Annus Mirabilis, the *locus classicus* of Dryden's "wit-writing," "seems to be the work of a man," says Macaulay, "who could never, by any possibility, write poetry." It is better to call it the work of a man who could never, by any possibility, write a certain kind of poetry—the luxuriant, splendid kind that is studded with significant allusions. No swarm of ideas has beset the imagination of Dryden here. He has had to make an effort for every image, proceeding with an almost childlike seriousness that is oddly accentuated by the halting cadence of his heroic stanza. For most of his happier strokes he has gone to the classics. He is proud to admit in his preface that many of his images are from Virgil, and his notes acknowledge debts not only to Virgil but to Petronius, Tacitus, Pliny, Statius, Horace, and Ovid as well. His notes also furnish scientific explanations for the more obscure allusions in the poem. Wishing in the third stanza to say that the Dutch have had the good fortune to discover jewels in the East Indies, he has written:

> For them alone the heavens had kindly heat;
> In eastern quarries ripening precious dew.

To this he appends a note: "Precious stones at first are dew, condensed and hardened by the warmth of the sun or subterranean fires." His images from the classics are generally happy. It is when he draws upon his own resources, or, which is little better, upon Waller, that he proves once and for all that his career must lie another way. Certain stanzas have been quoted by every commentator. Many remain.

On high-raised decks the haughty Belgians ride,
  Beneath whose shade our humble frigates go:
Such port the elephant bears, and so defied
  By the rhinoceros her unequal foe.

By viewing Nature, Nature's handmaid Art
  Makes mighty things from small beginnings grow;
Thus fishes first to shipping did impart
  Their tail the rudder, and their head the prow.

The gravity with which in these and similar cases the last two lines of a stanza are made to serve up an absurd simile for garnishing the first two is the most lamentable feature of *Annus Mirabilis*. The attention is drawn down full upon the unfortunate comparison, and Dryden has no way to conceal his fundamental weakness. A few figures are excellent; as when Prince Rupert comes upon the scene,

And his loud guns speak thick like angry men.

The Dutch ships retire, awed by the British cannon:

So reverently men quit the open air
  When thunder speaks the angry gods abroad.

But Dryden's strenuous efforts have thrown the balance the other way, and have made it plain, not that he was incapable of a single happy image, but that he was incapable of measuring his own success. Pepys took *Annus Mirabilis* home with him from a book stall, and found it "a very good poem." It is a spirited poem, and it is an admirable poem whenever Dryden forgets his spaniel long enough to speak with the purely metrical rush and emphasis which were eventually to win him his position in English verse:

There was the Plymouth squadron new come in,
  Which in the Straits last winter was abroad;
Which twice on Biscay's working bay had been,
  And on the midland sea the French had awed.

> Old expert Allen, loyal all along,
>   Famed for his action on the Smyrna fleet;
> And Holmes, whose name shall live in epic song
>   While music numbers, or while verse has feet;
>
> Now, anchors weighed, the seamen shout so shrill,
>   That heaven, and earth, and the wide ocean rings;
> A breeze from westward waits their sails to fill,
>   And rests in those high beds his downy wings.

Annus Mirabilis is by no means the first or the last poem in which Dryden reveals a fatal want of tact and subtlety in the use of figures. From his earliest piece, that on Lord Hastings, through the panegyrics written at the Restoration, through the *Threnodia Augustalis*, through the *Britannia Rediviva*, through the *Eleonora*, to his last translation from Ovid, he pursues with heavy steps the flashing heels of fancy. In Ovid, it may be remarked, he found a genius who invariably inspired him to excesses. Ovid's inexhaustible fund of grotesque and tasteless yet clear-cut scenes furnished Dryden with stuff he never failed to make the most of, and could not have embellished had he tried.

If Dryden should not be expected to compete with other poets on the score of delicacy in simile and metaphor, much less should he be required to display his powers of passionate utterance in drama and narrative. Here he is in competition with Shakespeare and the tragic poets of Greece, and here he fails once again to prove that he possesses discrimination. Not that he lacks assurance. No poet has talked at greater length about the passions, or about "sublimity." Yet no great poet has managed to acquire a firmer reputation as a bungler in these departments. It is another case of a man working with materials which are not gauged for him, and which to a certain extent are irreconcilable with the temper of his time.

Dryden lacks that whole conception of man and nature which gives what is called insight. He cannot compress a large amount of emotional experience into a single phrase. He is virtually barren of illuminating comments on human life which move a reader to take new account of himself. His passages on the soul are foolish, treating importantly as they do of something which is not important to him. And the pessimistic soliloquies which the characters in his plays deliver on the subjects of fate and deception are for the most part trash, though not a few of them have been quoted to prove that Dryden was a critic of life. The following lines from *Aureng-Zebe* are compact and bright:

> When I consider life, 'tis all a cheat;
> Yet, fooled with hope, men favour the deceit;
> Trust on, and think tomorrow will repay;
> Tomorrow's falser than the former day;
> Lies worse; and while it says we shall be blest
> With some new joys, cuts off what we possesst.
> Strange cozenage! None would live past years again,
> Yet all hope pleasure in what yet remain;
> And from the dregs of life think to receive
> What the first sprightly running could not give.
> I'm tired with waiting for this chemic gold,
> Which fools us young, and beggars us when old.

Yet there is nothing appalling in their revelation; and their felicity need disturb no one. They have done Dryden's reputation in the main more harm than good by being so often brought forward in a hopeless cause.

"It requires Philosophy," said Dryden, "as well as Poetry, to sound the depths of all the passions; what they are in themselves, and how they are to be provoked." Dryden did a great deal of experimenting in the depths he speaks of. Having little or no intuition, and being without discrimination, he was almost never successful. He had a lasting curiosity concerning what he called "those enthusiastic parts of poetry" which deal with love and hate, disaster and death. In the heroic plays, in the tragedies, and in the translations of classical narratives he labored to render desperate actions in fitting speech, remembering that the "sublimest subjects ought to be adorned with the sublimest . . . expressions." The results can rarely be placed to his credit. In the first part of *The Conquest of Granada*, the haughty Almanzor, after looking fixedly for a moment at Almahide's face, which she has just unveiled, turns aside and utters this humiliated confession:

> I'm pleased and pained, since first her eyes I saw,
> As I were stung with some tarantula.
> Arms, and the dusty field, I less admire,
> And soften strangely in some new desire;
> Honour burns in me not so fiercely bright,
> But pale as fires when mastered by the light;
> Even while I speak and look, I change yet more,
> And now am nothing that I was before.
> I'm numbed, and fixed, and scarce my eye-balls move;
> I fear it is the lethargy of love!
> 'Tis he; I feel him now in every part;
> Like a new lord he vaunts about my heart;
> Surveys, in state, each corner of my breast,
> While poor fierce I, that was, am dispossessed.

At the end of *Aureng-Zebe*, Nourmahal, distracted with poison she has swallowed, cries out in the face of death:

> I burn, I more than burn; I am all fire.
> See how my mouth and nostrils flame expire!
> I'll not come near myself——
> Now I'm a burning lake, it rolls and flows;
> I'll rush, and pour it all upon my foes.
> Pull, pull that reverend piece of timber near;
> Throw 't on—'tis dry—'twill burn—
> Ha, ha! how my old husband crackles there!
> Keep him down, keep him down: turn him about;
> I know him; he'll but whizz, and straight go out.
> Fan me, you winds; What, not one breath of air?
> I burn them all, and yet have flames to spare.

> Quench me: Pour on whole rivers. 'Tis in vain;
> Morat stands there to drive them back again;
> With those huge bellows in his hands he blows
> New fire into my head; my brain-pan glows.

These speeches are from the heroic plays, which in some measure were licensed to rave. Yet, with the one exception of *All for Love*, the maturest of the tragedies, those which are supposed to have been conceived in better taste under Greek, French, and Shakespearian influences are everywhere marred by mortal extravagances. Dorax, in *Don Sebastian*, believes he is poisoned:

> I'm strangely discomposed;
> Quick shootings through my limbs, and pricking pains,
> Qualms at my heart, convulsions in my nerves,
> Shiverings of cold, and burnings of my entrails,
> Within my little world make medley-war,
> Lose and regain, beat, and are beaten back,
> As momentary victors quit their ground.
> Can it be poison!

Cleonidas, in *Cleomenes*, doubts the immortality of the soul:

> Because I find, that, now my body starves,
> My soul decays. I think not as I did;
> My head goes round; and now you swim before me;
> Methinks my soul is like a flame unfed
> With oil, that dances up and down the lamp,
> But must expire ere long.

And Cleomenes himself, dying, announces:

> A rising vapor rumbles in my brains.

Dryden's excuse for every such passage was that "a man in such an occasion is not cool enough, either to reason lightly, or to talk calmly." Yet in his own cooler days, when he had Virgil and Boccaccio for guides, and less fortunately Ovid, he still guided his pen through love and death and regret with clumsy fingers. "With the simple and elemental passions, as they spring separate in the mind," said Dr. Johnson once and for all, "he seems not much acquainted."

Dryden's theory was that if one only entered in with enthusiasm and industrious abandon one could succeed as well as any in striking off brave, fine talk in verse. While occupied with writing heroic plays he was supported by the creed that a heroic poet "is not tied to a bare representation of what is true." Rather he is expected to be reckless.

Poets, like lovers, should be bold, and dare,

runs the prologue to *Tyrannic Love;* and in the preface to the same play scorn is expressed for him who "creeps after plain, dull, common sense." "A solid man is, in plain English, a solid, solemn fool," he was to observe to the Earl of Mulgrave six years later.

This rough-and-ready ardor soon found rare support in Longinus, whose treatise *On the Sublime* was translated by Boileau in France in 1674 and almost immediately taken up by Dryden. Horace had insisted that the poet should be more than correct, and the French critics generally had allowed for elevation in style. Thomas Rymer, in his translation of Rapin's *Reflections on Aristotle's Treatise of Poesie,* was writing this sentence in the same year that Boileau's *Longinus* appeared: "Of late some have fallen into another extremity, by a too scrupulous care of purity of language: they have begun to take from Poesie all its nerves, and all its majesty, by a too timorous reservedness, and false modesty." The true poet, says Rymer, will have "flame" as well as "phlegm." It was chiefly from Longinus himself, however, "who was undoubtedly, after Aristotle, the greatest critic among the Greeks," said Dryden, that Dryden derived the substance of his *Apology for Heroic Poetry and Poetic License* in 1677. He quoted Longinus on the meanness of a poet who will shun profuseness and write parsimoniously in order to secure safety from ridicule. And in the light of the famous Greek treatise he formulated a definition of poetic license. But it cannot be granted that he caught all or any of the subtlety of his master in sublimity. Certainly he received no inspiration that served later on to chasten or ripen his manner of dealing with the passions. He was attracted by his teacher's theory of images. "Imaging is, in itself," he wrote, "the very height and life of Poetry. It is, as Longinus describes it, a discourse, which, by a kind of enthusiasm, or extraordinary emotion of the soul, makes it seem to us that we behold those things which the poet paints, so as to be pleased with them, and to admire them." He was referring here to the distinction made by Longinus between poetical and oratorical images. The first, says Longinus, is achieved "when he who is speaking . . . imagines himself to see what he is talking about, and produces a similar illusion in his hearers." The second is merely "designed to give perspicuity, and its chief beauties are its energy and reality." The metaphor which Dryden brings forward from his own works to prove that he has approximated the poetical image of Longinus is unfortunately a typically bad one:

> Seraph and cherub, careless of their charge,
> And wanton, in full ease now live at large;
> Unguarded leave the passes of the sky,
> And all dissolved in hallelujahs lie.

Here if anywhere is final proof that Dryden lacked discrimination in executing and judging figures of speech. He feigns well enough the "enthusiasm, or extraordinary emotion of the soul," but he does not achieve the reality which is after all the end of any writing. He misses the chief point in Longinus, which is that sublimity is not a trick but a state of mind, is not mere fine writing but the expression of an important personality. The distinction made by Longinus between true sublimity and "amplification" reflects directly upon Dryden, and scarcely to his credit: "The sublime is often conveyed in a single thought, but amplification can only subsist with a certain prolixity and diffusiveness." Dryden spent energy on both his figures and his heroic declarations; but the effect is one of words rather than things. The words seem stark naked on the page; they throw off no enlarging rings of suggestion or illusion; there is no light behind.

Let Dryden pronounce the final verdict. "To speak justly of this whole matter," he wrote in the preface to *Troilus and Cressida,* " 'tis neither height of thought that is discommended, nor pathetic vehemence, nor any nobleness of expression in its proper place; but 'tis a false measure of all these, something which is like them, and is not them; 'tis the Bristol stone, which appears like a diamond; 'tis an extravagant thought, instead of a sublime one; 'tis roaring madness, instead of vehemence; and a sound of words, instead of sense. If Shakespeare were stripped of all the bombasts in his passions, and dressed in the most vulgar words, we should find the beauties of his thoughts remaining; if his embroideries were burnt down, there would still be silver at the bottom of the melting pot: but I fear (at least let me fear it for myself) that we, who ape his sounding words, have nothing of his thought, but are all outside; there is not so much as a dwarf within our giant's clothes." This handsome recantation was carried still further in the preface to *The Spanish Friar.* But no one should be deceived. Dryden was an incomparably better critic than he was a writer of tragedies. He never can be said to have "settled his system of propriety," as Dr. Johnson would say.

Dryden drew an interesting distinction between Shakespeare and Fletcher in the preface to *Troilus and Cressida.* "The excellency of that poet was, as I have said, in the more manly passions; Fletcher's in the softer: Shakespeare writ better betwixt man and man; Fletcher, betwixt man and woman; consequently, one described friendship better; the other love; . . . the scholar had the softer soul; but the master had the kinder." Here is offered an approach to Dryden's own peculiar triumph in the drama. Failing to distinguish himself in his accounts of love, he yet succeeded famously in showing friendships broken and mended. Taking for his model the quarrel between Brutus and Cassius in Shakespeare's *Julius Caesar*, he executed four admirable scenes in as many tragedies. One who would see him at his best in dialogue should go to the scenes between Antony and Ventidius in *All for Love*, Hector and Troilus in *Troilus and Cressida*, Sebastian and Dorax in *Don Sebastian*, and Cleomenes and Cleanthes in *Cleomenes*. Here he is straightforward, and he writes with his mind on the object. Here, in the most limited sense of the phrase, he shows the "manners of men." Almanzor's blunt direction to Almahide, given before she removes her veil, is worth all the pages of rant which follow upon her committing that indiscretion:

> Speak quickly, woman: I have much to ,do.

Dryden was at his best when describing a contest between two competent minds playing free of sentiment. It was in his true role of sensible observer that he wrote his quarrel scenes; as it was with his plainest vision that he watched those two astonishing beasts, the hind and the panther, in their endless game of crafty give and take:

> To this the Panther sharply had replied;
> But, having gained a verdict on her side,
> She wisely gave the loser leave to chide. . . .
> Yet thought it decent something should be said;
> For secret guilt by silence is betrayed.
> So neither granted all, nor much denied,
> But answered with a yawning kind of pride.

It is a commonplace of literary history that the seventeenth century in Europe saw an almost comical divergence between poetic theory and poetic practice, the heroic poem in France being the instance usually given of a type that failed to fulfill its promise. In England, as has been seen, the divergence was

very wide between Dryden's theory and practice in so far as
they involved a fancy operating over the face of nature and an
imagination operating among the human passions under dramatic strain; one reason beyond all doubt being that the sepa-
ration in current doctrine of wit from judgment, imagination
from reason, rendered it difficult or impossible to discriminate
between true and false expression and sanctioned a certain reck-
lessness which was mistaken for poetic rage. But there is another group of major defects in the poetry of Dryden and the
Augustans generally wherein form rather than substance is involved, and whence has resulted that artificiality of tone which
is the proverbial objection urged by modern critics. Here again
it is possible to find the poets controlled by theories, and here
again promise is hopelessly in advance of fulfillment owing
to the superficial character of the theories and the inadequacy
with which they are applied.

The theories are that poetry is like oratory, that poetry is
like painting, and that poetry is like music.* The aim is to
achieve the ends of those three parallel arts as well as the ends
of poetry, and thus enrich poetic expression. The problem is
purely one of expression, or as was said in the seventeenth century, of elocution. Art is the imitation of life. Each separate
art has means whereby it can accomplish direct imitation. If
poetry, in addition to its own direct means, can appropriate
the means of other arts and apply them obliquely to its material, why should not the eventual product be so much the fuller
of beauty and meaning? Actually the product as we now regard
it is less beautiful rather than more beautiful in consequence
of this confusion. Instead of deepening its own medium by contact with oratory, painting, and music, poetry became shallow;
instead of growing more eloquent, more picturesque, and more
harmonious, it only grew more rhetorical, more vague, and
more monotonous. That is to say, Augustan poetry at its worst

---

* "In it are assembled all the Powers of Eloquence, of Musick, and of
Picture." Sir William Temple. *Of Poetry.* 1690.

grew rhetorical, vague, and monotonous; at its best it was far different. As its worst has often been seized and unduly enlarged upon by contrary critics, and as only the worst of Dryden is being considered in the present chapter, it seems necessary to bestow considerable attention at this point upon these weaknesses which Dryden shared with all of his contemporaries and with most of his immediate followers.

Tacitus complained in his *Dialogus* that Roman oratory was being invaded by the dance; orations were being composed and delivered in dance measures; "orators speak voluptuously," he wrote with indignation, "and actors dance eloquently." Tacitus was not the first or the last to make objection to the mingling in spirit and technique of two distinct arts. *Laokoöns* were thought, even if they were not written, long before Lessing. But the confusion of poetry with eloquence that began to be current in the Italian Renaissance and persisted throughout the criticism of all Europe for at least two centuries aroused no Tacitus and was suffered to run its long course unchallenged. The original invasion of poetry by oratory was no less gradual and peaceable than the final withdrawal, if indeed the withdrawal can be said as yet to have reached a final stage, or can be expected or desired ever to be complete. The early Renaissance critics in Italy studied poetry and rhetoric together at a time when neither was in perfect health. Both were being made to serve the purposes of flattery in small despotic courts where a premium was placed on fullness and roundness and ordered pomp of elocution. The Italian critics originated parallels and confusions which were perpetuated by the French Pléiade and the English theorists of Elizabeth's time. These had mainly to do with rules for ornamentation and devices for securing striking effects. The classical critics had confined the application of their rules and devices to prose oratory, all of them agreeing that poetry had a style of its own which could not be taught. Aristotle had written separate treatises on rhetoric and poetry, and had treated of artifices in connection with the first which he would have denied could be applied to the second. Cicero, Quintilian, and Tacitus had discussed oratory, not poetry, although Cicero had raised his art both in theory and in practice to an exalted position. In all this body of doctrine there had been gradually developed and clearly explained numerous elaborate methods, not excluding assonance and rhyme, by which prose could be heightened in effect, made more symmetrical, and given a greater appearance of finality. Now when the Italians established their identification between the poet and the orator they were able to offer to the poet handsome if questionable assistance.

Poetry in Europe did not become rhetorical over night. In England, for example, the sixteenth century saw eloquence occupying the second place; Sidney, Webb, and Daniel denied it access to the highest levels. Yet Elizabethan criticism is curiously concerned with classical figures and decorations so far as they are applicable to the style of poetry; and George Puttenham finds one great difference between prose and poetry to be that poetry is the more "eloquent and rhetorical." "The poets," says Puttenham, "were . . . from the beginning the best persuaders, and their eloquence the first rhetoric of the world." Ben Jonson was thoroughly familiar with the works of the classical and post-classical rhetoricians, and helped to establish a tradition of their sacred efficacy which outlived him a hundred years. It was not until Dryden's time, when the inspiration of the Elizabethans had in a way given out, and the full body of modern classical doctrine was being received in its most systematic form from France, that eloquence came to feel completely at home in poetry. Then it was that sophistication, easy expertness, and obvious perfection of finish became of paramount importance in the manner of verse. A consciously "poetic" style was created. Poets called themselves "virtuosos." The secrets of individuality became obscure, while the conventions became easier each year to follow. It became less and less desirable to state things naïvely; the circumlocution was cherished for its elegance and the antithesis for its effect of completeness and finality even when nothing final was being said. It came to be expected that everything, whether important or not, should be said importantly. There was something not quite genuine about the poetry which was the ultimate product of these tendencies. Poetry at its best leaves the impression that there was something in the poet's head which must have been said, whatever the words at hand. The poetry which first of all was eloquence gave no such impression. "Modern poetry," complained Coleridge in 1805, "is characterized by the poets' anxiety to be always striking. . . . Every line, nay, every word, stops, looks full in your face, and asks and begs for praise! . . . There are no distances, no perspectives, but all is in the foreground; and this is nothing but vanity. . . . The desire of carrying things to a greater height of pleasure and admiration than . . . they are susceptible of, is one great cause of the corruption of poetry."

Dryden was peculiarly fitted to lead the rhetorical grand march in English poetry. Possessing all of Ovid's fondness for exhortation and pleading, he possessed in addition unexampled powers of classifying and dividing his thoughts, hitting upon happy generalities, thumping out bold, new epithets, and accumulating stores of rhetorical energy as he proceeded to build his resounding rhyme. He carried eloquence as high as it can go in poetry, which is not the highest, since eloquence is committed to dealing with effects rather than forces, with novelties and ardors rather than with truth. Not always sympathetic in theory with what he once condemned as "Ciceronian, copious, florid, and figurative," he yet was inclined by nature and by precept towards those very qualities. He was inclined to favor a diction that was even and dignified at the expense perhaps of piquancy. "Our language is noble, full, and significant," says Neander towards the end of the *Essay of Dramatic Poesy*, "and I know not why he who is master of it may not clothe ordinary things in it as decently as the Latin, if he use the same diligence in his choice of words. *Delectus verborum origo est elo-*

quentiae. . . . One would think, *unlock the door,* was a thing as vulgar as could be spoken; and yet Seneca could make it sound high and lofty in his Latin:

> *Reserate clusos regii postes laris.*
> Set wide the palace gates."

Dryden was also inclined to fall into an exalted antithetical tone of formal address which frequently suited his needs but which in many cases has rendered him unattractive to later generations. That tone was indispensable in the heroic plays, which were supposed by no one to be real. It was of enormous advantage in *Absalom and Achitophel,* where it erected great public personages to their proper height and gave to satire a strange epic importance; as may best be seen in Achitophel's address to Absalom beginning:

> Auspicious prince! at whose nativity
> Some royal planet ruled the southern sky,
> Thy longing country's darling and desire,
> Their cloudy pillar, and their guardian fire,
> Their second Moses, whose extended wand
> Divides the seas and shows the promised land,
> Whose dawning day in every distant age
> Has exercised the sacred prophet's rage,
> The people's prayer, the glad diviner's theme,
> The young men's vision, and the old men's dream,
> Thee, Saviour, thee the nation's vows confess,
> And, never satisfied with seeing, bless.

But it is not in the heroic plays or in the poems on public affairs that Dryden's rhetorical vein has failed to meet with approval; it is rather in those narrative poems where nothing short of exquisite variety and delicacy is demanded. Here Dryden, instead of proving himself sensitive to the demands made by the successive turns of his story and the altered dispositions of his characters, continues to speak in the cadence of the pulpit or the bar. It is this rigidity of manner which has

estranged fastidious readers from the *Virgil* and the *Fables*.
The pliancy of Virgil and Chaucer is not Dryden's. Arcite's
dying speech to Emily is one of Chaucer's directest and most
intimate passages:

> Naught may the woful spirit in myn herte
> Declare o poynt of alle my sorwes smerte
> To yow, my lady, that I love most;
> But I biquethe the service of my gost
> To yow aboven every creature,
> Sin that my lyf may no lenger dure.
> Allas, the wo! allas, the peynes stronge,
> That I for yow have suffred, and so longe!
> Allas, the deeth! Allas, myn Emelye!
> Allas, departing of our compaignye!
> Allas, myn hertes quene! allas, my wyf!
> Myn hertes lady, endere of my lyf!
> What is this world? What asketh men to have?
> Now with his love, now in his colde grave
> Allone, with-outen any compaignye.
> Fare-wel, my swete fo! myn Emelye!
> And softe tak me in your armes tweye,
> For love of God, and herkneth what I seye.

Dryden's Arcite speaks as follows:

> No language can express the smallest part
> Of what I feel, and suffer in my heart,
> For you, whom best I love and value most;
> But to your service I bequeath my ghost;
> Which from this mortal body when untied,
> Unseen, unheard, shall hover at your side;
> Nor fright you waking, nor your sleep offend,
> But wait officious, and your steps attend.
> How I have loved, excuse my faltering tongue,
> My spirit's feeble, and my pains are strong:
> This I may say, I only grieve to die,
> Because I lose my charming Emily:

> To die, when Heaven had put you in my power,
> Fate could not choose a more malicious hour!
> What greater curse could envious Fortune give,
> Than just to die, when I began to live!
> Vain men, how vanishing a bliss we crave,
> Now warm in love, now withering in the grave!
> Never, O never more to see the sun!
> Still dark, in a damp vault, and still alone!
> This fate is common; but I lose my breath
> Near bliss, and yet not blest before my death.
> Farewell; but take me dying in your arms,
> 'Tis all I can enjoy of all your charms;
> This hand I cannot but in death resign;
> Ah, could I live! but while I live 'tis mine.
> I feel my end approach, and thus embraced,
> Am pleased to die; but hear me speak my last.

Dryden has no equal in prayers, objurgations, politic addresses, and speeches of defiance; he wears the robes that he has borrowed from the orator with a splendid assurance; his accents, although they too are borrowed, ring true. But in poetic narrative his limits are firmly fixed. When the shades of the Forum cannot be beckoned to help him rise, he does not rise. He has always the appearance of being strong, but as Lowell has pointed out, there is stiffness, and there is coldness, in his strength. Taking him altogether, stiffness must be accounted one of his shortcomings.

Under Charles I, secular painting and music had come to England to stay. Van Dyck and Henry Lawes, to name no others, had won the enduring favor of courtiers and poets; and the technique of each of their arts had rapidly become familiar. Interest in those arts continued to increase after the Restoration and through the age of Dryden. It became a commonplace of aesthetics that poetry, painting, and music are allied. Congreve said, "Poetry includes Painting and Music." English and French writers throughout the eighteenth century carried forward the double parallel, so that when Friedrich Schlegel wrote in 1798, "Die Poesie ist Musik für das innere Ohr, und Malerei für das innere Auge," although he implied something that had not been implied a hundred years before, he yet was dealing with what might have been called an axiom. This axiom was to bear new and strange fruit in nineteenth-century literature. Upon Augustan verse its influence had been purely formal; it had established a diction and a scheme of numbers.

The single parallel between poetry and painting was already venerable in Dryden's day. It had first been drawn in Aristotle's *Poetics;* Horace and Plutarch had given it momentum; and it had been sanctioned by virtually every European critic during the sixteenth and seventeenth centuries. In England the Elizabethan theorists had touched upon it, and it had been ratified in turn by Ben Jonson, Cowley, Davenant, and Hobbes. It was cherished during the Restoration and the early eighteenth century, but it eventually lost its meaning, so that when Lessing attacked it in 1766, employing some of the weapons which Du Bos had used half a century earlier, it could offer only partial resistance. The parallel had not borne along any constant body of dogma. Aristotle had merely remarked that the poet, being an imitator, is therefore like a painter or any other artist; and it had occurred to him to compare the characters and plot of a tragedy to the colors and outline of a painting. Horace had suggested that poems and pictures are alike with respect to the circumstances under which spectators should judge them; some appear better at a distance than when closely observed, some require more lighting than others, some should be seen many times to be appreciated at their full value. Plutarch had called painting dumb poetry, and poetry a speaking picture. Lessing objected to the whole theory on the ground that it had led to a freezing of the drama; in striving to remove ugliness and suffering from the surface of their art so as to render it capable of comparison with the still surfaces of other arts, dramatists had thrown away their pity and their terror, and nothing was left. A stoic hero is not interesting since he cannot suffer. The bearings of the theory on dramatic construction are of no concern in the present connection. The parallel is important here for its bearing on the question of Dryden's diction.

Dryden was thoroughly familiar with the doctrine of the parallel and with its history. He first quoted the "Ut pictura poësis" of Horace in his *Defence of an Essay of Dramatic Poesy* in 1668. His works are loaded with references to technical points in painting, showing that he considered himself acquainted with the practical problems of the art. He draws the parallel, with applications of his own, no fewer than twenty times; and often he extends it. In the *Life of Plutarch* history is compared with painting. In the preface to *Sylvae* the shading of cadences in a Pindaric ode is found to be like the shading of colors in a picture. In the *Discourse Concerning Satire* a satirical "character" is compared to a portrait on canvas. It is in the *Parallel of Poetry and Painting*, however, which Dryden prefixed to his translation of Du Fresnoy's *De Arte Graphica* in 1695, that he elaborates the parallel to its fullest extent and explains its bearings on poetic diction. "Expression," he writes, "and all that belongs to words, is that in a poem which colouring is in a picture. The colours well chosen in their proper places, together with the lights and shadows which belong to them, lighten the design, and make it pleasing to the eye. The words, the expressions, the tropes and figures, the versification, and all the other elegancies of sound, as cadences, turns of words upon the thought, and many other things, which are all parts of expression, perform exactly the same office both in dramatic and epic poetry. . . . In poetry, the expression is that which charms the reader, and beautifies the design, which is only the outlines of the fable. . . . Amongst the ancients, Zeuxis was most famous for his colouring; amongst the moderns, Titian and Correggio. Of the two ancient epic poets, who have so far excelled all the moderns, the invention and design were the particular talents of Homer . . . but the *dictio Virgiliana,* the expression of Virgil, his colouring, was incomparably the better; and in that I have always endeavoured to copy him."

Expression, elocution, diction, were cardinal points with Dryden; they absorbed the greater part of his effort in virtuoso-works like the *Virgil* and the *Fables.* To be going hand in hand with Virgil and Titian, the supreme colorists, was a supreme privilege in his eyes. Yet he labored with a complacency that one does not expect in a conscientious painter. And his results are what one does not find in a conscientious poet. For the parallel he drew between diction in poetry and color in painting was superficial. He conceived color in painting as a kind of splendid wash applied after the drawing is done. It is decoration. So with elocution in poetry; it is, "in plain English," says Dryden, "the bawd of her sister, the design . . . ; she clothes, she dresses her up, she paints her, she makes her appear more lovely than naturally she is; she procures the design, and makes lovers for her." That is, diction in poetry is a splendid wash that is spread over the framework of the plot. Words have no more function than the painter's pigments; the imagination is nothing but camel's hair.

The diction of the *Virgil* and the *Fables* is always vigorous and smooth, and at its best it is magnificent. But the poet has laid it on from without. At its best it is gilt rather than gold, and at its worst it is tinsel. The tinsel is what modern readers have found difficult to accept in Dryden. Dryden applied his elocution with a hasty hand, and one that rarely showed discrimination. He has been called the Rubens among English poets because of his lavishness and gusto; surely he can deserve the title for no other reason. He has boundless gusto; but he is almost incorrigibly vague. His vagueness is partly the result of a theory, partly the result of defective vision. The theory is the theory of idealized or generalized Nature. He makes much of it in the *Parallel,* where he shows that the poet and

the painter alike should form ideas of a perfect nature in which
all eccentricities are corrected and all vulgarities pared away.
The surface of a poem or a painting should be smooth and
beautiful and decorous; no word or phrase should be inserted
which it might strain the intelligence of elegant readers or
spectators to understand. Technical diction is barred for the
benefit of "those men and ladies of the first quality, who have
been better bred than to be too nicely knowing in the terms."
Here is the source of that generalizing frame of mind which
created the poetry and the painting of the next century; that
frame of mind which made Sir Joshua Reynolds most of what
he was as artist or as critic, but which eventually moved Ruskin
and Blake to awful wrath. "To generalize," said Blake, "is to
be an idiot." Dryden generalized. His feeling for details was
not keen, and his interest in them was nil. He used a broad
brush, and painted swiftly. He did not mind repeating himself.
He would have been pleased had he been called conventional.
Virgil had conventionalized Homer. Dryden conventionalized
Virgil. In the thirteenth book of the *Odyssey* Homer describes
the harbor in Ithaca where Odysseus landed:

> There is in the land of Ithaca a certain haven of Phorcys, the
> ancient one of the sea, and thereby are two headlands of sheer cliff,
> which slope to the sea on the haven's side and break the mighty
> wave that ill winds roll about, but within, the decked ships ride
> unmoored when once they have reached the place of anchorage.
> Now at the harbor's head is a long-leaved olive tree, and hard by is
> a pleasant cave and shadowy, sacred to the nymphs, that are called
> the Naiads. And therein are mixing bowls and jars of stone, and
> there moreover bees do hive. And there are great looms of stone,
> wherein the nymphs weave raiment of purple stain, a marvel to
> behold, and therein are waters welling evermore.*

This is the work of a poet who would always rather insert a
detail than leave it out. Virgil's description of the Libyan

* Translation of Butcher and Lang. Oxford, 1879.

harbor where Aeneas landed (I, 159ff.) is the work of a poet who cares somewhat less for the concrete than he does for the beautiful:

There, in a deep bay, is a roadstead, which an island forms by its jutting sides. On those sides every wave from the deep breaks, then parts into the winding hollows: on this hand and that are vast rocks, and twin cliffs frowning to heaven; and beneath their peaks, far and wide, the peaceful seas are silent. From the height hangs a background of waving forests, and a grove of dim and tangled shadows. Under the fronting crags is a rock-hung cave—haunted by nymphs—and, within it, sweet water and seats from the living rock.*

Dryden's account is the work of a man who altogether lacks fondness for particulars:

> Within a long recess there lies a bay;
> An island shades it from the rolling sea,
> And forms a port secure for ships to ride;
> Broke by the jutting land, on either side,
> In double streams the briny waters glide;
> Betwixt two rows of rocks a sylvan scene
> Appears above, and groves forever green:
> A grot is formed beneath, with mossy seats,
> To rest the Nereids, and exclude the heats.
> Down through the crannies of the living walls
> The crystal streams descend in murmuring falls.

In these "briny waters," "sylvan scenes," and "crystal streams" are the beginnings of the stereotyped Nature which graced the verse of England for at least two generations. No one can be held more strictly accountable for its vogue than Dryden, whose *Virgil* was read by every poet and served as a storehouse, like Pope's *Homer*, of cultivated phrases. Dryden supplied himself with a kind of natural furniture with which he could stock any house of verse that seemed to him bare. He laid in a fund

* Translation of John Jackson. Oxford, 1908.

of phrases with which he could expand any passage that seemed
to him curt. Thus in the fifth *Aeneid*, when Virgil writes

> ferit aethera clamor
> Nauticus, adductis spumant freta versa lacertis,

Dryden goes beyond him and whips the sea into a more suitable froth:

> With shouts the sailors rend the starry skies;
> Lashed with their oars, the smoky billows rise;
> Sparkles the briny main, and the vexed ocean fries.

One word in Chaucer's *Knight's Tale*, "huntyng," becomes four
lines in Dryden's *Palamon and Arcite:*

> A sylvan scene with various greens was drawn,
> Shades on the sides, and in the midst a lawn;
> The silver Cynthia, with her nymphs around,
> Pursued the flying deer, the woods with horns resound.

Three words in *The Flower and the Leaf*, "the briddes songe,"
become sixteen in Dryden:

> The painted birds, companions of the Spring,
> Hopping from spray to spray, were heard to sing.

Nor did young poets in the time of Queen Anne need to go
further than Dryden for models of periphrasis. The circumlocution, that pale ghost of the Roman epithet, that false pig-
ment bound to fade even before its poet-painter could apply
it, was everywhere in the later Dryden. In the *Aeneis*, an arrow
is a feathered death; in the *Georgics*, honey is liquid gold,
tenacious wax, ambrosial dew, gathered glue; and always the
fish are finny.

"Music and Poetry have ever been acknowledged Sisters,"
said Henry Purcell, the greatest English musician of Dryden's
time. He had the Greeks for his authority, as well as every
Englishman who had ever written either about music or about

poetry. The intimacy of the two arts may be said to have seemed self-evident to the Elizabethans, Gascoigne, Sidney, Puttenham, Daniel, Campion, and to writers of the seventeenth century. Davenant confessed that he had composed the cantos of his *Gondibert* with "so much heat . . . as to presume they might (like the works of *Homer* ere they were joined together and made a volume by the Athenian king) be sung at village feasts, though not to monarchs after victory, nor to armies before battle. For so (as an inspiration of glory into the one, and of valour into the other) did *Homer's* spirit, long after his body's rest, wander in musick about Greece." Sir William Temple derived music and poetry from a single source, a certain heat and agitation of the brain. The parallel had and always will have multitudinous phases, of which the opera and the song and the ballad suggest the most obvious. The connection which Dryden and others made between the two arts purported, however, to be a more subtle one than that which is involved in the accompaniment of words by music. It involved the arrangement of words in such a succession that they themselves should produce the effects of music. This is an important theory, which in different guises and in the hands of different men has been productive of genuine results; for no one will deny that the most moving poetry has been in some way musical. But it is not a simple theory, and it cannot be applied complacently or mechanically. In so far as Dryden and his followers applied it complacently and mechanically they failed to produce poetry that moves. As in the case of the analogy from painting they failed to perceive that it is only the color of a distinguished mind that can lend distinctive shades of beauty to a poem, so in the case of the analogy from music they were not always aware that it is only the tone of a composed imagination which can give important harmonies to verse. They relied upon a kind of musical attachment, both to furnish them with a constant pitch and to ring occasional changes suited to the sense.

"I do not hesitate to say," wrote Leigh Hunt in the preface to his *Story of Rimini* in 1816, "that Pope and the French school of versification have known the least on the subject of any poets perhaps that ever wrote. They have mistaken mere smoothness for harmony." This is perhaps the most absolute condemnation which the music of Augustan verse has received. But it is by no means the earliest. Hunt was capping a commonplace of criticism with his climax. Milton, in his preface to *Paradise Lost*, had categorically denied the possibility of true music to heroic verse, with its "jingling sound of like endings." Augustan poets and critics themselves had inveighed against "mere harmony." The Earl of Mulgrave, in his *Essay upon Poetry* of 1682, had observed that

> Number, and Rime, and that harmonious sound
> Which never does the Ear with harshness wound,
> Are necessary, yet but vulgar Arts.

The preface to that remarkable anthology, the *Poems on Affairs of State* (1697), had contained a robust protest against mere regularity: "There are a sort of men, who having little other merit than a happy chime, would fain fix the Excellence of Poetry in the smoothness of the Versification, allowing but little to the more Essential Qualities of a Poet, great Images, good sense, etc. Nay they have so blind a passion for what they excel in, that they will exclude all variety of numbers from English Poetry, when they allow none but Iambics, which must by an identity of Sound bring a very unpleasant satiety upon the Reader." Pope, in his *Essay on Criticism*, had disposed very neatly of

> these tuneful fools . . .
> Who haunt Parnassus but to please their ear.

And finally, Cowper in *Table Talk* had found Pope wanting because he

> Made poetry a mere mechanic art,
> And every warbler has his tune by heart.

So that from the beginning there had been no lack of consciousness that heroic verse tended towards monotony. Yet in general the claim of the couplet writers that their essential contribution to English poetry was in the way of harmony went without serious challenge for a good hundred years after Waller and Denham first "came out into the world," as the saying was, "forty thousand strong." It was precisely the music of the couplet, easy and continuous rather than intricate and intermittent, that won the couplet its prestige at the start.

> The relish of the Muse consists in rhyme;
> One verse must meet another like a chime.
> Our Saxon shortness hath peculiar grace
> In choice of words fit for the ending place:
> Which leave impression in the mind as well
> As closing sounds of some delightful bell.

So wrote Sir John Beaumont early in Dryden's century, in his *Concerning the True Form of English Poetry*. Not only delightful rhymes but flawless "numbers" as well became the aim of successive generations of versifiers. At the close of the sixteenth century in France, Malherbe, in his commentary on Desportes, had laid down rules for a kind of negative harmony, a mere smoothness, in French verse. The only distinction between prose and verse, said Malherbe, was to be *nombre*. "Numbers" became paramount both in England and in France. "The music of numbers . . . ," wrote Cowley, "almost without anything else, makes an excellent poet." The preface * to Joshua Poole's *English Parnassus* (1657), an enterprising forerunner of the handbooks on poetry which Bysshe, Gildon, and others were to issue in the eighteenth century, placed particular emphasis upon the "Symphony and Cadence" of poesy;

* Signed "J. D."

right accent, "like right time in Music, produces harmony";
rhyme is the "symphony and music of a verse." It became easy,
by Pope's time, to write in flawless cadence. Pope himself,
despising as he did the tuneful poetasters, tuned his own instrument with great pains. "The great rule of verse," he told
Spence, "is to be musical." Within their narrow range, it must
be granted, the Augustan poets were able to achieve a much
greater variety of tone than it now is the custom to recognize,
and it never is necessary to remind a knowing reader that the
best of these poets were anything but slaves to numbers. But
no one will deny that their range was narrow, and that their
energies were directed too much into the mechanics of their art.

Dryden, who was considered in his own day to be unrivaled
anywhere for diversity, and who must always be prized for his
genuine melody, lived also under the spell of numbers, believing in them with his whole mind and communicating his faith
with a proselyting zeal. Such monotony and such glibness as
he has result from the conviction which he never abandoned
that a poet's best powers should go into the perfecting of his
verse instrument. Aristotle had not denied to the music of the
flute and the lyre the capacity for imitating life, but he had
observed that the medium through which musical instruments
may function in their imitation of life is restricted to "harmony
and rhythm alone." Dryden, believing always that "versification and numbers are the greatest pleasures of poetry," tended
to cherish heroic verse as a musical instrument, and to work
for "harmony and rhythm alone." He thought that "well-
placing of words, for the sweetness of pronunciation, was not
known till Mr. Waller introduced it." He never doubted that
English could be rendered more liquid than it was, so that in
time it might even compete with Virgil's Latin and with Tasso's
Italian, "the softest, the sweetest, the most harmonious" of all
tongues, a tongue which seemed to him "to have been invented
for the sake of Poetry and Music." His desire was always for
more "even, sweet, and flowing" lines. His objection to English

consonants and monosyllables was that they obstructed the flow of verse. His fondness for latinistic polysyllables arose from the capacity which they seemed to have for "softening our uncouth numbers," for suppling the heroic line, and imparting to it an undulating grace. Circumlocutions recommended themselves to him and to all Augustans as much for their sound as for their ingenuity. "Periphrasis," Longinus told them, "tends much to sublimity. For, as in music the simple air is rendered more pleasing by the addition of harmony, so in language periphrasis often sounds in concord with a literal expression, adding much to the beauty of its tone—provided always that it is not inflated and harsh, but agreeably blended. Plato . . . takes . . . words in their naked simplicity and handles them as a musician, investing them with melody,—harmonizing them, as it were,—by the use of periphrasis."

Dryden was well aware at all times that it is possible to become smooth at the expense of more important qualities. "I pretend to no dictatorship," he confessed in his dedication of the *Aeneis*, "among my fellow poets, since, if I should instruct some of them to make well-running verses, they want genius to give them strength as well as sweetness." Dryden can rarely be said to have had the appearance of weakness, either in his *Virgil* or elsewhere. Yet it was just in his *Aeneis* that he surrendered most completely to the tyranny of numbers. His boundless admiration for Virgil's metrical and verbal genius led him to toy with strange devices. Recognizing clearly enough that Virgil's haunting melody was well beyond his reach, he endeavored to compensate the readers of his translation with obvious and sensational substitutes. For the effect of fluency and for "softening" his numbers he depended upon polysyllables; dissyllabic adjectives he simply could not resist, as witness heapy, spiry, sluicy, sweepy, forky, fainty, spumy, barmy, beamy, roofy, flaggy, ropy, dauby, piny, moony, chinky, pory, and hugy. Not finding a sufficient stock of long Latin words in English, he brought many of Virgil's abundant phrases

straight over, rendering them for what they appeared rather
than for what they meant. It is impossible to quote any one
passage from the *Aeneis* which will adequately reveal the
virtuoso temper in which Dryden composed it. But it is no
exaggeration to say that it shows better than any other Augustan
poem the effects of musical principles applied mechanically to
verse.

Pope, as is well known, had in mind two kinds of tuneful
fools when he was writing his *Essay on Criticism*.

> 'Tis not enough no harshness gives offense,
> The sound must seem an echo to the sense.

The second line of his couplet referred to the Dick Minims
who insisted that "imitative harmony," or "representative harmony," or "representative versification," as it was variously
called, was an indispensable ingredient in poetry. Dionysius of
Halicarnassus was perhaps the parent of the creed. Vida had
echoed him in his *De Arte Poetica,* and the dogma had settled
gradually down through various Italian and Spanish rhetoricians to Cowley, who in a note to his *Davideis* declared that
"the disposition of words and numbers should be such, as that
out of the order and sound of them, the things themselves may
be represented." The Earl of Roscommon, in his *Essay on
Translated Verse* (1684), wrote:

> The Delicacy of the nicest Ear
> Finds nothing harsh or out of Order there.
> Sublime or low, unbended or Intense,
> The sound is still an echo to the Sense.

Pope's lines, which derived no doubt from Roscommon's, gave
the doctrine especial currency, and to echo sense with sound
became a pleasant duty of versifiers. Pope himself told Spence
that he "followed the significance of the numbers, and the
adapting them to the sense, much more even than Dryden."
Later in the eighteenth century there grew up a rather fine

distinction between what Dr. Johnson called the imitation of
sound and the imitation of motion in verse. Daniel Webb, in
his *Observations on the Correspondence between Poetry and
Music* (1769), claimed that the use of words to represent
sounds was an inferior artifice, not comparable to the important
art of communicating emotion through cadences. James Beattie,
in his *Essay on Poetry and Music as They Affect the Mind*
(1776), followed Webb; and Dr. Johnson, in his lives of
Cowley and Pope, enunciated the distinction most forcibly of
all. At its highest, imitative harmony cannot be said to have
attained the dignity of an art. It was always a cheap and easy
artifice not to be associated with that mysterious power, possessed in abundance by Virgil, Shakespeare, Milton, and Wordsworth, which works its mighty will among the emotions through
sound *and* sense.

"The chief secret," confided Dryden in the preface to *Albion
and Albanius,* "is the choice of words; and, by this choice, I do
not here mean elegancy of expression, but propriety of sound,
to be varied according to the nature of the subject. Perhaps a
time may come when I may treat of this more largely out of
some observations which I have made from Homer and Virgil,
who, amongst all the poets, only understood the art of numbers." Dryden never treated of the matter on the scale he
promised, nor had he done so is it likely that his treatise would
have been profound. He was not only intrigued, he was baffled
by the harmonies of Virgil, whose verse, he observed in the
preface to *Sylvae,* "is everywhere sounding the very thing in
your ears, whose sense it bears." His own *Virgil* is nothing more
or less than an extensive proving-ground for imitative harmony. It is a huge temple of sound, not beautiful on the whole,
but sturdy and imposing. Dryden attempts in it to represent
both noises and movements, if Dr. Johnson's distinction may
be employed once more. The first he accomplished without
any subtlety at all. He is particularly fond of storms that

churn the seas and shake the shores. Our ears grow accustomed
to windy caverns echoing thunder. Time and again

> The impetuous ocean roars,
> And rocks rebellow from the sounding shores.

There are no gradations of violence in Dryden's weather, and
there is rarely more than an obvious and general fitness in
Dryden's language. He is much more cunning when he is representing movements of animals or persons. The fifth book of his
Aeneis is particularly noteworthy for this. The serpent which
issues from Anchises' tomb while Aeneas is praying before it
moves with writhing splendor:

> Scarce had he finished, when with speckled pride
> A serpent from the tomb began to glide;
> His hugy bulk on seven high volumes rolled;
> Blue was his breadth of back, but streaked with
>   scaly gold;
> Thus riding on his curls, he seemed to pass
> A rolling fire along, and singe the grass.
> More various colours through his body run
> Than Iris when her bow imbibes the sun.
> Betwixt the rising altars, and around,
> The sacred monster shot along the ground;
> With harmless play amidst the bowls he passed,
> And with his lolling tongue essayed the taste.
> Thus fed with holy food, the wondrous guest
> Within the hollow tomb retired to rest.

The funeral games are presented in plunging, roughly felici-
tous cadences. The boxers Dares and Entellus seem to strike
real blows and fall their actual heavy lengths in Dryden's
verse; and the young horsemen perform their evolutions without a metrical flaw:

> The second signal sounds, the troop divides
> In three distinguished parts, with three distin-
>   guished guides.

> Again they close, and once again disjoin;
> In troop to troop opposed, and line to line.
> They meet; they wheel; they throw their darts afar
> With harmless rage, and well-dissembled war:
> Then in a round the mingled bodies run;
> Flying they follow, and pursuing shun;
> Broken, they break; and, rallying, they renew
> In other forms the military shew.
> At last, in order, undiscerned they join
> And march together in a friendly line.
> And, as the Cretan labyrinth of old,
> With wandering ways and many a winding fold,
> Involved the weary feet, without redress,
> In a round error, which denied recess;
> So fought the Trojan boys in warlike play,
> Turned and returned, and still a different way.

Dryden's *Virgil* served Pope and many other successors as a sample-book wherein both representative cadences and representative words could be found. Pope's famous lines on Camilla in the *Essay on Criticism* come from Dryden's portrait of Camilla at the end of the seventh *Aeneis* more directly than from Virgil himself. Dryden's virago

> Outstripped the winds in speed upon the plain,
> Flew o'er the fields, nor hurt the bearded grain;
> She swept the seas, and as she skimmed along,
> Her flying feet unbathed on billows hung.

Pope's *Homer* owes much to the *Virgil* in this as well as in other departments. Gray's *Progress of Poesy* borrows Dryden's most sounding diction, as in the lines

> Now rolling down the steep amain,
> Headlong, impetuous, see it pour;
> The rocks and nodding groves rebellow to the roar.

From Cowley to Dick Minim, Dryden was the great example

of the imitative versifier, as he was also the great example of
most of what the Augustans believed to constitute a poet.

It seems never to have been suspected that Dryden was
speaking with his most communicative cadences in the satires
and the epistles. But nothing is more natural than that his best
music should be heard in the poems which he most meant. It
was when he was most oblivious of the problem of adapting
sound to sense, when he was fullest of the scorn or the admiration which he knew better than any other poet to express, that
he fell into his properest rhythms. These two utterly contemptuous lines from *Absalom and Achitophel*,

> A numerous host of dreaming saints succeed,
> Of the true old enthusiastic breed,

are perfectly tuned; the vowels and the consonants, whether or
not they were thoughtfully chosen, are steeped in disdain. This
gracious triplet from the poem *To the Memory of Mr. Oldham*,

> Thy generous fruits, though gathered ere their prime,
> Still shewed a quickness; and maturing time
> But mellows what we write to the dull sweets of rhyme,

is otherwise attuned, but its attunement too is perfect. The
acceleration in the second line speaks eagerness to praise whatever can be praised; the long, ripe cadence of the close breathes
consolation. Such passages are worth, as poetry, a thousand
Camillas and all the rocks that ever were heard rebellowing to
the roar. It is in them that the true fire of Dryden's genius will
be found to burn.

III

THE TRUE FIRE

THE ONLY qualities which Wordsworth could find in Dryden deserving to be called poetical were "a certain ardour and impetuosity of mind" and "an excellent ear." Whether or not Wordsworth stopped short of justice in his enumeration, he hit upon two virtues which are cardinal in Dryden, and confined himself with proper prudence to what in Dryden is more important than any other thing, his manner. His manner, embracing both an enthusiastic approach to any work and a technical dexterity in the performance of it, was constant. The channels through which his enthusiasm drove him were not always fitted for his passage, as we have been seeing; nor was his ease of motion always an advantage, inasmuch as his metrical felicity served at times only to accentuate his original error in choice of province. But when his material was congenial, and when he himself was thoroughly at home in his style, he was unexceptionable.

Dryden was most at home when he was making statements. His poetry was the poetry of statement. At his best he wrote without figures, without transforming passion. When Shakespeare's imagination was kindled his page thronged with images.

When Donne was most genuinely possessed by his theme he departed in a passionate search for conceits. When Dryden became fired he only wrote more plainly. The metal of his genius was silver, and the longer it was heated the more silver it grew. Nausicaa fell in love with Odysseus because the goddess Athene had shed a strange grace about his head and shoulders and made him seem more presentable than he was. No one can be impressed by Dryden who sees him in disguise. One must see him as he is: a poet of opinion, a poet of company, a poet of civilization. It is not to be inferred that he was without passion; but it is true that he never got outside himself. His passion was the passion of assurance. His great love was the love of speaking fully and with finality, his favorite subjects being persons and books.

Persons he treated from a variety of motives, but always with honest delight. He celebrated public heroes real or supposed, sketched the characters of men in high places and in low, addressed elaborate compliments to benefactors or friends, described minds and actions both in fact and in fable with an endless relish. Books he treated from a single motive, admiration for them and their makers. Dryden was above all things a literary man. His mind could best be energized by contact with other minds; he himself could become preoccupied most easily with other poets. He sat down with indubitable pleasure to write his addresses to Howard, to Roscommon, to Lee, to Motteux, his laments for Oldham and Anne Killigrew, his prologues and epilogues on Shakespeare, Jonson, and the present state of poetry. He was partial to literary history and literary parallels as subjects for poems, and no one in English, not even Pope, has done better criticism in meter. In verse as in prose he earned Dr. Johnson's judgment that "the criticism of Dryden is the criticism of a poet." Personalities, actions, ideas, and art were Dryden's best material.

But let it be said again, the story of Dryden's conquest of English poetry for the most part is the story not of his material but of his manner. It is the story of a poet who inherited a medium, perfected it by long manipulation, stamped it with his genius, and handed it on. That medium was heroic couplet verse.

The utility of the heroic couplet had been established for all time in England by Chaucer. Spenser, Marlowe, and Shakespeare had made various uses of it at the end of the sixteenth century, as had also the group of satirists which included Hall, Lodge, Marston, and Donne. It had grown more and more in favor during the early years of Dryden's century, and had begun to adapt itself to the type of mind which Dryden represents long before he became of age poetically. This adaptation involved a number of characteristics, of which the end-stop, the best known, was only one; the others were a conformation of the sentence-structure to the metrical pattern, a tendency towards polysyllables within the line, a tendency towards emphatic words at the ends of lines, and a frequent use of balance with pronounced caesura. The end-stop, and the modification of sentence-structure to suit the length of measure, made for pointedness if not for brevity, and provided in the couplet a ratiocinative unit which served admirably as the basis for declarative or argumentative poems. The polysyllables made for speed and flexibility, and encouraged a latinized, abstract vocabulary. The insistence upon important words for the closing of lines meant that the sense was not likely to trail off or be left hanging; and the use of balance promoted that air of spruce finality with which every reader of Augustan verse has long been familiar.

Just when and in whom the couplet first reached a stage something like this is a matter that has not been settled. In France a similar development can be traced back pretty clearly to Malherbe, whose formula for perfect rhetorical poetry called, among other things, for a caesura which would cut every verse into two equal parts. "As for the pauses," said Dryden in the dedication of the *Aeneis*, "Malherbe first brought them into

French within this last century; and we see how they adorn
their Alexandrines." No formula like Malherbe's was contrived
in England, but the first half of the seventeenth century there
saw couplet verse invaded and conquered by the principles just
specified. Credit for the innovation has been given to a number
of different poets, none of whom can be said to deserve it
wholly. Edward Fairfax, the translator of Tasso's *Godfrey of
Bulloigne* (1600), is the earliest whom Dryden himself named
among the reformers of English versification; in the preface
to the *Fables* Waller is declared the "poetical son" of Fairfax.
The stanzas of the *Tasso* end in couplets which often have the
accent of the Augustans, but which more often have it not,
tending less towards a monotony of balance than towards a
monotony of series or "triplets" of adjectives and nouns.
Michael Drayton at various times during his long career wrote
couplets which come very near to having Dryden's ring; his
England's Heroical Epistles (1597) afford the best examples.
Drayton was a good Elizabethan, which suggests that there
were many Elizabethans who could write Augustan couplets.
Spenser did so in his *Mother Hubberds Tale;* the closing
couplets of Shakespeare's sonnets are curiously like Dryden and
Pope, as here:

> For we, which now behold these present days,
> Have eyes to wonder, but lack tongues to praise.

The Elizabethan satirists, particularly Joseph Hall, whose
Virgidemiarum appeared in 1597-8, spoke occasionally in clear
tones, though in general their expression was uneven, and such
felicity as they permitted themselves to achieve was not contagious. Ben Jonson's influence on seventeenth-century poetry
was immense, and he was in large part responsible for the new
form of heroic verse; but his chief influence was rather upon
diction than upon meter. Sir John Beaumont, who died in
1627, wrote his *Bosworth Field* and other poems in couplets
which not only for their own time but for any time are models

of sweetness and clarity. The *Metamorphoses* of George Sandys (1621-6) was for a hundred years after its publication a landmark to all who would trace poetical genealogies. Dryden called Sandys "the best versifier of the former age" in the preface to the *Fables,* and Pope paired him with Dryden's Fairfax as a "model to Waller" in versification. The couplets of Sandys were what Drayton called them, "smooth-sliding," but they were neither as uniform nor as brisk as the new poetry was to require. Milton wrote four of his Cambridge poems in couplets which are not significant here. The speech of the Genius in *Arcades* begins like one of Dryden's prologues:

> Stay, gentle swains, for though in this disguise,
> I see bright honour sparkle through your eyes;

but it does not continue in that vein.

It was Waller who the Augustans themselves, from Dryden on, declared had been the parent of their line. Francis Atterbury, in his preface to the 1690 edition of Waller's poems, gave a detailed account of what he believed Waller's innovations to have been. "Before his time," said Atterbury, "men rhymed indeed, and that was all; as for the harmony of measure, and that dance of words which good ears are so much pleased with, they knew nothing of it. Their poetry then was made up almost entirely of monosyllables; which, when they come together in any cluster, are certainly the most harsh, untuneable things in the world. . . . Besides, their verses ran all into one another, and hung together, throughout a whole copy, like the hooked atoms that compose a body in Descartes. There was no distinction of parts, no regular stops, nothing for the ear to rest upon. . . . Mr. Waller removed all these faults, brought in more polysyllables, and smoother measures, bound up his thoughts better, and in a cadence more agreeable to the nature of the verse he wrote in; so that wherever the natural stops of that were, he contrived the little breakings of his sense so as to fall in with them; and, for that reason, since the stress of our verse lies commonly upon the last syllable, you will hardly ever find him using a word of no force there." Atterbury was inventing the chaotic state of English verse before Waller, and he attributed innovations to Waller that really should be credited to Marlowe, Sandys, and others; yet he analyzed with particular delicacy the salient points in which Dryden's versification differs, for instance, from Donne's.

Cowley's *Davideis* was composed in heroic couplets which could teach Dryden nothing after Waller and Denham. Cowley handled this measure less felicitously than he handled any other; the *Davideis* does not chime. Cleveland's political poems, which Dryden must have read before the Restoration, were not smooth or sweet, but they had another quality which was important for Dryden, the quality of momentous directness. Such pauseless lines as these,

> Encountering with a brother of the cloth,
>
> Who used to string their teeth upon their belt,
>
> Religion for their seamstress or their cook,

gave Dryden his metrical cue on more than one occasion.

Dryden wrote altogether, over a period of exactly fifty years, some thirty thousand heroic couplets. The stream of English verse, flowing through him thus for half a century, both sustained him and was sustained by him. His achievement was to make of it a strong yet light vehicle for miscellaneous loads, a medium for the poetry of statement. He learned to say anything in it that he liked, high or low, narrow or broad. Earlier in the century John Selden had written in his *Table Talk:* " 'Tis ridiculous to speak, or write, or preach in verse. As 'tis good to learn to dance, a man may learn to leg, learn to go handsomely; but 'tis ridiculous for him to dance when he should go." Dryden showed how one might speak, and write, and preach, and how one might "go" in verse. Verse became for him a natural form of utterance. "Thoughts, such as they are, come crowding in so fast upon me," he wrote in the preface to the *Fables*, "that my only difficulty is to choose or to reject, to run them into verse, or to give them the other harmony of prose; I have so long studied and practiced both, that they are grown into a habit, and become familiar to me."

Dryden's style was a constant delight to his contemporaries because it was unfailingly fresh; new poems by Mr. Dryden meant in all likelihood new cadences, new airs. He was perpetually fresh because he perpetually studied his versification. He perhaps was not a laborious student of metrics; the *Prosodia* for which he said in the dedication of the *Aeneis* he had long ago collected the materials, but which he never published, might have been anything but exhaustive. Yet there can be no question that he experimented freely and was always sensitive to novel demands that novel subjects might make upon his medium. He generally knew beforehand what effects he should gain; and he had a happy faculty for hitting at once upon rhythms which would secure those effects. His was not, like Doeg's, "a blundering kind of melody." "There is nobody but knows," declared John Oldmixon in 1728, "that it was impossible for Dryden to make an ill verse, or to want an apt and musical word, if he took the least care about it." He was always conscious that rhyme was a handicap, but he accepted it without prolonged protest; and within the bounds imposed by it he obtained a surprising diversity of accent. He defended rhyming plays against Sir Robert Howard in the dedication of *The Rival Ladies*, in the *Essay of Dramatic Poesy*, and in the *Defence of the Essay*, taking occasion by the way to declare against the inversions and the strained diction into which the exigencies of rhyme tend to force even good poets. But in the prologue to *Aureng-Zebe* he repudiated his "long-loved Mistress"; in both the epistle to Roscommon and the epistle to Sir Godfrey Kneller he damned her as a barbaric fraud foisted upon Europe by the Goths and Vandals; and in the dedication of the *Aeneis* he admitted that "Rhyme is certainly a constraint even to the best poets."

Dryden did not always make his principles of versification clear, nor did he ever follow any of them scrupulously. A good case is that of the monosyllables. The Elizabethans had not been moved to inveigh against monosyllables. "The more . . . that you use," said Gascoigne, "the truer Englishman you shall seem." But the new versifiers found them clogging, and spoke against them with great frequency. Dryden was especially resentful of "our old Teuton monosyllables." Yet he employed the "low words," as Pope called them, time and again with excellent effect. He began his *Aeneis* with ten of them:

> Arms and the man I sing, who, forced by fate;

and some of his most telling passages have twenty in succession. He told the young poet Walsh that he was often guilty of them "through haste." It should be understood that his quarrel was only with monosyllabic lines that are heavy with consonants, like this from Creech's *Lucretius:*

> Thee, who hast light from midst thick darkness brought,

or this from Ben Jonson's poem to Camden,

> Men scarce can make that doubt, but thou canst teach.

He gladly allowed such open, liquid lines as this from the same poem of Jonson's:

> All that I am in arts, all that I know.

Of course, both easy polysyllabic and difficult monosyllabic lines can be effective in ways of their own; no more compendious example of which could be cited than these two from Hamlet's dying speech:

> Absent thee from felicity awhile,
> And in this harsh world draw thy breath in pain.

Dryden was probably not always aware of the extent to which he relied upon mechanical devices. Alliteration seems to have been instinctive with him, as indeed it is with most rapid and powerful English writers. It played an integral part in his versification, assisting both sense and sound. Scarcely ten consecutive lines can be found in him wherein alliteration is not conspicuous. It serves a variety of purposes. In satire it is either corrosive in its contemptuousness:

> In *f*riendship *f*alse, implacable in hate,
> *R*esolved to *r*uin or to *r*ule the state;

or simply derisive and pelting:

> And *p*ricks up his *p*redestinating ears,
>
> And *p*opularly *p*rosecutes the *p*lot.

In ratiocination it quietly weaves phrases into a firm texture of thought:

> This general worship is to *p*raise and *p*ray,
> One *p*art to *b*orrow *b*lessings, one to *p*ay;
> And when *f*rail nature slides into o*ff*ense,
> The sa*cr*ifice for *cr*imes is penitence.
> Yet, since the e*ff*ects of providence, we *f*ind,
> Are variously dispensed to humankind;
> That *v*ice triumphs, and *v*irtue suffers here,
> (A *b*rand that sovereign justice cannot *b*ear;)
> Our reason prompts us to a future state,
> The last appeal *f*rom *f*ortune and *f*rom *f*ate.

In narrative it lends luxuriance and momentum where it does not lend speed:

> Down fell the beauteous youth; the gaping wound
> *G*ushed out a crimson *s*tream, and *s*tained the *g*round.
> His *n*odding *n*eck reclines on his white breast,
> Like a *f*air *f*lower, in *f*urrowed *f*ields oppressed
> By the keen share; or *p*oppy on the *p*lain,
> Whose *h*eavy *h*ead is overcharged with rain.

> Dis*d*ain, *d*espair, and *d*eadly *v*engeance *v*owed,
> Drove Nisus *h*eadlong on the *h*ostile crowd.

Dryden's gift for adapting his rhythmical emphasis to his meaning amounted to genius. Alliteration, effective rhyme, antithesis, and the use of polysyllables were only auxiliaries to that. It was that which gave him rapidity without the appearance of haste and flexibility without the loss of strength. Bound by the laws of a syllabic system of versification and condemned to a narrow metrical range, he succeeded in manipulating his measures so that he could speak· directly and easily yet with dignity. He was more than a believer in mere variety of accent, though he stressed that too as early as the *Essay of Dramatic Poesy,* where Neander observed: "Nothing that does *perpetuo tenore fluere,* run in the same channel, can please always. 'Tis like the murmuring of a stream, which not varying in the fall, causes at first attention, at last drowsiness. Variety of cadences is the best rule." Dryden was a believer in significant variety of accent. Pope, in a letter to his friend Henry Cromwell, recognized three places within the heroic line where pauses might come: after the fourth, after the fifth, and after the sixth syllables. Dryden knew no limits of the kind. The freedom of blank verse seems to have been in his thoughts. His pauses come anywhere; and often they do not come at all, as in these lines:

> Drawn to the dregs of a democracy,
> Of the true old enthusiastic breed,
> To the next headlong steep of anarchy,
> But baffled by an arbitrary crowd.

He kept himself free to distribute his emphasis where the sense demanded it. The result was a speaking voice. Someone seems actually to be reciting *Absalom and Achitophel:*

> Others thought kings an useless heavy load,
> Who cost too much, and did too little good;

> They were for laying honest David by,
> On principles of pure good husbandry.

And the voice in this prologue is plainly to be heard:

> Lord, how reformed and quiet are we grown,
> Since all our braves and all our wits are gone! . . .
> France, and the fleet, have swept the town so clear
> That we can act in peace, and you can hear. . . .
> 'Twas a sad sight, before they marched from home,
> To see our warriors in red waistcoats come,
> With hair tucked up, into our tiring-room.
> But 'twas more sad to hear their last adieu:
> The women sobbed, and swore they would be true;
> And so they were, as long as e'er they could,
> But powerful guinea cannot be withstood,
> And they were made of playhouse flesh and blood.

Everywhere Dryden's personal presence can be felt. Pope lurks behind his poetry; Dryden stands well forward, flush with his page and speaking with an honest voice if not always an honest heart.

The most speaking lines in the last passage quoted are the two which close their respective triplets. Dryden's triplets and Alexandrines have been sources of worry to critics and of satisfaction to enemies. Inheriting the triplet from Chapman and Waller, the Alexandrine from Spenser and Hall, and the two in combination from Cowley, he took these devices to himself and made them into important metrical instruments. He did not always succeed in rendering them organic to his verse structure; often they were excrescences. The Earl of Rochester was thinking of this when he spoke of Dryden's "loose slattern muse," and Tom Brown, that excellent fooler, made fine fun of the laureate's long lines. Swift was angered at the currency which Dryden had given to triplets and Alexandrines, and Dr. Johnson condemned such of them as were not justified by the general tenor of the passages in which they occurred. Macaulay disposed of them as "sluttish." Dryden put them to various uses. Sometimes his Alexandrines and fourteeners served little or no purpose, being most likely unconscious echoes of the French heroic line. At other times they contributed a flourish of burlesque grandeur, as in the epistle to John Driden of Chesterton:

> But Maurus sweeps whole parishes, and peoples every grave.

Elsewhere, and particularly in the translations, they were calculated to yield an effect of splendor. Dryden counted on them, when he was putting Lucretius into English, to represent what he called "the perpetual torrent of his verse." A passage in the dedication of the *Aeneis* described how they were used in that work: "Spenser has . . . given me the boldness to make use sometimes of his Alexandrine line. . . . It adds a certain majesty to the verse, when it is used with judgment, and stops the sense from overflowing into another line. . . . I take another license in my verses: for I frequently make use of triplet rhymes, and for the same reason, because they bound the sense. And therefore I generally join the two licenses together, and make the last verse of the triplet a Pindaric; for, besides the majesty which it gives, it confines the sense within the barriers of three lines, which would languish if it were lengthened into four. Spenser is my example for both these privileges of English verses; and Chapman has followed him in his translation of Homer. Mr. Cowley has given in to them after both; and all succeeding writers after him. I regard them now as the *Magna Charta* of heroic poetry, and am too much an Englishman to lose what my ancestors have gained for me. Let the French and Italians value themselves on their regularity; strength and elevation are our standard." They were not always used with judgment in the *Virgil*, their frequency being a root of weakness rather than of strength. At certain junctures, in the *Virgil* and elsewhere, they discharged Dryden's accumulated poetic energy in passages that partook of the nature of the ode.*

There remains to be pointed out a function of the triplet which is different from the rest and which has not been emphasized before. It is a function that may have been discerned in the prologue from which the last quotation was made; it operates everywhere in the occasional poems; it consists in the supplying of a colloquial, first-hand note. The third line of a triplet in Dryden frequently represents a lowering of the voice to the level of parenthesis or innuendo, as in the *Epilogue Spoken at the Opening of the New House, March 26, 1674:*

> A country lip may have the velvet touch;
> Tho' she's no lady, you may think her such;
> A strong imagination may do much;

or in the prologue to *Troilus and Cressida:*

> And that insipid stuff which here you hate,
> Might somewhere else be called a grave debate;
> Dulness is decent in the Church and State;

or in the prologue to *Love Triumphant:*

> The fable has a moral, too, if sought;
> But let that go; for, upon second thought,
> He fears but few come hither to be taught.

Also, triplets closing with Alexandrines frequently succeed in imparting a compendiousness to compliment, as in the epistle to Congreve:

> Firm Doric pillars found your solid base;
> The fair Corinthian crowns the higher space;
> Thus all below is strength, and all above is grace.

> In him all beauties of this age we see,
> Etherege his courtship, Southerne's purity,
> The satire, wit, and strength of Manly Wycherley.

* See Chapter VI.

This is your portion; this your native store;
Heaven, that but once was prodigal before,
To Shakespeare gave as much; she could not give him more.

Lines like these represent Dryden's metrical license at its safest and best; he could not always be trusted to employ it sanely when describing storms of Nature or of passion in Virgil and Lucretius; when he used it to stamp a statement of his own, as here, he was well within his province and could not go wrong.

A triplet-and-fourteener which appears in the *Cymon and Iphigenia* leads the way to another metrical device of which Dryden pretended to be fond. The triplet runs:

The fanning wind upon her bosom blows,
To meet the fanning wind the bosom rose;
The fanning wind and purling streams continue her repose.

This is one of those "turns" which Dryden in the *Discourse Concerning Satire* said he had been led by Sir George Mackenzie twenty years before to study in Waller, Denham, Spenser, Tasso, Virgil, and Ovid. A "turn" involved the musical repetition of a phrase with variations of meaning. Dryden had a good deal to say about "turns" from time to time, but in general he thought them below his dignity, and worthy of no greater geniuses than those of Ovid and the French, or of such minor versifiers of the day as pleased themselves with translating Virgil's fourth Georgic and wringing all the possible echoes out of the name Eurydice. The sleeping Iphigenia occurred to him as a pretty enough subject upon which to try one of the metrical toys. He tried few others, though in general he was perhaps too fond of playing with words for their own sake, so that he exposed himself to the censure of Luke Milbourne, to name an enemy, and John Oldmixon, to name an admirer, for "turning the Epick style into Elegiack." Virgil's turn in the seventh Eclogue,

Fraxinus in silvis pulcherrima, pinus in hortis,
Populus in fluviis, abies in montibus altis;
Saepius at si me, Lycida formose, revisas,
Fraxinus in silvis cedat tibi, pinus in hortis,

he rendered thus:

The towering ash is fairest in the woods;
In gardens pines, and poplars by the floods;
But, if my Lycidas will ease my pains,
And after visit our forsaken plains,
To him the towering ash shall yield in woods,
In gardens pines, and poplars by the floods.

"He was an improving writer to the last," said Congreve. What Dryden improved in most steadily was the texture of his verse. The difference in respect of texture between the poem on the death of Hastings and *The Hind and the Panther*, to go no further, is enormous; that the author of one should have grown out of the author of the other seems now a kind of miracle. The transformation, which was gradual, involved the discovery and the exploitation of a fundamental rhythm, and it progressed with the adaptation of that rhythm, through modification or enrichment, to widely varying themes. Dryden's metrical evolution began with his earliest verses and proceeded through the plays, through the poems on public affairs, and through the translations.

He scored no decisive technical triumph before the period of the heroic plays. The early poems, distinguished though they are in spots, and approaching Dryden's best manner though they do at times, cannot be supposed to have encouraged the poet to believe he had caught his stride. The first one, the elegy on Hastings (1649), was done, it must be remembered, before he was eighteen. Metrically it was chaos. Gray remarked to Mason that it seemed the work of a man who had no ear and might never have any. Gray probably had in mind such lines as those addressed to Hastings's "virgin-widow":

> Transcribe the original in new copies; give
> Hastings o' th' better part; so shall he live
> In's nobler half; and the great grandsire be
> Of an heroic divine progeny.

There is nothing of the future Dryden there. But in the preceding outburst against old age there is an enthusiasm which warms the verse; and certain other lines have a readiness to run:

> But hasty winter, with one blast, hath brought
> The hopes of autumn, summer, spring, to naught.
> Thus fades the oak i' th' sprig, i' th' blade the corn;
> Thus without young, this Phoenix dies, new-born.

The *Heroic Stanzas* appeared ten years later, after what must have been a period of frequent experiments in more than one kind of meter. The poems to John Hoddesdon (1650) and to Honor Dryden (1655) had not told of any advance. But in this poem, as in the *Annus Mirabilis* eight years later still, Dryden wielded with positive assurance a mighty line which was much his own. Spenser in *Colin Clout,* Sir John Davies, Donne, and Ben Jonson had written heroic stanzas before Davenant; and Davenant, wishing to adapt his utterance "to a plain and stately composing of music," had interwoven his long-falling, leaden-stepping lines to form what Dryden and Soame called "the stiff formal style of *Gondibert.*" But no elegiac quatrains before 1659 had contained verses more emancipated or more confident than these on Cromwell:

> His grandeur he derived from Heaven alone;
>   For he was great ere fortune made him so:
> And wars, like mists that rise against the sun,
>   Made him but greater seem, not greater grow.

> By his command we boldly crossed the line,
>   And bravely fought where southern stars arise;
> We traced the far-fetched gold into the mine,
>   And that which bribed our fathers made our prize.

His ashes in a peaceful urn shall rest;
  His name a great example stands to show,
How strangely high endeavors may be blessed,
  Where piety and valour jointly go.

Each quatrain developed a proposition of its own, and usually, as in the first two which have been quoted, a distinction was stated. It is interesting to see Dryden's earliest fluency coming to him in the exercise of ratiocination. The heroic stanza with its leisurely authority continued to fascinate him even when he resorted to other forms. His next poem, *Astraea Redux* (1660), started off with twenty-eight lines sharply divided into groups of four and developing seven distinct propositions. The brief series of complimentary poems which began with the *Astraea* were quickened and sweetened by the influence of Waller, although Dryden in them did not attain to his eventual flow. The heroic stanza motif was quickly silenced, but no other motif was as yet distinguishable. The close of the *Astraea* had what must have seemed a new sort of drive; and passages like the following from the poem *To His Sacred Majesty, a Panegyric on His Coronation* (1661), must have struck the ears even of Waller's readers as novel in their strength and smoothness:

The grateful choir their harmony employ,
Not to make greater, but more solemn joy;
Wrapped soft and warm your name is sent on high,
As flames do on the wings of incense fly;
Music herself is lost, in vain she brings
Her choicest notes to praise the best of kings;
Her melting strains in you a tomb have found,
And lie like bees in their own sweetness drowned.
He that brought peace, and discord could atone,
His name is music of itself alone.

In the poem *To My Lord Chancellor* (1662) there were lines somewhat similar on the subject of Charles I, "our setting sun." Dryden in them is seen to be at least partially a master of his medium; his voice is becoming a more important instrument than his pen. The poem *To The Lady Castlemaine, Upon Her Incouraging His First Play* (c. 1663) both began and ended with skillfully modulated tones and happily emphatic stresses; the *Verses to Her Highness the Duchess* (1665), prefixed to the first edition of *Annus Mirabilis,* rode pleasantly on the wings of Waller:

> While, from afar, we heard the cannon play,
> Like distant thunder on a shiny day.

Certain of the stanzas in *Annus Mirabilis,* as has been said, struggled not unsuccessfully to surmount the rubbish that lay about them:

> The moon shone clear on the becalmèd flood,
>   Where, while her beams like glittering silver play,
> Upon the deck our careful General stood,
>   And deeply mused on the succeeding day.
>
> That happy sun, said he, will rise again,
>   Who twice victorious did our navy see;
> And I alone must view him rise in vain,
>   Without one ray of all his star for me.
>
> Yet like an English general will I die,
>   And all the ocean make my spacious grave;
> Women and cowards on the land may die,
>   The sea's a tomb that's proper for the brave.
>
> Restless he passed the remnants of the night,
>   Till the fresh air proclaimed the morning nigh;
> And burning ships, the martyrs of the fight,
>   With paler fires beheld the eastern sky.

"The composition and fate of eight-and-twenty dramas include too much of a poetical life to be omitted," remarked Dr. Johnson. The dramas which Dryden wrote in verse were of the first importance in his metrical development; for it was in them that he became fully aware of the energy which is latent in the heroic couplet, and it was in them that he cut the rhythmical pattern which was to serve him during the remainder of his career. He recognized that a writer of verse plays had first of all to write swiftly; for "all that is said is supposed to be the effect of sudden thought; which . . . admits . . . not anything that shows remoteness of thought, or labour in the writer." He learned to adjust his load while the load was light. Some of his plays were largely dependent for their success upon the quality of their meter, or perhaps the quantity. Writing them with a flesh-and-blood audience, an actually hearing audience in mind, he could not be inattentive to the claims of the ear. His dramatic triumph, such as it was, was a triumph chiefly of the ear. He won his way to fame through sheer metrical genius, this metrical genius first manifesting itself in the heroic plays.

> You in the people's ears began to chime,
> And please the Town with your successful Rime,

grudgingly admitted Shadwell in *The Medal of John Bayes*.

The heroic plays, generally speaking, were of manifold origin; they derived from English tragicomedy, from French romance, and from French tragedy. Their verse too derived from more than a single source, perhaps; but Corneille stands forth as a great progenitor of English heroic versifiers for the stage. Dryden adduced "the example of Corneille and some French poets" when in the essay *Of Heroic Plays* he was explaining the pieces which Davenant had produced under the Commonwealth; and Dryden himself knew a good deal about the French dramatist, both as critic and as poet. He found in Corneille a vein of oratory which was effective for verse no less than for drama; like Corneille he had a fondness for stage argument and stoic declamation, and from him he learned the value of an obvious, unbroken melody. Dryden was fascinated

at an early point by rhymed argumentation. He spoke in the
Essay of Dramatic Poesy of "the quick and poynant brevity"
of repartee; "and this," he said, "joined with the cadency and
sweetness of the rhyme, leaves nothing in the soul of the hearer
to desire." He employed the give-and-take of rhymed repartee
chiefly in the heroic plays, but strains of it also appeared amidst
his blank verse and his prose, at such times as he could not
resist the temptation to chime. Dryden was fascinated again
by the possibilities of mere rhyme, possibilities which are naturally very great in English. The heroic plays were staged with
an elaborate musical accompaniment, and it is certain that the
audiences accepted the verse as only a portion of a greater
ensemble. As the authors of *The Censure of the Rota* less
charitably put it, "An heroic poem never sounded so nobly, as
when it was heightened with shouts, and clashing of swords;
. . . drums and trumpets gained an absolute dominion over
the mind of the audience (the ladies, and female spirits); . . .
Mr. Dryden would never have had the courage to have ventured on a Conquest had he not writ with the sound of drum
and trumpet." *The Indian Emperor* (1665) made the first great
impact upon English ears. *The Wild Gallant* (1663), in prose,
and *The Rival Ladies* (1664), in glib Fletcherian blank verse,
had contained only a few perfunctory couplets; and *The Indian
Queen* (1664), almost entirely the work of Sir Robert Howard, had lacked rhythmical energy although it was composed
throughout in couplets or quatrains.

The Indian Emperor must have sounded suddenly and
loudly like a gong. Dryden broke forth in it with consummate
rhetoric, consummate bluff, and consummate rhyme. The secret
of the spell which it cast lay in its pounding regularity of
cadence and its unfailing emphasis upon the rhyme even at the
expense of sense and natural word order. Whether a scene is
being sketched from Nature after the manner of some Latin
poet or whether a nervous argument is being thrummed out of
Dryden's own vocabulary, the accents never cease to pound

or the rhymes to ring. Montezuma demands of his son Guyomar:

> I sent thee to the frontiers; quickly tell
> The cause of thy return; are all things well?

Guyomar describes the appearance of the Spanish vessels:

> I went, in order, sir, to your command,
> To view the utmost limits of the land;
> To that sea-shore where no more world is found;
> But foaming billows breaking on the ground;
> Where, for a while, my eyes no object met,
> But distant skies that in the ocean set;
> And low-hung clouds that dipt themselves in rain
> To shake their fleeces on the earth again.
> At last, as far as I could cast my eyes
> Upon the sea, somewhat methought did rise,
> Like bluish mists, which still appearing more,
> Took dreadful shapes, and moved towards the shore.

There is not a single departure here from the iambic norm; the diversity which Dryden had already achieved in the early complimentary poems is thrown away. But we are compensated by a more powerful ground-rhythm than has been heard before. This metrical plunge and bound was the discovery and glory of the heroic plays. It was exactly this which was to give spring to Augustan heroic verse. The theological disputation between Montezuma and the Christian priests in Act V is a good example of Dryden's controversial rhyme; and the second scene of the first act sees Cydaria and Cortez falling in love in heroic quatrains:

> *Cydaria.* My father's gone, and yet I cannot go;
> Sure I have something lost or left behind!
>   (*Aside*)
> *Cortez.* Like travellers who wander in the snow,
> I on her beauty gaze till I am blind.
>   (*Aside*)

The Maiden Queen (1667), in excellent prose and decent blank verse, admitted a few rhymes which were out of place and in no way impressive. *Tyrannic Love* (1669) brought back the old rage. In the preface to the printed version of 1670 Dryden described the effect which he believed his verse to have: "By the harmony of words we elevate the mind to a sense of devotion, as our solemn music, which is inarticulate poesy, does in churches." In the second act there is a doctrinal war between St. Catherine and Maximin the Tyrant, and in general there is a vast deal of splendid absurdity.

The two parts of *The Conquest of Granada* (1670), which drew Dryden out to his fullest length, are justly famous. They are *The Indian Emperor* in full and double bloom. It is unnecessary to quote more than a dozen lines: four to show the hero and the heroine in give-and-take:

> *Almahide.* My light will sure discover those who talk—
> Who dares to interrupt my private walk?
> *Almanzor.* He, who dares love, and for that love must die,
> And, knowing this, dares yet love on, am I;

and eight to illustrate a new cumulative energy in Dryden which demands *enjambement* and elevates the verse to another level of music: Almanzor replies to Lyndaraxa, who has made advances,

> Fair though you are
> As summer mornings, and your eyes more bright
> Than stars that twinkle in a winter's night;
> Though you have eloquence to warm and move
> Cold age, and praying hermits, into love;
> Though Almahide with scorn rewards my care;
> Yet, than to change, 'tis nobler to despair.
> My love's my soul; and that from fate is free;
> 'Tis that unchanged and deathless part of me.

There is a rise here, with no corresponding fall, that denotes new technical powers. The next rhyming play, or "opera," as it was called, *The State of Innocence,* carried on further experiments in architectural verse.* Triplets and Alexandrines added embroidery to the old pattern, which perhaps now seemed a little plain. Raphael tells Adam of the home he is to find in Paradise:

> A mansion is provided thee, more fair
> Than this, and worthy Heaven's peculiar care;
> Not framed of common earth, nor fruits, nor flowers
> Of vulgar growth, but like celestial bowers;
> The soil luxuriant, and the fruit divine,
> Where golden apples on green branches shine,
> And purple grapes dissolve into immortal wine;
> For noon-day's heat are closer arbours made,
> And for fresh evening air the opener glade.
> Ascend; and, as we go,
> More wonders thou shalt know.

The well-known prologue to *Aureng-Zebe* (1675), Dryden's last heroic tragedy, struck off the fetters of rhyme in drama, and thereafter no more rhyme was used, except for a few tail-speeches in *Oedipus* (1679) and *The Duke of Guise* (1682), until the last three plays of all, *Amphitryon* (1690), *Cleomenes* (1692), and *Love Triumphant* (1694), into each of which a few rocking scenes were allowed to enter. "According to the opinion of Harte," said Dr. Johnson, "who had studied his works with great attention, he settled his principles of versification in the . . . play of *Aureng-Zebe.*" What this means is not clear; nor is it true to the extent that it can be used to explain the versification of a poem like *The Hind and the Panther. Aureng-Zebe* still comes short of the political poems in pliability. Yet advances have been made over *The Indian Emperor.* Under the influence of Shakespeare's blank verse, and following up the various licenses which had distinguished *The State of Innocence,* Dryden has arrived in *Aureng-Zebe* at a limper, more

* See Chapter **VI**.

natural texture of rhyme than he had achieved before in any play. Nourmahal tells the hero:

> I saw with what a brow you braved your fate;
> Yet with what mildness bore your father's hate.
> My virtue, like a string wound up by art
> To the same sound, when yours was touched, took part,
> At distance shook, and trembled at my heart.

The rhymed plays alone did not bring Dryden to his metrical maturity. The prologues and epilogues which he wrote to accompany them contributed an important, racy, vocal note which their dialogue never contained. And blank verse, though the connection between it and Dryden's rhyme is not easy to make, was also a valuable school for style. His earlier blank verse is not significant, being easy and banal in the late Elizabethan way, so that the printer was as likely as not to set it up for prose; verse of this sort may be found in *The Rival Ladies*, *The Maiden Queen*, *The Tempest* (1667), *An Evening's Love* (1668), *Marriage à la Mode* (1672), *The Assignation* (1672), and *Amboyna* (1673). It was not until *All for Love* (1678), and the ensuing pair of tragedies composed in the light of French ideals, *Oedipus* and *Troilus and Cressida* (1679), that Dryden attained to any remarkable justice or roundness in his blank verse. The style of *All for Love* is virtually impeccable; it has made the play. It is richly and closely woven, but it is absolutely clear, and it bears no traces of complacency in composition. *The Spanish Friar* (1681) sought again the Fletcherian levels of conversation, as did *Amphitryon* in 1690. In *Don Sebastian* (1690) and *Cleomenes* (1692) Dryden reverted to what he believed to be an Elizabethan "roughness of the numbers and cadences," even departing here and there into a veritable Marstonian crabbedness. In general, all that can be said of his blank verse is that it gave him ample training in the manipulation of phrases. It made no direct contribution to what is after all of most consequence in him, his fund of knowledge about the heroic couplet.

It is not a simple matter to calculate the influence of France on Dryden's style after about 1675, but one may be sure that the influence was real. During the Commonwealth the Royalist exiles to France had seen a good deal of the best refinement which the continent possessed. And with the Restoration there had flooded back across the Channel a strong tide of Gallic modernism, involving new fashions in costume, carriage, conduct, cooking, new ideas of medicine, painting, architecture, music, dancing, new accents in cultivated speech, and a new impatience with heavy learning and staid chivalry. Most of what was impossible in the new fashions soon disappeared from English life under the pressure of ridicule. The best remained; and beginning about 1675 solid improvements were made in taste and speech under the triple guidance of the French formal criticism of men like Le Bossu, the French good sense of Rapin and Boileau, and the French "taste" of which Longinus had been found to be the best expression.

As far back as 1668 Dryden had shown himself in the *Essay of Dramatic Poesy* to be familiar with the critical works of Sarrasin, Le Mesnardière, Chapelain, and Corneille; and it is to be supposed that subsequently he kept well abreast of literary developments in France, for he was one of the first Englishmen during the following decade to acclaim Rapin and Boileau.

Rapin seems to have found at all times a ready audience in England. His *Reflections upon the Use of the Eloquence of These Times* appeared at Oxford in 1672, his *Comparison of Plato and Aristotle* at London in 1673, and his *Reflections on Aristotle's Treatise of Poesie* at London in 1674, the same year that it was published in Paris. Dryden drew upon the last work for the famous definition of wit with which he closed his *Apology for Heroic Poetry and Poetic License* in 1677: "a propriety of thoughts and words." Thomas Rymer was Rapin's translator; the Frenchman and the Englishman between them gradually led Dryden to give a classical turn to tragedy and to renounce his pristine "bladdered greatness."

The year 1674 was remarkable in France for the publication of five new works by Boileau: the second and third Epistles, the first four books of the *Lutrin*, the *Art Poétique*, and the translation of Longinus. Dryden became acquainted with at least the fourth and fifth of these almost immediately upon their appearance. He was powerfully moved by the *Longinus*, which it seems he had not known in John Hall's English translation of 1652; and the *Art Poétique* never ceased to appeal to him as a magazine of maxims. Dryden was in an important degree responsible for Boileau's vogue in England through his collaboration with Sir William Soame in 1680-1 upon a translation of the *Art of Poetry*. Until then Boileau's effect had been felt chiefly in satire; Etherege, Buckingham, Rochester, Butler, and Oldham in turn had imitated him in that department. Now it was Boileau's whole outlook which was transferred to England. Now it was that the accepted meanings of "wit" and "sense" and "nature" and "the classics" began to draw together; now it was that English speech and English writing in all their parts began to seem nearly civilized. The Earl of Mulgrave's *Essay upon Poetry* (1682) and the Earl of Roscommon's *Essay on Translated Verse* (1684), two sensible poems in the manner of Horace and Boileau, stamped aristocratic approval upon the Frenchman's creeds at the same time that they spoke his language and breathed his spirit. Almost the first of English verse-essays, they set the standard of decency and urbanity to which Augustans were continually returning over the next three or four decades.

St. Evremond, the French exile who spent the greater part of his life in London, was another Gallic influence on Dryden. In 1683, in the *Life of Plutarch*, Dryden remarked that he had been "casually casting [his] eye on the works of a French gentleman, deservedly famous for wit and criticism." This was St. Evremond, who began in 1685 to make his appearance in English print. St. Evremond was not a profound gentleman, but he was a believer in conversation, and his emphasis upon the choicer phases of intercourse went not without its effect on Dryden, who, it will be remembered, "was not a very genteel man."

Dryden's best style, then, the style of the 1680's, the style of *Absalom and Achitophel*, the *Religio Laici*, and *The Hind and the Panther*, owed a good deal to France. The debt was to French criticism and to French ideals exquisitely expressed rather than to any French poetry that Dryden read. The thinking he was led by Rapin and Boileau and Longinus to do, and the conviction they forced upon him that adequacy of expression is the first and last rule of writing, bore fruit, if only directly, in the great satires and ratiocinative poems. But French poetry itself never had Dryden's respect. "Impartially speaking," he wrote in the dedication of the *Aeneis*, "the French are as much better critics than the English as they are worse poets." His habit of depreciation he had contracted in the *Essay of Dramatic Poesy*, where the regularity of the French had been declared too thin for English blood. A number of prologues in the next decade cordially damned French farce and opera. Doralice, in *Marriage à la Mode*, says to Palamede: "You are an admirer of the dull French poetry, which is so thin, that it is the very leaf-gold of wit, the very wafers and whipped cream of sense, for which a man opens his mouth and gapes, to swallow nothing; and to be an admirer of such profound dulness, one must be endowed with a great perfection of impudence and ignorance." In the Argument to his Sixth *Juvenal* Dryden compared the French affectations of his England to the Greek affectations of the early Roman empire. In the dedication of the *Aeneis* he made the comparison between the French greyhound and the English mastiff which already has been quoted.* "The affected purity of the French has unsinewed their heroic verse," he declared. He was by no means alone in this dislike. The distaste

* See page 33.

for French "thinness" was common. Oldham condemned it in
his poem on Ben Jonson, and Roscommon wrote in his *Essay:*

> But who did ever in French authors see
> The comprehensive English Energy?
> The weighty Bullion of one Sterling Line,
> Drawn to French Wire, would thro' whole Pages shine.

The French themselves were ready to admit a distinction.
Rymer's translation of Rapin's *Reflections* in 1674 contained a
confession, taken literally from Rapin, that the "beauty" of
"number and harmony" is "unknown to the French tongue,
where all the syllables are counted in the verses, and where
there is no diversity of cadence." Englishmen have always been
proud of the difference between French verse and their own, a
difference which has been used at various times to point various morals; in Dryden's time it was the last refuge of those
who, like Dryden himself, leaned upon the tradition of English
magnificence and steadfastly refused to recognize a thinning in
the contemporary product.

Two-thirds of Dryden's non-dramatic verse consisted of
translations from the classics. It is not to be supposed that so
much labor was without important result. The sheer experience
involved in composing some twenty thousand couplets was
bound either to intrench him in whatever ground of style he
already occupied or to draw him forward on to new surfaces of
expression. It did both things; but more often it did the first.
More often than not Dryden failed to learn anything by his
translating. Doing most of it under pressure from the printers,
he missed that margin of leisure which allows reflection and ex-
perimentation. As a rule Dryden performed well under pressure; but there are limits, which in Dryden's case meant that
he was reduced to turning out a great number of stale and
undistinguished lines. Yet in a respectable number of instances
he did unquestionably enlarge himself through his identification

with ancient masters, so that in translating them he produced what cannot be considered other than great original poems.

Domestication of Greek and Roman writers was the order of the day in England. A society whose cultivated members lived exclusively, without warm vision and without much concern for problems that pressed, was pleased to feed on echoes of past grandeur and to take frequent account of that "stock of life," as St. Evremond affectionately called it, which the classics furnished in circumscribed and compendious form. Thomas Creech's *Lucretius, Horace,* and *Theocritus* in 1682 and 1684 were marks of the rising tide in translation which was to sweep Dryden and Jacob Tonson on to their great successes. Dryden believed that a translator was bound in all honor to enter generously into the spirit of his original and present him fairly as the individual which he once had been. His prefaces abound in distinctions nicely maintained between Homer and Virgil, Juvenal and Persius, Juvenal and Horace, Virgil and Ovid, and so on. He had a true translator's conscience, and liked to think that for the time being he and his masters were "congenial souls." But he seldom succeeded in bestowing individuality anywhere; his translations read very much alike; only his Juvenal and his Lucretius are really living men. Altogether he turned his hand to eight of the ancients: Ovid, Theocritus, Lucretius, Horace, Juvenal, Persius, Virgil, and Homer.

He began with Ovid in 1680, when he contributed three pieces to a volume of *Translations from Ovid's Epistles.* He was always an admirer of Ovid's fertility, and of his faculty for "continually varying the same sense an hundred ways," but his admiration in general was tempered by a conviction that the author of the *Metamorphoses* was a cheaper man than Virgil. He lacked taste; "he never knew how to give over, when he had done well." Only rarely did Dryden translate him with distinction. The three Epistles of 1680 were loose and latinistic. A brisker piece, the nineteenth elegy of the second book of the *Amores,* appeared in Tonson's first *Miscellany* in 1684. The

third *Miscellany,* called *Examen Poeticum,* which was published in 1693, contained Dryden's version of the entire first
book of the *Metamorphoses* and the "fables" of *Iphis and
Ianthe* and *Acis, Polyphemus and Galatea,* from the ninth and
thirteenth books respectively. From only one passage in the
three poems does genius emerge; the impassioned speech of
Polyphemus to Galatea is in Dryden's best vein of suasion. The
Art of Love and the first and fourth elegies of the first book
of the *Amores* were done by Dryden while he was occupied with
his *Virgil;* they were not printed during his lifetime. The
Fables found him in better form, yet even in that venerable
volume the Ovidian poems are the least engaging. Dryden
learned speed and audacity from Ovid, but nothing richer. It
has been Ovid's narrative materials rather than his personal
qualities that have fired the modern poets; his stories are inexhaustible, but his exterior too often glitters and leaves the lis-
tener cold.

Dryden's four Idylls from Theocritus, the third, the eighteenth, the twenty-third, and the twenty-seventh, printed in the
first and second *Miscellanies* of 1684 and 1685, professed to
speak in the "Doric dialect" which Dryden thought had "an
incomparable sweetness in its clownishness, like a fair shepherdess in her country russet, talking in a Yorkshire tone."
The dialect is difficult to distinguish from Dryden's customary
language. When Theocritus writes simply, "O dark-eyebrowed
maiden mine," Dryden writes,

> O Nymph, . . .
> Whose radiant eyes your ebon brows adorn,
> Like midnight those and these like break of morn.

This is handsome, but its sound is that of a trumpet rather than
a shepherd's pipe. Dryden never can he said to have expanded
his poetic personality so as to include the rare Sicilian.

Dryden's *Lucretius* is another story. What he tried to reproduce in Lucretius was a certain "noble pride, and positive asser-

tion of his opinions." His success was signal in at least two out
of the five selections which he chose to translate for the second
Miscellany in 1685. His passages from the second and third
books of the *De Rerum Natura* must be numbered among the
most convincing specimens of ratiocinative poetry in any language. The spirit of the Roman has invaded and actually moved
the Englishman; for a time he is another person. These lines
on the fear of death are executed with a new delicacy and a new
precision:

> We, who are dead and gone, shall bear no part
> In all the pleasures, nor shall feel the smart
> Which to that other mortal shall accrue,
> Whom of our matter time shall mold anew.
> For backward if you look on that long space
> Of ages past, and view the changing face
> Of matter, tossed and variously combined
> In sundry shapes, 'tis easy for the mind
> From thence t' infer, that seeds of things have been
> In the same order as they now are seen;
> Which yet our dark remembrance cannot trace,
> Because a pause of life, a gaping space,
> Has come betwixt, where memory lies dead,
> And all the wandering motions from the sense are fled.
> For whosoe'er shall in misfortunes live,
> Must be, when those misfortunes shall arrive;
> And since the man who is not, feels not woe,
> (For death exempts him, and wards off the blow,
> Which we, the living, only feel and bear,)
> What is there left for us in death to fear?
> When once that pause of life has come between,
> 'Tis just the same as we had never been.

The skill with which the movement of the verse is made to
correspond to the progress and the outline of the idea can be
called inspired. Dryden has learned much from Lucretius. This
poem on the fear of death is his very own.

It is rather to be regretted that Dryden never imitated the satires of Horace as Pope did. He touched only three odes and an epode, versions of which appeared under his name in the second *Miscellany* of 1685. The pieces are of no consequence in connection with the present inquiry. Dryden could not possibly succeed in miniatures. The twenty-ninth ode of the third book he made one of his masterpieces, but only by transforming it into a Pindaric ode and so egregiously distending it.* He required more space than Horace ever would allow.

The five satires of Juvenal which Dryden published in 1693 along with the whole of Persius are a triumph comparable to the *Lucretius*. In the *Discourse* with which he prefaced the volume he analyzed what he had found to be the distinction of Juvenal, his impetuosity. The five satires as he gave them are not only impetuous; they are close and powerful. A full weight of brutal wrath bears down upon the antitheses and the rhymes. There is no tender *enjambement;* the couplets thump and crackle. The sixth, against women, is one of the grandest and most terrible poems in English.

> In Saturn's reign, at Nature's early birth,
> There was that thing called Chastity on earth;
> When in a narrow cave, their common shade,
> The sheep, the shepherds, and their gods were laid;
> When reeds, and leaves, and hides of beasts were spread
> By mountain huswifes for their homely bed,
> And mossy pillows raised, for the rude husband's head.
> Unlike the niceness of our modern dames,
> (Affected nymphs with new affected names,)
> The Cynthias and the Lesbias of our years,
> Who for a sparrow's death dissolve in tears;
> Those first unpolished matrons, big and bold,
> Gave suck to infants of gigantic mold;
> Rough as their savage lords who ranged the wood,
> And fat with acorns belched their windy food.

* See Chapter VI.

The largeness of these opening lines is not specious. Dryden has
developed another voice while in the company of Juvenal.

Dryden began to work with Virgil as early as the first *Miscellany* in 1684, when he contributed to that volume translations
of the fourth and ninth Pastorals. The fourth Pastoral as he
allowed it to be printed was metrically licentious, and an unworthy performance. The ninth was full of a fresh melody
which at once cast a shade over John Ogilby's *Virgil*, a respectable and often sumptuously printed work which had appeared
first in 1649 and which until Dryden's folio was not superseded.
Ogilby had been stingy and literal. Where Virgil's Moeris says
regretfully:

> Omnia fert aetas, animum quoque; saepe ego longos
> Cantando puerum memini me condere soles:
> Nunc oblita mihi tot carmina, vox quoque Moerim
> Iam fugit ipsa; lupi Moerim videre priores,

Ogilby's says:

> Age all things wastes, and spends our lively heat.
> I but a boy, could singing set the sun.
> Now all those notes are lost, and my voice gone;
> A wolf saw Moeris first;

while Dryden's shepherd sings:

> The rest I have forgot; for cares and time
> Change all things, and untune my soul to rhyme.
> I could have once sung down a summer's sun;
> But now the chime of poetry is done;
> My voice grows hoarse; I feel the notes decay,
> As if the wolves had seen me first today.

Dryden seems keenly to have relished his occupation with the
pastorals of Virgil, and it was by no means seldom that he
achieved therein a sweet and shining clarity. In the second
eclogue his Corydon thus runs over the favors which the
nymphs will bestow upon Alexis:

White lilies in full canisters they bring,
With all the glories of the purple spring.
The daughters of the flood have searched the mead
For violets pale, and cropped the poppy's head,
The short narcissus and fair daffodil,
Pansies to please the sight, and cassia sweet to smell;
And set soft hyacinths with iron-blue,
To shade marsh marigolds of shining hue;
Some bound in order, others loosely strewed,
To dress thy bower, and trim thy new abode.
Myself will search our planted grounds at home,
For downy peaches and the glossy plum;
And thrash the chestnuts in the neighbouring grove,
Such as my Amaryllis used to love;
The laurel and the myrtle sweets agree;
And both in nosegays shall be bound for thee.

The second *Miscellany* in 1685 contained versions by Dryden
of three episodes from the *Aeneid:* the episode of Nisus and
Euryalus, from the fifth and ninth books, the episode of
Mezentius and Lausus from the tenth, and the speech of
Venus to Vulcan from the eighth. The third Georgic was inserted in the fourth *Miscellany* of 1694; and three years later
the complete folio itself issued from Jacob Tonson's shop with
all the pomp of a state event. Dryden had come very near to
despair more than once while he was engaged with Virgil.
"Some of our countrymen," he explained to the Earl of Mulgrave, "have translated episodes and other parts of Virgil,
with great success; . . . I say nothing of Sir John Denham,
Mr. Waller, and Mr. Cowley; 'tis the utmost of my ambition
to be thought their equal . . . but 'tis one thing to take pains
on a fragment, and translate it perfectly; and another thing to
have the weight of a whole author on my shoulders." "I do
not find myself capable of translating so great an author," he
wrote to Tonson; and in the dedication of the *Aeneis* he admitted that he had done "great wrong to Virgil in the whole

translation," offering as reasons "want of time, the inferiority of our language, the inconvenience of rhyme." By his own confession, he kept the manuscript of the Earl of Lauderdale's translation by him and "consulted it as often as I doubted of my author's sense," or as often, more likely, as he felt pressed for time. Some two hundred lines of that nobleman's version he appropriated without any alteration at all, and some eight hundred came over only slightly recast. The readiness of the Earl to place his work at the poet's disposal may be accounted for by the fact that he himself had made free with the translations of the episodes of Nisus and Euryalus and Mezentius and Lausus as they had stood under Dryden's name since the *Miscellany* of 1685. There is a tradition that Dryden regretted before he was through that he had not chosen blank verse for his medium. An *Aeneid* in the style of *All for Love* might be a truly superb performance. He had been advised to make the attempt. Thomas Fletcher, in the preface to his *Poems* of 1692, had repeated Roscommon's condemnation of rhyme, and had suggested that "If a Dryden (a master of our Language and Poetry) would undertake to translate Virgil in blank Verse, we might hope to read him with as great pleasure in our Language as his own." But it is likely that Dryden on the whole was satisfied with his couplets. He had reasons for dissatisfaction with the poem on other grounds. It is vastly imperfect. The Cyclops, the funeral games, and the gathering of the clans in the *Aeneis* are handled in a manner worthy of the best heroic tradition, and every page without exception bristles with energy. Yet in the main the texture of the verse is coarse; Dryden has made no advance in subtlety of speech, he is only applying standard formulas and securing standard results. Virgil has eluded him as Lucretius and Juvenal did not.

Dryden was "fixing his thoughts" on Homer in his last years and halfway projecting a new folio which should stand as a companion to the *Virgil*. He had a notion that Homer was more suited to his genius than Virgil, since he was more "violent, impetuous, and full of fire." He had done into English *The Last Parting of Hector and Andromache* for the third *Miscellany* in 1693, and he included in the *Fables* a complete version of the first book of the *Iliad*. He got no further with Homer, which is to be regretted; for although the two specimens he left behind are neither violent, impetuous, nor full of fire in a preternatural degree, they are honest and various as few translations are.

It is not to be supposed that Dryden had been without his English masters all along. Shakespeare, Spenser, and Milton were constantly enriching him, if not with direct gifts then with less tangible inspirations. His unqualified admiration for Shakespeare scarcely needs to be cited; the tributes he paid in the *Essay of Dramatic Poesy*, the dedication of *The Rival Ladies*, the prologue to the *Tempest*, and the prologue to *Troilus and Cressida* are *loci classici* of criticism. He knew the text of Shakespeare's major dramas as well as he knew his own works; his plays are reminiscent, often only trivially, in word and phrase of *Hamlet*, *King Lear*, *Macbeth*, and *Julius Caesar*. But imitation of Shakespeare on a significant scale was out of the question, as it must be always. Spenser offered gifts of style which were easier to accept and put in use. "I must acknowledge," wrote Dryden in the dedication of the *Aeneis*, discussing the general problem of "numbers," "that Virgil in Latin, and Spenser in English, have been my masters." Spenser he considered in a degree the creator of English harmony, and Spenser's fluency seemed to him to the last a glorious marvel. Fluency as such is a quality which cannot be fingered over by a follower of influences; hence its passage from Spenser into Dryden can be better announced than proved. The passage did occur, Spenser's broad current eventually enveloping the little stream of Waller that flowed to Dryden. Dryden seems to have been thoroughly versed in *The Faerie Queene*. Occasional lines clearly recall its sensitive author, as these two from the Episode of Nisus and Euryalus:

> Black was the brake, and thick with oak it stood,
> With fern all horrid, and perplexing thorn.

The accounts of the fairies at the beginning of *The Wife of Bath, Her Tale* and in *The Flower and the Leaf*, in the *Fables*, are Chaucer plus Spenser plus Shakespeare. And Thomas Warton pointed out that the sleeping Iphigenia in *Cymon and Iphigenia* owes certain of her beauties to the Elizabethan who best of all could paint enchanting forms.

Milton's impact upon Dryden was not sudden, nor was his influence of a permeating kind. The two poets were worlds apart. Yet Dryden was among the first Englishmen who conferred important honors upon Milton dead; and his works reflect careful reading not only of *Paradise Lost* but of the minor poems, the prose, and *Samson Agonistes* as well. Milton's *Ode on the Morning of Christ's Nativity*, as has been remarked, is probably responsible for Dryden's thirty-fifth stanza on Cromwell.* Stanza 232 of *Annus Mirabilis*, which Settle declared was stolen from Cowley, vaguely recalls *Lycidas* as well as the *Davideis*,

> Old Father Thames raised up his reverend head,
>   But feared the fate of Simoeis would return;
> Deep in his ooze he sought his sedgy bed,
>   And shrunk his waters back into his urn,

and stanza 293 certainly suggests the *Areopagitica*:

> Methinks already, from this chymick flame,
>   I see a city of more precious mold;
> Rich as the town which gives the Indies name,
>   With silver paved, and all divine with gold.

That the *State of Innocence* is a tagged *Paradise Lost* needs no mention; though the proverbial corollary that it is a wretched poem calls for emphatic denial. Langbaine pointed out a borrowing in *Aureng-Zebe* from *Samson Agonistes*. "Now give

* See page 2.

me leave," he asked in his *Account of the English Dramatick Poets* (1691), "to give you one Instance . . . of his borrowing from Mr. Milton's *Samson Agonistes:*

> Dal.   I see thou art implacable, more deaf
> To Prayers than winds and seas; yet winds to seas
> Are reconcil'd at length, and sea to shore;
> Thy anger unappeasable still rages,
> Eternal Tempest never to be calm'd.
>
> Emp.   *Unmov'd she stood, and deaf to all my prayers,*
> *As Seas and Winds to sinking Mariners;*
> *But Seas grow calm, and Winds are reconcil'd;*
> *Her Tyrant Beauty never grows more mild.*"

A still more interesting levy on Milton's tragedy was made by Dryden in the first act of *Oedipus.* The blind Tiresias comes upon the stage led by his daughter Manto and addressing her as follows:

> A little farther; yet a little farther,
> Thou wretched daughter of a dark old man,
> Conduct my weary steps. . . . Now stay;
> Methinks I draw more open, vital air.
> Where are we?
>
> Manto: Under covert of a wall;
> The most frequented once, and noisy part
> Of Thebes; now midnight silence reigns even here,
> And grass untrodden springs beneath our feet.
>
> Tiresias: If there be nigh this place a sunny bank,
> There let me rest awhile.

Dryden may have had in mind here at least five different scenes in classical tragedy. The spectacle of a blind old man being led upon the stage was familiar to Greek audiences. In the *Oedipus Tyrannus* of Sophocles Tiresias appears hand in hand with a boy; in the *Oedipus Coloneus* Oedipus follows after Antigone, whom he pities as "the wretched child of a blind old man," and who conducts him to a rocky seat. In the *Phoenissae* of Euripides Tiresias is conducted upon the scene by Manto, "the eye of his feet." Seneca begins his *Phoenissae* with Antigone leading Oedipus, and in his *Oedipus* Manto guides Tiresias along. Dryden may have had any of these scenes vividly in his memory. Yet the opening of *Samson Agonistes* must have furnished him with certain of his words, and must have suggested two details for his tableau which neither the Greeks nor Seneca had provided: the sunny bank and the draughts of fresh air. Milton's lines run thus:

> *Samson:*   *A little onward* lend thy guiding hand
>   To these dark steps, *a little further on;*
>   *For yonder bank hath choice of sun or shade.*
>   There I am wont to sit, when any chance
>   Relieves me from my task of servile toil,
>   Daily in the common prison else enjoined me,
>   Where I, a prisoner chained, *scarce freely draw*
>   *The air imprisoned also, close and damp,*
>   Unwholesome draught; but here I feel amends,
>   The breath of Heav'n fresh blowing, pure and sweet,
>   With day-spring born.

The parallel is of interest only as showing that Dryden knew Milton well. The poems on public affairs drew heavily upon *Paradise Lost* for epic machinery and accent. The speeches in *Absalom and Achitophel* are Satanic or Godlike much in Milton's way, and the account in *The Hind and the Panther* (II., 499-514) of Christ's accepting in Heaven the burden of man's sin follows Milton's recital in his third book with remarkable fidelity. Instances might be multiplied without establishing further types of obligation. The obligation was never spiritual; it was rarely that Dryden was moved by anything other than the diction of a great poet. Shakespeare, Spenser, Milton remain on the other side of the world from Dryden; but he visits them and takes from them whatever he can carry away.

By dint of manifold experience, then, and manifold discipleship, Dryden rolled and beat into shape the poetic medium which had descended to him. But he did more than make that medium perfectly clear and strong. He stamped it peculiarly with himself. His genius was for grouping; his passion was for form. He had above most poets "that energy," as Dr. Johnson put it, "which collects, combines, amplifies, and animates." He had a mind; he had grasp; he could follow a subject home. His poems lived. He loved to see things take shape. At the beginning of his dedication of *The Rival Ladies* he told the Earl of Orrery in words which later haunted the imagination of Lord Byron that his play had once been "only a confused mass of thoughts, tumbling over one another in the dark; when the fancy was yet in its first work, moving the sleeping images of things towards the light." As many as a dozen times throughout his works he played with the notion of a world of scattered atoms, rejecting it for the image of a world composed with care. He wrote to Sir Robert Howard in 1660:

> This is a piece too fair
> To be the child of chance, and not of care;
> No atoms casually together hurled
> Could e'er produce so beautiful a world.

He insisted that a good play could not be a heap of "huddled atoms"; an epic could never succeed if "writ on the Epicurean principles." This genius of his took effect in two ways. It made him a master in the art of grouping and throwing swiftly together statements, reasons, instances, implications; it made him the most irresistible discursive and ratiocinative poet in English. And it supplied him with a powerful rhythmical pulse; it established the paragraph, the passage, as his unit of metrical advance, not the line or the couplet; it made him a mighty metrist. Such was Dryden's best manner. Dryden's best material, it has been said, lay in personalities, actions, ideas, art. The two in conjunction brought forth his best poetry, occasional, journalistic, lyric, or narrative.

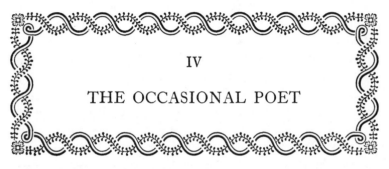

IV

THE OCCASIONAL POET

THERE is a sense in which every poem that Dryden wrote was occasional. Not sudden convictions, or happy perceptions of identities in the world of nature and man, but circumstances were required to draw him out on paper. Births, deaths, literary events, political incidents tapped in him the richest commenting mind that English poetry has known. He is the celebrant, the signalizer *par excellence*. He succeeded Ben Jonson, the other great occasional poet of the seventeenth century, in a kind of writing that was peculiarly Augustan. Jonson had created the kind in England, clearing off a broad field for it and practicing it with rare compactness and rightness. He had planted every variety of it which was to have a successful growth: the official panegyric, the complimentary epistle, the epigram, the epitaph, the elegy, the prologue, the epilogue. The growth had been rapid before Dryden. The temper of the century had swiftly become suited to a sort of expression aiming "rather at aptitude than altitude," as Thomas Jordan put it in the dedication of his *Poems and Songs* in 1664. It had become more and more agreeable to read and write verses that suavely wreathed themselves around plain, social facts. The main line

of descent from Jonson to Dryden was through men like Cartwright and Waller. Most of Milton's sonnets had been occasional poems of another order, instinct with the passions of
ambition, anger, or worship. True Augustan verse was to be
impersonal, containing no bursts that might embarrass. Even
Milton had approximated the type in his sonnets to Lawes, to
Lawrence, and to Cyriack Skinner. The type was to be first of
all civil.

Every year of the world will see occasional poetry; but
fashions vary, and only at intervals is hard civility the mode.
Poets since Dryden have been softer, and have expressed themselves upon more precious occasions: upon receiving a mother's
picture, upon turning up a field mouse with a plow, upon hearing a lass sing at her reaping, upon spying a primrose by a
river's brim or a violet by a mossy stone, upon seeing a peasant
bent hopelessly over his hoe, upon looking into the eyes of a
harlot, upon dreaming weird dreams, upon thinking fine
thoughts. The Augustans kept such experiences, if they had
them, to themselves. Their subjects were prescribed and clas-
sified. Their minds were formal, stored with categories and
properties. Writing upon a subject meant turning it over casually in the mind and exposing it to preconceptions. The aim
was not at revelation or surprise but at the satisfaction which
comes from a topic perfectly covered.

Dryden was a great occasional poet because he was more
than merely that. He was more than equal to his occasions, few
of which moved him. He condescended to them, brought to
them richer stores of thought and melody than were adequate.
He operated with self-control, he was generally discreet and
right; yet there are overtones to be distinguished in all his
pieces. He was a large poet writing largely about medium
things. His genius for grouping and shaping was of extraordinary consequence here. More easily than any other English
poet he could assemble ripe clusters of apposite ideas, rounding

them off by the pressure of his swift, disciplined mind and welding them into their true proportions with rhythm.

If we disregard for a moment the satires and the ratiocinative poems, which can better be considered by themselves in connection with a study of Dryden as a journalist in verse, it appears that Dryden's occasional pieces fall into four divisions: the panegyrics, celebrating public events and complimenting public characters; the epistles and personal addresses; the epigrams, epitaphs, and elegies; and the prologues and epilogues.

The ten years between 1660 and 1670 saw in England a flowering of panegyric that sends the memory back to several distant periods in the world's literature. Greeks and Italians have a well-known capacity for voluble laudation; the classics are replete with praise. "The inimitable Pindar" needs only to be mentioned. Isocrates and Demosthenes in ancient Greece and Cicero in ancient Rome wrote in a golden age of panegyrical prose. Rome saw a silver age in the famous twelve *Panegyrici Veteres* of later days, among whom was Pliny the Younger; Pliny's oration on Trajan Dryden knew and quoted in *Annus Mirabilis*. The last great Roman poet, Claudian, was a professional panegyrist; his verses in praise of Honorius and Stilicho at the end of the fourth century look forward to the poetry of Dryden in respect of their fertility, ingenuity, and general temper. The fifteenth century in Italy was a century of adulation. A dark period of latinity that interposed itself between the brilliant times of Dante, Petrarch, and Boccaccio and the brilliant times of Ariosto and Tasso, it witnessed the reigns of petty despots who called themselves descendants of the Roman Emperors and thirsted for a Roman kind of praise. The praise was forthcoming, in prose and verse; the great Poliziano expended as much effort upon Lorenzo de Medici as he did upon the Greek and Roman poets whom he so intensely admired. In England, Queen Elizabeth received at least her meed of formal flattery, and Prince Henry's death in 1612 was the occasion for a veritable Augustan abundance of eulogy. Upon the occa-

sions of visits by James I to the universities, the learned outdid
themselves in hyperbole of welcome. Cromwell had his Marvell
as well as his Dryden. But it was only with the return of
Charles II from France and the setting up of what was believed
would be a permanent little social court that literary England
came for a while to be something like literary Rome in the
fourth century or like literary Italy in the fifteenth. The conditions of such a becoming include a certain pettiness, a certain
exclusiveness, a certain blindness, and a certain pretentious un-
reality in the official psychology. England during the first
decade after the Restoration supplied all these conditions. London was intoxicated with peace, and with what it greeted as an
established order. Not until after Clarendon's fall, not until
after confidence in Charles began to be less general, were larger
perspectives opened up. Not that panegyrics ever stopped altogether. Southey and Byron were still to have their turns with
George the Third. But this particular Stuart decade must remain unique in English history.

Dryden never ceased to exercise his panegyrical vein while
Charles and James were in power. But what may more specifi-
cally be called his panegyrical period extended only from 1660
to 1666. The model of all then, including Dryden, was Waller.

> He best can turn, enforce, and soften things,
> To praise great Conquerors or to flatter Kings,

wrote Rochester in his *Allusion to Horace;* and when Dryden
inserted his English names in Soame's Boileau he substituted
"Waller" for "Malherbe" in the line,

> Malherbe, d'un héros peut vanter les exploits.
> Waller a hero's mighty acts extol.

Waller could be rapt and smooth and fatuous in pleasant
proportions. Dryden added other qualities to those three. His
official praise rings with a round Roman grandeur. He writes as
if he lived to praise, not praised to live. His lines speak con-

tempt for all things small—small passions, small deeds, small wit. He is warm yet decorous; he is effectual because of his great confidence and his unremitting eloquence. And his resources are infinite. "He appears never to have impoverished his mint of flattery by his expenses, however lavish," says Dr. Johnson. "He had all the forms of excellence, intellectual and moral, combined in his mind, with endless variation . . . and brings praise rather as a tribute than a gift, more delighted with the fertility of his invention than mortified by the prostitution of his judgment." The *Heroic Stanzas* would seem to have been written in an age rather remote from the *Astraea Redux,* although only a year separated them. The difference in quality is the difference between Marvell and Waller, or better yet, the difference between Cromwell and Charles. The one has symmetry and sinewy calm, the other slips along with a kind of tepid abandon. The *Astraea* is more shapeless and profuse than Dryden usually is in his occasional poetry; he has not yet learned his grouping. Yet the peroration is well gathered up. The poem *To His Sacred Majesty, a Panegyric on His Coronation,* composed about a year after the *Astraea,* is an improvement with respect to form. The ideas are fewer, but each in its turn is rounded out. The poem climbs in a series of flights, with intervals or landings between, the melody mounting continuously and tending to be cumulative within the flights. The poem *To My Lord Chancellor, Presented on New Year's Day* (1662) is profuse and tepid again except for one nobly concentrated passage on Charles I and Clarendon. The *Annus Mirabilis,* published in 1667, is Dryden's most ambitious official compliment, being dedicated "to the Metropolis of Great Britain," and celebrating both a naval war and a great fire. The prophecy with which it ends continues the central motif of his occasional work in that it is collected and sustained. The last twelve stanzas pile themselves up like the Theban stones that obeyed Amphion's lyre.

Dryden's panegyrical period now came to a close. The Stuart

spell was broken, Clarendon fled to France, and Marvell, bitterly loyal to the best interests of England, answered the vapid
flatteries of Waller and his train with exposures which made
such men as Pepys weep because they were so true. Nearly
twenty years passed before Dryden performed again on his
official pipes. This was at the death of Charles II when he
wrote his *Threnodia Augustalis,* a "Funeral-Pindaric" which
will be considered more fully elsewhere, along with the other
Pindarics.* The poem lies loosely about for want of any sin-
cere motive that can knit it together. The best-constructed passage is that which summons up Dryden's happiest memories,
his memories of peace:

> For all those joys thy happy restoration brought,
> For all the miracles it wrought,
> For all the healing balm thy mercy poured
> Into the nation's bleeding wound,
> And care that after kept it sound,
> For numerous blessings yearly showered,
> And property with plenty crowned;
> For freedom still maintained alive,
> Freedom, which in no other land will thrive,
> Freedom, an English subject's sole prerogative,
> Without whose charms even peace would be
> But a dull quiet slavery:
> For these, and more, accept our pious praise.

Britannia Rediviva (1688), on the birth of an heir to James II,
is a dull conclusion to the least distinguished division of Dryden's occasional poetry. Like the *Threnodia* it lacks that san-
guineness which alone had justified the pieces of the 1660's
and which had given them a metrical structure interesting
enough to study now. These last two poems lack what it is fatal
for Dryden ever to lack, drive.

Dryden's personal epistles and complimentary addresses
bring us into a different world. Here he is at home, for here

* See Chapter VI.

he is speaking to private persons and he is praising books. Three
kinds of poetical epistles gained currency during the seventeenth
century. The Horatian or didactic kind began with Daniel,
Drayton, Donne, and Jonson, and culminated in Pope. The
Ovidian or "voluptuous" kind got a start in volumes like Drayton's *Heroical Epistles* and ran on to Pope's *Eloisa to Abelard*.
The third kind, the complimentary, was more peculiarly modern and local. Rooted in Jonson, it flowered in Dryden, who
practiced virtually no other sort. Having to praise both men
and books, he was never in want of excellent models. Jonson's
epistles to the owner of Penshurst and to Elizabeth, Countess of
Rutland, Drayton's to Sandys and Reynolds, and Waller's to
Falkland had established a distinguished line of personal compliment. Waller's verses to the young Viscount as he left for
war are among the most genuine which he composed, one in-
dication of which may be found in their radical *enjambement*,
as in this passage:

> Ah, noble friend! with what impatience all
> That know thy worth, and know how prodigal
> Of thy great soul thou art (longing to twist
> Bays with that ivy which so early kissed
> Thy youthful temples), with what horror we
> Think on the blind events of war and thee!
> To fate exposing that all-knowing breast
> Among the throng, as cheaply as the rest;
> Where oaks and brambles (if the copse be burned)
> Confounded lie, to the same ashes turned.

The line of literary compliment which descended to Dryden
was more distinguished still. The more firmly literary standards
became fixed the readier men were to praise whatever writing
they approved, and the more copious too became critical vocabu-
laries. In the seventeenth century praise of books might be
either interested or disinterested. It might be motivated by
actual enthusiasm; but it also might be motivated by personal

friendship, by hope of patronage, by party feeling, by the fee of a printer, or by something more canny yet, the expectation that the author commended would reciprocate when next he published a volume. Authors, at the instigation of publishers, traded compliments as freely as boys trade marbles, and a book was very poor which could not appear prefaced by at least two poetical puffs. Whatever the motives, the practice itself produced some of the best occasional poetry of the century; and there is surely something logical about the predilection of a critical age for critical verse. The line, to resume, came down through such poems as Jonson's to Shakespeare and Sir Henry Savile, through the *Jonsonus Virbius* of 1638, and through Waller's and Cowley's prefaces to *Gondibert*. Running into Dryden it found itself in the control of a great man who was fond of bestowing judgments and who was possessed of unexampled gifts in casual criticism.

Shortly after Dryden entered Trinity College, Cambridge, in 1650, he contributed some commendatory verses to a volume of "divine Epigrams" published by his friend John Hoddesdon. The verses have a Puritan tinge and are clumsy in their approbation. Ten years later he opened a freer vein of compliment in the piece which he prefixed to a volume of Sir Robert Howard's poems published by Henry Herringman. Probably the applause he gave to Howard, who after another three years was to become his brother-in-law, was not disinterested; possibly Herringman engaged him to deliver it. At any rate, he wrote the lines with real relish, achieving in a slight measure the felicity, the fluency, and the plenitude of praise which marked his maturest compliments. He also indulged in a little general criticism, incidentally announcing some literary ideals of his own. He denounced conceits, for instance, and informed Howard that

> To carry weight, and run so lightly too,
> Is what alone your Pegasus can do.

So firm a strength, and yet withal so sweet,
Did never but in Samson's riddle meet.

In 1663 he furnished an epistle to Dr. Charleton for insertion
in his treatise on Stonehenge, which Herringman was publishing. The epistle was the first of Dryden's that set out to
examine a literary or philosophical point. It is virtually an
essay on the conquest of Aristotelianism by experimental science. The address to Lady Castlemaine which Dryden probably
made soon after the failure of his first play in 1663 shows him
fairly emancipated from the pedantry and miscellaneity of the
poems that preceded it. It runs straight on, swiftly and sweetly,
quickened into life by the sun of gallantry which shines upon it.

What further fear of danger can there be?
Beauty, which captives all things, sets me free.
Posterity will judge by my success,
I had the Grecian poet's happiness,
Who, waiving plots, found out a better way;
Some god descended, and preserved the play.
When first the triumphs of your sex were sung
By those old poets, Beauty was but young,
And few admired the native red and white,
Till poets dressed them up to charm the sight;
So Beauty took on trust, and did engage
For sums of praises till she came of age.
But this long-growing debt to poetry
You justly, Madam, have discharged to me,
When your applause and favor did infuse
New life to my condemned and dying Muse.

It will be observed that no accent here is in the smallest degree misplaced. Another epistle did not appear until 1677,
when Dryden supplied a puff for Lee, to go in front of his
printed play, *The Death of Alexander the Great*. The epistle
begins with an interesting reference to the practice of poetical
log-rolling already described. Lee had puffed Dryden's *State of
Innocence*. Now, begins Dryden,

> The blast of common censure could I fear,
> Before your play my name should not appear;
> For 'twill be thought, and with some colour too,
> I pay the bribe I first received from you;
> That mutual vouchers for our fame we stand,
> And play the game into each other's hand;

but he proceeds to disclaim any other than the purest motives in praising Lee's tragedy. He ends with a defense of Lee's mad way of writing which in seven sharply distinct couplets proves that Dryden has mastered Ovid's art of "varying the same sense an hundred ways":

> They only think you animate your theme
> With too much fire, who are themselves all phle'me.
> Prizes would be for lags of slowest pace,
> Were cripples made the judges of the race.
> Despise those drones, who praise while they accuse
> The too much vigour of your youthful muse.
> That humble style which they their virtue make,
> Is in your power; you need but stoop and take.
> Your beauteous images must be allowed
> By all, but some vile poets of the crowd.
> But how should any signpost dauber know
> The worth of Titian or of Angelo?
> Hard features every bungler can command;
> To draw true beauty shows a master's hand.

The Earl of Roscommon prefixed a complimentary poem to a new issue of the *Religio Laici* in 1683. Dryden came back the next year with some lines applauding Roscommon's *Essay on Translated Verse*. The opening furnishes the most handsome example in all Dryden of a piece of versified literary history. The progress of rhyme from ancient Athens to modern London is represented by a metrical progression which must have been the despair of all living poets:

Whether the fruitful Nile, or Tyrian shore,
The seeds of arts and infant science bore,
'Tis sure the noble plant translated, first
Advanced its head in Grecian gardens nursed.
The Grecians added verse; their tuneful tongue
Made nature first and nature's God their song.
Nor stopped translation here; for conquering Rome
With Grecian spoils brought Grecian numbers home,
Enriched by those Athenian Muses more
Than all the vanquished world could yield before;
Till barbarous nations, and more barbarous times,
Debased the majesty of verse to rhymes;
Those rude at first: a kind of hobbling prose,
That limped along, and tinkled in the close.
But Italy, reviving from the trance
Of Vandal, Goth, and monkish ignorance,
With pauses, cadence, and well-vowelled words,
And all the graces a good ear affords,
Made rhyme an art, and Dante's polished page
Restored a silver, not a golden age.
Then Petrarch followed, and in him we see
What rhyme improved in all its height can be;
At best a pleasing sound, and fair barbarity.
The French pursued their steps; and Britain, last,
In manly sweetness all the rest surpassed.
The wit of Greece, the gravity of Rome,
Appear exalted in the British loom;
The Muses' empire is restored again,
In Charles his reign, and by Roscommon's pen.

Roscommon here, however much as an anticlimax he may come to a modern reader, comes at least metrically as a true and stately climax. The manner if not the matter of this sketch, which Dryden enjoyed doing if he ever enjoyed doing anything at all, is without flaw. The next epistle, *To My Friend, Mr. J. Northleigh, Author of the Parallel, On His Triumph of the British Monarchy* (1685), is short and of no account. A year

or two after this Dryden wrote for the Earl of Middleton a
letter in octosyllabic couplets to Sir George Etherege, who had
sent a similar piece to Middleton from Ratisbon. It was for
Dryden a *tour de force*. He was not fond of the octosyllabic
measure, nor was he temperamentally equipped for a species
of verse which seemed to fall somewhere between Butler and
Prior. His epistle *To My Ingenious Friend, Henry Higden,
Esq., on His Translation of the Tenth Satire of Juvenal* (1687)
contained like the poem to Roscommon a literary discussion, this
time on the subject of ancient and modern satire. In 1692 he
consoled Southerne for the failure of his comedy called *The
Wives' Excuse* with an epistle that closed on a note of sage and
compendious counsel. The famous lines to Congreve on his
Double-dealer (1694), and those to Sir Godfrey Kneller of the
same year, probably in acknowledgment of a portrait of
Shakespeare which Kneller had given him, represent a more
reflective stage in the progress of Dryden's epistolary manner.
They do not charge upon their subjects with the breathless
speed of the early addresses; their discourse, which in one case
is upon the dramatic poetry of the last age and in the other case
is upon the history of painting, seems packed and ripe. The
poem to Congreve opens on a theme Dryden had often discussed in prose and once had covered in an epilogue, the superiority of Restoration wit to Jacobean humor. The handling
here is marked by rare composure; the edifice of modern wit
rises steadily and surely:

> Well then, the promised hour is come at last;
> The present age of wit obscures the past:
> Strong were our sires, and as they fought they writ,
> Conquering with force of arms and dint of wit;
> Theirs was the giant race before the flood;
> And thus, when Charles returned, our empire stood.
> Like Janus he the stubborn soil manured,
> With rules of husbandry the rankness cured;

Tamed us to manners, when the stage was rude,
And boisterous English wit with art indued.
Our age was cultivated thus at length,
But what we gained in skill we lost in strength.
Our builders were with want of genius curst;
The second temple was not like the first:
Till you, the best Vitruvius, come at length,
Our beauties equal, but excel our strength.
Firm Doric pillars found our solid base;
The fair Corinthian crowns the higher space;
Thus all below is strength, and all above is grace.

The poem ends with a touching last will and testament which
has never had to beg for praise, but which borders, it must be
admitted, upon the maudlin. In the epistles to Granville and
Motteux in 1698 Dryden returned more or less to the glibness
of poems like the *Roscommon*. The verses to Motteux the
Frenchman, affixed to his tragedy called *Beauty in Distress*, begin with a reply to the newly arisen moral censor of the stage,
Jeremy Collier, and end with a tribute to Motteux's powers
which affords another example of Dryden's facility in turning
over an idea and extracting from it all that can be extracted:

Let thy own Gauls condemn thee, if they dare;
Contented to be thinly regular.
Born there, but not for them, our fruitful soil
With more increase rewards thy happy toil.
Their tongue, infeebled, is refined so much,
That, like pure gold, it bends at every touch;
Our sturdy Teuton yet will art obey,
More fit for manly thought, and strengthened with allay.
But whence art thou inspired, and thou alone,
To flourish in an idiom not thy own?
It moves our wonder, that a foreign guest
Should overmatch the most, and match the best.
In underpraising thy deserts, I wrong;
Here, find the first deficience of our tongue;

Words, once my stock, are wanting to commend
So great a poet and so good a friend.

The last two epistles of all appeared with considerable pomp in
Dryden's last volume, the *Fables*. The *Palamon and Arcite*
was preceded by a dedicatory poem to the Duchess of Ormond
and was followed by a piece upon which Dryden expended a
great deal of effort and of which he was justly proud: *To My
Honored Kinsman, John Driden, of Chesterton, in the County
of Huntingdon, Esquire*. The lines to "illustrious Ormond,"
though tawdry in a few places, are suffused with a fine old
man's gallantry; the medieval luster of the *Fables* has lent
them a new light. Their rapture has all the old pulse, but it is
chastened and poised:

> O daughter of the rose, whose cheeks unite
> The differing titles of the red and white;
> Who heaven's alternate beauty well display,
> The blush of morning, and the milky way;
> Whose face is paradise, but fenced from sin:
> For God in either eye has placed a cherubin.
> All is your lord's alone; e'en absent, he
> Employs the care of chaste Penelope.
> For him you waste in tears your widowed hours,
> For him your curious needle paints the flowers;
> Such works of old imperial dames were taught;
> Such, for Ascanius, fair Elisa wrought.

Only the most frigid reader would take exception to the
cherubim which God has stationed in the Duchess's eyes. The
poem to Driden of Chesterton is the most Horatian of all the
epistles. It is a eulogy of country life in general and a com-
mendation of the kinsman's own rural regimen in particular,
with digressions more or less sardonic upon marriage, medicine, and the present state of Europe. The closing paragraph is
mathematically final:

O true descendant of a patriot line,
Who, while thou shar'st their luster, lend'st 'em thine,
Vouchsafe this picture of thy soul to see;
'Tis so far good as it resembles thee.
The beauties to the original I owe;
Which when I miss, my own defects I show;
Nor think the kindred Muses thy disgrace;
A poet is not born in every race.
Two of a house few ages can afford;
One to perform, the other to record.
Praiseworthy actions are by thee embraced;
And 'tis my praise, to make thy praises last.
For ev'n when death dissolves our human frame,
The soul returns to heaven, from whence it came;
Earth keeps the body, verse preserves the fame.

Dryden paraded a distaste for epigrams which was consonant with the contemporary worship of epic poetry; for from Bacon to Temple the heroic poem crowded out of the general estimation all forms that were less pretentious. "From Homer to the *Anthologia*, from Virgil to Martial and Owen's Epigrams, and from Spenser to Fleckno; that is, from the top to the bottom of all poetry," wrote Dryden in the *Discourse of Satire*. Yet he proved upon a few occasions to have an epigrammatic turn of some distinction. His epigram on Milton, which appeared in Tonson's 1688 folio edition of *Paradise Lost*, is neatly put together. Its shape alone has given it currency. Few have observed that it seems to say more than it does. "Loftiness of thought" and "majesty" seem to make a better antithesis than in truth they do. De Quincey, in a shrewd essay on this poem, which he calls "the very finest epigram in the English language," marvels at the perfection of form which could intrigue a whole century of readers into accepting as profound a half dozen lines which really say nothing. Dryden was probably drawn to the Greek Anthology long before 1683, when he closed his *Life of Plutarch* with this translation of the epigram by Agathias:

> Cheronean Plutarch, to thy deathless praise
> Does martial Rome this grateful statue raise;
> Because both Greece and she thy fame have shared,
> (Their heroes written, and their lives compared;)
> But thou thyself couldst never write thy own;
> Their lives have parallels, but thine has none.

Dryden's eight epitaphs all derive a certain pointedness and sufficiency from the shining Anthology, although in the main their author tends to weave a heavier burial cloth than that which was woven by Antipater, Leonidas, and Simonides. He stiffens his texture by means of conceits and antitheses, with the result that his effect is likely to be one of rectangularity. His epitaphs by no means lack that seventeenth-century largeness which the next few generations could not muster, and the absence of which in contemporary burial verses Dr. Johnson wrote an essay to lament. Dryden shows best in his lines on John Graham of Claverhouse, Viscount Dundee, and those on the Marquis of Winchester. Both poems celebrate the lives and deaths of loyalists who supported lost causes. The Marquis of Winchester had fought for Charles I, and the great Graham of Claverhouse had been killed at Killiecrankie in 1689. The epitaph on Winchester begins with four couplets which draw or imply four distinctions:

> He who in impious times undaunted stood,
> And midst rebellion durst be just and good;
> Whose arms asserted, and whose sufferings more
> Confirmed the cause for which he fought before,
> Rests here, rewarded by an heavenly prince,
> For what his earthly could not recompense.
> Pray, reader, that such times no more appear;
> Or, if they happen, learn true honour here.

The epitaph on Dundee is a translation from a Latin poem by
Dr. Archibald Pitcairne. It follows its original closely enough,
but at the end it makes a characteristic departure towards a
greater profuseness in antithesis:

> O last and best of Scots! who didst maintain
> Thy country's freedom from a foreign reign;
> New people fill the land now thou art gone,
> New gods the temples, and new kings the throne.
> Scotland and thee did each in other live;
> Thou wouldst not her, nor could she thee survive.
> Farewell, who living didst support the State,
> And couldst not fall but with thy country's fate.

The epitaphs on Lady Whitmore, on "A Fair Maiden Lady
Who Died at Bath," on "Young Mr. Rogers of Gloucester-
shire," on Mrs. Margaret Paston, on Sir Palmes Fairborne (in
Westminster Abbey), and on Erasmus Lawton have no special
significance.

"We have been all born; we have most of us been married;
and so many have died before us, that our deaths can supply
but few materials for a poet," wrote Dr. Johnson; and Goldsmith thought there was nothing new to be said upon the death
of a friend after the standard classical elegies. Dryden's temper
seems anything but elegiac if in connection with elegiac we
think of Theocritus, Bion, Moschus, Ovid, Dante, Petrarch,
Spenser, and Donne. The more mystical of the Elizabethan
sonnets on the subject of death, and the exquisite dirges in
Shakespeare, Beaumont and Fletcher, and Webster were keyed
above him, or at least keyed in another sphere of poetry than
his. He is not a prober among mysteries; he is not exquisite. He
is sober and symmetrical, and pays his tribute to the dead with
plain, manly melodies. His elegies and Donne's are poles apart.
His demand to be read aloud, there being no reason why the
music in them should be subdued. Donne's take effect only
upon an inner ear and eye, back behind the curtain of the senses,

where they stage their dark, fierce little dramas with Love and Hate and Fear and Jealousy and Death in the leading roles.

Dryden's first elegy happens to be his worst poem. It is scarcely necessary to say that when writing the *Hastings* he was not much concerned either about the young departed lord or about the idea of death in general. His next elegy might well be called his best poem.

If one is not pleased by the lines *To the Memory of Mr. Oldham* one will not be pleased by anything in Dryden; they are his touchstone. They appeared in 1684 among several laments which prefaced a volume of Oldham's remains. That wrathful young satirist had died the previous year at the age of thirty. Dryden had owed him no trifling literary debts. He discharged them posthumously as follows:

> Farewell, too little and too lately known,
> Whom I began to think and call my own:
> For sure our souls were near allied, and thine
> Cast in the same poetic mold with mine.
> One common note on either lyre did strike,
> And knaves and fools we both abhorred alike.
> To the same goal did both our studies drive;
> The last set out the soonest did arrive.
> Thus Nisus fell upon the slippery place,
> Whilst his young friend performed and won the race.
> O early ripe! to thy abundant store
> What could advancing age have added more?
> It might (what nature never gives the young)
> Have taught the numbers of thy native tongue.
> But satire needs not those, and wit will shine
> Through the harsh cadence of a rugged line:
> A noble error, and but seldom made,
> When poets are by too much force betrayed.
> Thy generous fruits, tho' gathered ere their prime,
> Still shewed a quickness; and maturing time
> But mellows what we write to the dull sweets of rhyme.

> Once more, hail and farewell; farewell, thou young,
> But ah too short, Marcellus of our tongue;
> Thy brows with ivy and with laurels bound;
> But fate and gloomy night encompass thee around.

This poem is artificial, like *Lycidas*; it is full of echoes; and its subject is literary. But the melody is round and sure; every couplet sounds "like a great bronze ring thrown down on marble"; and the ideas erect themselves without commotion into a perfectly proportioned frame of farewell. There is not an original word in the work. It is a classical mosaic, pieces of which Dryden had had by him for a long time. It is precisely as a mosaic, as a composition, that it is triumphant. The passionate farewell, the *ave atque vale*, had been a favorite motif in Greek and Latin elegy. Dryden begins with a line that savors of Juliet's bewildered outburst when she discovers Romeo's full identity at the ball:

> My only love, sprung from my only hate!
> Too early seen unknown, and known too late!

Virgil had been fond of celebrating two souls that were "near allied"; and Persius in the fifth Satire had drawn a parallel between himself and his tutor Cornutus of which Dryden's third and fourth lines are reminiscent. The story of Nisus seems never to have been out of Dryden's mind. As early as *The Indian Emperor* he had made Guyomar declare to Odmar, his rival for Alibech:

> It seems my soul then moved the quicker pace;
> Yours first set out, mine reached her in the race.

And very recently he had been translating the episode of Nisus and Euryalus from Virgil for the second *Miscellany*, which was to appear in a few months. He had written then for Virgil:

> One was their care, and their delight was one;
> One common hazard in the war they shared.

And he had spoken for Ascanius to Euryalus thus:

> But thou, whose years are more to mine allied. . . .
> One faith, one fame, one fate, shall both attend.

"Young Marcellus" was the dead nephew of Augustus whom Virgil had mourned in the sixth Aeneid. Dryden had inserted a similar lament for the Duke of Ormond's (Barzillai's) son in *Absalom and Achitophel* (ll. 830-855). The ivy, the laurel, the fate, and the gloomy night encompassing around were venerable adornments which could scarcely be avoided. Additional parallels can be of no consequence; these in themselves are enough to show how Dryden was able to pour his memories out upon an occasion. Nothing except his genius can explain the precision with which he grouped those memories in this case, or the harmony with which his feeling suffused them.

He never succeeded so well in elegy again. The ode in memory of Anne Killigrew is more interesting as an ode than as an elegy, and is reserved for consideration as such.* *Eleonora* (1692), composed for a fat fee in honor of the late Countess of Abingdon, whom Dryden had never seen, was declared by Sir Walter Scott, the gentlest critic whom the poet has had, to be "totally deficient in interest." It is a catalogue of female Christian virtues, virtues which Dryden was not much moved by. It suffers from a threadbare piety everywhere except at the end, in what Dryden calls the "Epiphonema, or close of the poem." Here, as usual, he quickens his pulse and gathers his powers. He is probably inspired in this case by Ben Jonson, who began an epigram to the Earl of Pembroke with the lines,

> I do but name thee, Pembroke, and I find
> It is an epigram on all mankind.

Dryden writes:

> Let this suffice: nor thou, great saint, refuse
> This humble tribute of no vulgar muse;

* See Chapter VI.

Who, not by cares, or wants, or age depressed,
Stems a wild deluge with a dauntless breast;
And dares to sing thy praises in a clime
Where vice triumphs, and virtue is a crime;
Where ev'n to draw the picture of thy mind
Is satire on the most of humankind;
Take it, while yet 'tis praise; before my rage,
Unsafely just, break loose on this bad age;
So bad, that thou thyself hadst no defense
From vice, but barely by departing hence.
    Be what, and where thou art; to wish thy place
Were, in the best, presumption more than grace.
Thy relics (such thy works of mercy are)
Have, in this poem, been my holy care;
As earth thy body keeps, thy soul the sky,
So shall this verse preserve thy memory;
For thou shalt make it live, because it sings of thee.

An elegy of uncertain date *On the Death of a Very Young Gentleman* is even less interesting than *Eleonora*. The account may close with Dryden's only attempt at a pastoral elegy, a poem *On the Death of Amyntas*, also undated. It is a dialogue between Damon and Menalcas. It opens with a fine rush of melody:

'Twas on a joyless and a gloomy morn,
Wet was the grass, and hung with pearls the thorn;
When Damon, who designed to pass the day
With hounds and horns, and chase the flying prey,
Rose early from his bed; but soon he found
The welkin pitched with sullen clouds around,
An eastern wind, and dew upon the ground.
Thus while he stood, and sighing did survey
The fields, and cursed th' ill omens of the day,
He saw Menalcas come with heavy pace;
Wet were his eyes, and cheerless was his face;
He wrung his hands, distracted with his care,
And sent his voice before him from afar.

But it soon ceases to give out sound, proceeding through some of the flattest moralizing in Dryden and ending with a very inferior conceit.

As a class, the prologues and epilogues of Dryden are the richest and best body of his occasional verse. There is no surer way to become convinced of his superbly off-hand genius than to read the ninety-five pieces which he is known to have composed for delivery from the front of the Restoration stage. They give, more adequately than any other division of his work, a notion of his various powers: his speed, his precision, his weight, his melody, his tact. He seems to have been braced in writing them by his consciousness that they would be heard by acute and critical ears in actual playhouses; for he has purged himself of conceits, bombast, and mannered elegance. They are his most speaking poems; they have the warmth of flesh and blood. He has written some of them as much for fun as for money, and consciously or unconsciously he has revealed himself in them all to an important extent. They are a running commentary on forty years of his life, as well as a living mirror in which the tiny theatrical world of Charles and James is shrewdly reflected.

Dryden is the master of the prologue and epilogue in English. His peculiar authority was felt in his own day before even a dozen of his supple, terse addresses had been delivered by members of the King's Company; and eventually he was acknowledged to be without rival in the art of presenting new dramas to old audiences. It came to be understood that a prologue by Mr. Dryden might mean the making of a green playwright or the saving of an unprepossessing play. Spectators relished his confidences and his innuendoes; often there was more real meat in his forty lines of introduction than the whole ensuing tragedy or comedy could furnish forth. The secret of his success lay in the intimacy yet dignity of his harangue. He was both easy and important; he was fluent, but he was also condensed. There was something peculiarly satisfying in his form; he rounded off his little speeches as though they were clay and his brain were a potter's wheel. The final impression was one of many riches casually summoned but faultlessly disposed.

There is nothing exactly like these pieces of Dryden's in any literature. The classical drama approximated them nowhere except in the *parabases* of Aristophanes, when the Chorus came forward for the author and delivered torrents of audacious remarks to the audience. Greek tragedies might be prefaced with prologues, but these were more or less integral to the action, and were not personal. Plautus and Terence used prologues mainly to explain the events which were to follow, though Terence in his conducted mild literary quarrels around charges of plagiarism; their epilogues were only perfunctory bids for applause. The French drama never developed either form extensively; the English drama began at an early stage to cultivate both, scarcely, however, in the direction of Dryden. Marlowe introduced his *Tamburlaine* with high astounding terms. Shakespeare preserved a chaste anonymity in the playhouse; his Prologue in *Henry V* is strictly necessary; only in the epilogue to *As You Like It* and in the prologue and epilogue to *Henry VIII* does he take his audience into his confidence, and even there he has his reserves. Ben Jonson opened a vein which was followed along by none of his contemporaries or immediate successors. He was the first English playwright to harangue the pit; he was the father of the militant prologue. He first showed how literary criticism could be run serially, preceding plays; his prologue to *Every Man in His Humour* sounds like Dryden. Dekker and Heywood were more modest; Beaumont and Fletcher did much to discourage altogether the bold, direct address to the audience.

The Restoration brought in a new mode. Theater-goers were now more sophisticated and belonged more clearly to a single class; being somewhat familiar as well with the fashionable literary canons, they liked an occasional dash of criticism from a poet not too pedantic to be interesting or even saucy. As time went on, more intimate relations came to be established among dramatists, players, and spectators within the four walls of the theaters; the fortunes of both authors and actors came to be of real concern to a now well-seasoned public; a greater body of common knowledge took shape; it became possible for audiences to be addressed on special subjects. Prologues and epilogues were poems now that could stand alone; often it made very little difference at what play or in what order they were spoken. "Now, gentlemen," says Bayes in *The Rehearsal*, "I would fain ask your opinion of one thing. I have made a Prologue and an Epilogue, which may both serve for either; that is, the prologue for the epilogue, or the epilogue for the prologue; (do you mark?) nay, they may both serve too, 'egad for any other play as well as this." Bayes was right; prologues and epilogues had become social events. Etherege helped to set the tone of Restoration performances in this kind, with his pungent reflections on the tastes of the pit and his cavalier trick of speaking of his Muse as his mistress; but Etherege wrote little at the most. Outside of Dryden the best Restoration performers were Lee, Mrs. Behn, Otway, and Congreve, with their varying degrees of sprightliness and authority. Dryden could stand against them all; they could please, but he could take by storm. The Restoration saw the prologue and the epilogue at their height. The revolutions in taste which introduced the new age of Steele and Cibber and Lillo brought more heterogeneous crowds to the theaters, and it seemed less important to hear what the author, whoever he might be, had to say each day. Yet so old a habit could not be broken at once, and many excellent sets of verses continued to precede and follow plays, particularly farces, throughout the eighteenth century. Pope, Thomson, Goldsmith, and Johnson wrote respectable pieces; but the masters in this century were Fielding and Garrick. Fielding had all of Dryden's energy and wickedness, if not his richness and his form. He pretended to write prologues under protest,

> As something must be spoke, no matter what;
> No friends are now by prologues lost or got. . . .
> I wish with all my heart, the stage and town
> Would both agree to cry all prologues down,
> That we, no more obliged to say or sing,
> Might drop this useless, necessary thing.

Garrick has more of the useless things to his credit than has any other Englishman; he is always dexterous, but he does not carry a considerable weight.

It is likely that Dryden began to write prologues and epilogues perfunctorily, without any notion of their possibilities; and to the end he maintained a certain nonchalance with reference to them that he could not easily muster for other forms. He felt free in them, for instance, to indulge in feminine rhymes, which elsewhere he renounced as too familiar. Yet he came early to see that some of these poems were almost his best writing. He arranged for the first *Miscellany* in 1684 to include eighteen of the riper specimens; and his relish for the exercise steadily increased. He was under no obligations in this form; he could damn the small critics of the pit and he could pour no end of ridicule upon the general taste. Yet he could exercise his gifts of compliment too if he liked. Tom Brown affected to believe that Dryden's flattery of Oxford was very gross, and Dryden himself wrote to Rochester remarking "how easy 'tis to pass any thing upon an university, and how gross flattery the learned will endure." He took increasing pains to render himself effective, and to make it clear to all that he excelled. He compared the prologue in his hands to a church-bell in the hands of the sexton:

> Prologues, like bells to churches, toll you in
> With chiming verse, till the dull plays begin;

> With this sad difference, tho', of pit and pew,
> You damn the poet, but the priest damns you; *

or to a military assault conducted on a large and fierce scale. He compared the epilogue to a benediction:

> As country vicars, when the sermon's done,
> Run huddling to the benediction;
> Well knowing, tho' the better sort may stay,
> The vulgar rout will run unblest away;
> So we, when once our play is done, make haste
> With a short epilogue to close your taste.†

He selected the most intelligent and vivacious players as his spokesmen, and adapted his lines to their known dispositions: Nell Gwynn could do the surprising, saucy things; Mrs. Bracegirdle, Mrs. Mountfort, and Mrs. Marshall could deliver more scurrilous and scandalous messages; Mr. Betterton could be infinitely grave, as when he impersonated the ghost of Shakespeare; and Mr. Hart could be choice and elegant, for the prologues at Oxford. Nell Gwynn was twice called upon to succeed by sensational means: in the prologue to the first part of *The Conquest of Granada*, which she recited wearing a hat as broad as a coach-wheel, and in the epilogue to *Tyrannic Love*, which she spoke only after resisting the efforts of the bearers to convey her dead body off the stage:

> (*To the Bearer*):   Hold, are you mad, you damned confounded dog,
>   I am to rise, and speak the epilogue.
> (*To the Audience*): I come, kind gentlemen, strange news to tell ye,
>   I am the ghost of poor departed Nelly.

Dryden came also more and more to pack his pieces with criticism and allusion. His serried dialectic flattered the audience

---

* Prologue to *The Assignation*.
† Epilogue to *Sir Martin Mar-All*.

which was expected to follow it; though the following was made somewhat easier by the practice of circulating folio copies of the prologue and epilogue before the play began, so that the hearers could be familiar with the lines when it came time for them to be recited. If Dryden wrote his first prologues and epilogues perfunctorily, it is plain that he wrote his later ones both with instinctive delight and with due attention to the precautions necessary for insuring their success.

For his measure he has confined himself almost wholly to the heroic couplet; though the prologues to his *Wild Gallant* and to Joseph Harris's *Mistakes* are in part prose dialogues; and the prologue to *The Maiden Queen,* the epilogue to *The Tempest,* the prologue to *Limberham,* and the prologue to the King and Queen (1682) are in triplets, the effect of which is often slily jovial:

> Old men shall have good old plays to delight 'em;
> And you, fair ladies and gallants, that slight 'em,
> We'll treat with good new plays; if our new wits can write 'em.

He is fond of leading off with a simile or metaphor and elaborating it throughout the length of the piece; as witness the prologue to *The Wild Gallant, Revived,* where the author's dramatic muse is compared to a raw young squire who has come up to London bent on making an impression swiftly. He falls at times, for the sake of emphasis, into aphorism, as here in the prologue to *All for Love:*

> Errors, like straws, upon the surface flow;
> He who would search for pearls must dive below;

or here in the epilogue to Lee's *Mithridates:*

> Love is no more a violent desire;
> 'Tis a mere metaphor, a painted fire. . . .
> Let honour and preferment go for gold,
> But glorious beauty is not to be sold.

Only in the satires is his pen as pointed; and indeed it was largely from the sixty-five prologues and epilogues which he had written by 1681 that the author of *Absalom and Achitophel* had learned to wield irresistible satiric cadences. Scorn for French farces and for Whig reformers had been sharpening Dryden's claws during the late 1670's. He had learned the accents of mockery in such lines as these from the prologue to Carlell's *Arviragus:*

> If all these ills could not undo us quite,
> A brisk French troop is grown your dear delight,
> Who with broad bloody bills call you each day
> To laugh and break your buttons at their play;
> Or see some serious piece, which we presume
> Is fallen from some incomparable plume.

He had taken his turn at the Popish Plot in the prologues to Lee's *Caesar Borgia* and Tate's *Loyal General.* Always there had been his audience at which he could rail.

> The most compendious method is to rail;
> Which you so like, you think yourselves ill used
> When in smart prologues you are not abused.
> A civil prologue is approved by no man;
> You hate it as you do a civil woman,

he had declared as early as 1667, in the epilogue to *The Maiden Queen.* The fun he was to have with Og and Doeg was very much like the fun he had had with the yawning faces in the stalls at *Caesar Borgia:*

> You sleep o'er wit, and by my troth you may;
> Most of your talents lie another way.
> You love to hear of some prodigious tale,
> The bell that tolled alone, or Irish whale.

Roughly speaking, there are nine subjects treated in Dryden's prologues and epilogues, or nine reasons for their being. These will not serve as the basis for an exact classification, because certain pieces turn on more than one point; but an enumeration of those prologues and epilogues which play notably on each of the nine strings may stand as a guide through this most miscellaneous department of Dryden's poetry.

First, there are those which celebrate theatrical occasions, such as the "Prologue Spoken on the First Day of the King's House Acting after the Fire," the "Prologue for the Women when they Acted at the Old Theatre in Lincoln's Inn Fields," the prologue and epilogue to "The Maiden Queen, when Acted by the Women Only," and the prologues and epilogue "Spoken at the Opening of the New House" in 1674.

Second, there are those which compliment distinguished spectators or flatter special audiences, like the prologues and epilogues spoken at Oxford, the prologue and epilogue for *The Unhappy Favourite* "Spoken to the King and the Queen at their Coming to the House," the "Prologue to His Royal Highness [the Duke of York], Upon His First Appearance at the Duke's Theatre Since His Return from Scotland," the "Prologue to the Duchess [of York] on Her Return from Scotland," and the prologue and epilogue "To the King and Queen at the Opening of their Theatre upon the Union of the Two Companies in 1682." Of all these the prologues spoken at Oxford are deservedly the best known, containing as they do some of Dryden's most genial verse. One, which is seldom quoted, shows him in a particularly merry humor. It is the prologue spoken at the University during the Duke of York's residence in Scotland in 1681. Certain members of the company, it seems, had followed the Duke up to Holyrood House:

> Our brethren are from Thames to Tweed departed,
> And of our sisters all the kinder-hearted
> To Edenborough gone, or coached, or carted.
> With bonny bluecap there they act all night
> For Scotch half-crown, in English threepence hight.
> One nymph, to whom fat Sir John Falstaff's lean,
> There with her single person fills the scene;

Another, with long use and age decayed,
Dived here old woman, and rose there a maid.
Our trusty doorkeepers of former time
There strut and swagger in heroic rhyme.
Tack but a copper lace to drugget suit,
And there's a hero made without dispute;
And that which was a capon's tail before
Becomes a plume for Indian Emperor.

Mrs. Marshall took this pretty farewell of the learned in 1674:

Such ancient hospitality there rests
In yours, as dwelt in the first Grecian breasts,
Whose kindness was religion to their guests.
Such modesty did to our sex appear,
As had there been no laws we need not fear,
Since each of you was our protector here.
Converse so chaste, and so strict virtue shown,
As might Apollo with the Muses own.
Till our return, we must despair to find
Judges so just, so knowing, and so kind.

Third, there are those which deal in literary criticism, such
as the first prologue to *The Maiden Queen,* on the French and
English rules, the epilogue to *The Wild Gallant, Revived,* on
the difficulties of writing comedy, the prologue to *The Tempest,*
on Shakespeare, the prologue to *Albumazar,* on plagiarism, the
prologue to *Tyrannic Love,* on poetic license, the epilogue to
the second part of *The Conquest of Granada,* on Elizabethan
and modern wit, the famous prologue to *Aureng-Zebe,* on rhyming plays, the prologue and epilogue to *Oedipus,* on anglicizing
Greek tragedy, the prologue to *Troilus and Cressida,* on
Shakespeare again, and the prologue to *Amphitryon,* on the
subject of contemporary satire. The epilogue to the second part
of *The Conquest of Granada* is as a whole the most perfect of
these poems. The contrast between Jonson's humor and King
Charles's wit is developed with economy and precision and yet

with a staggering copiousness. The subject is turned every possible way; the seventeen couplets lay on seventeen different pieces of fuel to brighten the fire. Dryden exhausts the subject without exhausting the reader. He varies one sense seventeen ways, but each of the ways is fresh and contributive.

Fourth, there are those which introduce young playwrights, such as the prologue to *Circe*, introducing Charles Davenant, the epilogue to *Tamerlane*, commending Charles Saunders, the prologue and epilogue to *The Loyal Brother*, introducing Thomas Southerne, and the epilogue to *The Husband His Own Cuckold*, introducing Dryden's own son John.

Fifth, there are those which berate the audience for its low taste, for its preferring French farce to English comedy, and for the fools and critics that largely compose it. These railing prologues and epilogues are legion. The general taste is lamented the most reproachfully in the prologue to *The Rival Ladies*, the epilogue to *Aureng-Zebe*, the prologue to *Limberham*, the prologue to Lee's *Caesar Borgia*, the prologue to Tate's *Loyal General*, and the prologues to *King Arthur* and *Cleomenes*. The weakness for French literary goods is hit the best blows in the epilogue to *An Evening's Love*, the prologue to Carlell's *Arviragus*, the epilogue to Etherege's *Man of Mode*, the prologue to *The Spanish Friar*, and the prologue to *Albion and Albanius*. Critics and fools are both abhorred alike in the prologue to *The Rival Ladies*, the epilogue to *The Indian Emperor*, the second prologue to *The Maiden Queen*, the prologue to the second part of *The Conquest of Granada*, the prologue to *All for Love*, and the epilogue to *The Man of Mode*.

Sixth, there are those which play with contemporary manners in the town and in the theaters; like the prologues written for the women only, the prologue to *Marriage à la Mode*, which makes out a pitiful case for "poor pensive punk" now that the braves are all gone off to war, the prologue to Shadwell's *True Widow*, on certain familiar vices, the prologue to *The Spanish Friar*, the prologue to Lee's *Princess of Cleves*, the epilogue to the King and Queen, and the prologue to Southerne's *Disappointment*.

Seventh, there are those which seem to have been calculated to please through sheer brutal innuendo. These are incontestably expert at the game they play. They are the exercises of an adroit and tireless imagination which hesitated at nothing. The prologues and epilogues for the women only, the prologue to *The Wild Gallant, Revived*, the prologue to *An Evening's Love*, the epilogue to *The Assignation*, the epilogue to *Limberham*, the prologue and epilogue to Lee's *Princess of Cleves*, the prologue to *The Disappointment*, the epilogue to Lee's *Constantine the Great*, the epilogue to *Don Sebastian*, the epilogue to *Amphitryon*, the epilogue to *Cleomenes*, the epilogue to Bancroft's *Henry II*, and in fact almost every prologue or epilogue thereafter, must be dispatched to this category.

Eighth, there are the political prologues and epilogues. *A Lenten Prologue* of 1683, probably by Shadwell, pointed the way to the new type:

> Our prologue wit grows flat; the nap's worn off,
> And howsoe'er we turn and trim the stuff,
> The gloss is gone that looked at first so gaudy;
> 'Tis now no jest to hear young girls talk bawdy,
> But plots and parties give new matters birth,
> And state distractions serve you here for mirth.

Shadwell, if Shadwell it was, referred to Dryden and Lee's *Duke of Guise* (1682). A prologue at Oxford in 1680 had compared critics in the theater to Whigs in the state. During the next ten years almost every prologue or epilogue of Dryden's bore more or less directly upon the constitutional conflict of that decade; the series closing in 1690 with the prologue to Fletcher's *Prophetess*, which contained covert sneers at the Revolution and presented King William's Irish campaign in a ludicrous light.

Ninth, there are those which are personal or controversial,

and take the audience into the poet's confidence. The epilogue to *Marriage à la Mode* is an apology for a chaste play. The epilogue to Fletcher's *Pilgrim* (1700) is a none too sober moral recantation following the attacks of Collier and others upon the manners of the stage. The prologue to *Don Sebastian*, Dryden's first play after the Revolution, asks that civil grudges be forgotten, and begs forgiveness for supposed political sins. The prologue to *Love Triumphant*, Dryden's last play of all, is a will and testament bequeathing his various dramatic gifts to the critics and the beaux. It is a sly, ripe piece of raillery, a portion of which should be fitting as tailpiece to a chapter which has aimed to convey a sense of Dryden's occasional riches. The lines were spoken by Mr. Betterton:

> So now, this poet, who forsakes the stage,
> Intends to gratify the present age.
> One warrant shall be signed for every man.
> All shall be wits that will, and beaux that can. . . .
> He dies, at least to us, and to the stage,
> And what he has he leaves this noble age.
> He leaves you first, all plays of his inditing,
> The whole estate which he has got by writing.
> The beaux may think this nothing but vain praise;
> They'll find it something, the testator says;
> For half their love is made from scraps of plays.
> To his worst foes he leaves his honesty,
> That they may thrive upon 't as much as he.
> He leaves his manners to the roaring boys,
> Who come in drunk, and fill the house with noise.
> He leaves to the dire critics of his wit
> His silence and contempt of all they writ.
> To Shakespeare's critic, he bequeaths the curse,
> To find his faults, and yet himself make worse. . . .
> Last, for the fair, he wishes you may be,
> From your dull critics, the lampooners, free.
> Tho' he pretends no legacy to leave you,
> An old man may at least good wishes give you.

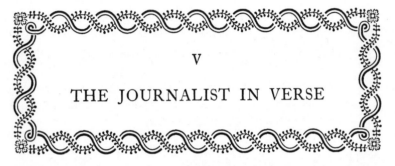

V

THE JOURNALIST IN VERSE

I s IT not great pity to see a man, in the flower of his romantic conceptions, in the full vigour of his studies on love
and honour, to fall into such a distraction, as to walk
through the thorns and briers of controversy?" So Tom Brown,
in his *Reflections on the Hind and Panther*, pretended to lament Dryden's defection from the theaters in the 1680's and
his alliance with the new powers of politics and religion. The
change, as is well known, meant relief to Dryden from modes
of expression which were not altogether adapted to his
disposition and by his subjection to which over a period of
approximately twenty years he had become bored. There were
a number of reasons, as a matter of fact, for the new departure.
Not all of the plays had been successful. "I gad," Bayes had
said in *The Rehearsal*, "the Town has used me as scurvily, as
the Players have done. . . . Since they will not admit of my
Plays, they shall know what a Satyrist I am. And so farewell
to this stage forever, I gad." In the dedication of *Aureng-Zebe*
to Lord Mulgrave in 1676, Dryden had confessed to his patron
that he was weary of play-writing and had asked that the King
be sounded on the question of an epic, for which leisure and

hence a pension would be required. In 1690, in the preface to *Don Sebastian,* he recalled further reasons why he had deserted the stage ten years before. "Having been longer acquainted with the stage than any poet now living, and having observed how difficult it was to please; that the humours of comedy were almost spent; that love and honour (the mistaken topics of tragedy) were quite worn out; that the theaters could not support their charges; that the audience forsook them; that young men without learning set up for judges, and that they talked loudest who understood the least; all these discouragements had not only weaned me from the stage, but had also given me a loathing of it."

Still another set of circumstances must have been impressing themselves upon him during the half-dozen years that preceded *Absalom and Achitophel.* The Court, which had served as a setting and a justification for the heroic drama and which in its self-sufficiency had tended to cramp the imagination and restrict the field of literary enterprise, had begun to lose something of its significance; politics had grown more complicated; the formation of parties was imminent; and journalism promised new rewards to men who could comment with effect upon topics absorbing the general attention. The Popish Plot injected new fevers into the general blood; violent ups and downs in public fortunes came again, as during the Civil War, to seem matters of course; dramatic reversals of position like those of Titus Oates, who was in glory in 1679, was flogged almost to death in 1685, but was set up with a pension in 1689, were now quite regularly to be looked for. The climax of Dryden's career was coincident with these new crises. The poems on public affairs which he wrote during the six years between *Absalom and Achitophel* in 1681 and *The Hind and the Panther* in 1687 furnished him as a class with his best opportunities and must always, as a class, deserve to be the best known of his work.

Throughout the closing years of his main dramatic period Dryden had been wont to express a strong dislike for those "abominable scribblers," the pamphleteers. It was not only that the pamphleteers of the country party in particular offended his sense of political propriety; pamphleteering in general offended his sense of the dignity of literature and poetry. Meanwhile he was developing a public voice of his own. The prologues and epilogues, the controversial prefaces, and both the rhymed tragedies and the prose comedies in so far as they involved exercise in repartee, had trained his powers of attack, had taught him the damage that might be done with cool, insulting analysis and loaded innuendo. All the while, as it has been seen, he had been discovering important new resources in the heroic couplet, and he had been suppling his medium so that a great variety of materials could be run through it. The new materials were to make severe demands upon his verse, but he came equipped to meet any demand. He came with unexampled stores of energy and with an incorruptible literary conscience that scorned the trivial, the feeble. "If a poem have genius," he remarked in the preface to *Absalom and Achitophel,* "it will force its own reception in the world." Dr. Johnson's father, the bookseller, has attested the reception which *Absalom and Achitophel* forced in its world; genius paid in that one case at least. Dryden came also with an abiding sense of his superiority; he arrived on a high level from which he looked down not only upon other controversialists but even upon the events which he was to treat; he maintained that elevation and that composure which are never found except in the company of an artistic confidence. He came finally with his most valuable gift of all, his gift of shaping thoughts and composing full, round pictures of men and principles.

He came, it must be admitted at once, without conspicuous principles of his own concerning Church or State. Bishop Burnet denied him religious convictions of any complexion whatsoever, and his name has always been synonymous with turncoat in politics. First of all, as he himself said, he was "naturally inclined to scepticism"; it is not to be believed that he was con-

verted to Catholicism by the works of Bossuet at the age of
fifty-four in the same sense that Gibbon was converted at the
age of sixteen, though Gibbon thought he was following in
Dryden's tracks; nor is it to be believed that he ever possessed
a set of nicely distinguished, carefully pondered political ideas.
In the second place, he was not so much convinced that principles were necessary as it is generally assumed he should have
been; he was not a prophet or a hero, but a party writer, writing
at a time when a comparatively neutral field of public opinion
had not as yet been cleared. In the third place, such principles
as he did possess were not so much principles as prejudices, all
of which can be summed up by saying that he hated and feared
disturbance of any kind.

By temperament a firm believer in order, he learned from
Hobbes to set a peculiar value on "peaceable, social, and com-
fortable living" even at the expense of justice and the general
health. He was absorbed in the *status quo,* and his instinct was
to strike desperately at whatever new thing threatened a dis-
sipation of authority.

> All other errors but disturb a state,
> But innovation is the blow of fate,

he wrote in *Absalom and Achitophel.* He had all of Hobbes's
distrust of the multitude, "that numerous piece of monstrosity,"
as Sir Thomas Browne put it, "which, taken asunder, seem men,
and reasonable creatures of God; but, confused together, make
but one great beast." He declined to believe that the crowd
knew what it wanted.

> The tampering world is subject to this curse,
> To physic their disease into a worse.

What it needed, he said, was "common quiet," and common
quiet could only be imposed by a single authority, the King. He
had no superstitions about the divine right, but he had no faith
in democracy. "Both my nature, as I am an Englishman, and

my reason, as I am a man, have bred in me a loathing to that specious name of a Republick," he told the Earl of Danby in the dedication of *All for Love* three years before the appearance of *Absalom and Achitophel:* "that mock-appearance of a liberty, where all who have not part in the government are slaves; and slaves they are of a viler note than such as are subjects to an absolute dominion." Where power already was, there were his sympathies. Any priest or any politician who questioned that power or offered to repair the machinery of state was an enemy of mankind. Dryden's dread of change was neither reasonable nor noble, but it was consistent.

Given a consistent outlook, it was not required that a seventeenth-century journalist in verse be a subtle scholar. When journalism becomes subtle, it must go over into prose. It being desirable in that day to work in plain blacks and whites, a type of expression such as Dryden was master of could not fail to be effectual. Both in satire and in ratiocination he wrote with a pulse that could be distinctly felt. His political poems and his religious poems beat against whatever consciousness there was with a regular and powerful rhythm.

Testimony is varied as to Dryden's satirical temper. "Posterity is absolutely mistaken as to that great man," ran an octogenarian's letter in the *Gentleman's Magazine* in 1745; "tho' forced to be a satirist, he was the mildest creature breathing. . . . He was in company the modestest man that ever conversed." It is recorded that latterly at least he was short, fat, florid, had "a down look," and could be "easily discountenanced." He spoke in the preface to the second *Miscellany* of his "natural diffidence," and in the dedication of *Troilus and Cressida* he said, no doubt facetiously in part: "I never could shake off the rustic bashfulness which hangs upon my nature." It was notorious that he could not read his own lines aloud without hesitation and embarrassment. "He had something in his nature," asserted Congreve, "that abhorred intrusion into any society whatsoever . . . and, consequently, his character might become liable both to misapprehensions and misrepresentations." George Granville, Lord Lansdowne, defended him thus against Bishop Burnet's charge that he had been "a monster of immodesty": "modesty in too great a degree was his failing. He hurt his fortune by it; he was sensible of it; he complained of it, and never could overcome it." All this does not consort with the notion one is likely to have entertained that Dryden was personally formidable, even overbearing. The scourge of Shaftesbury, Buckingham, Shadwell, and Settle by rights should have been towering and scowling; the man who is said to have sent a messenger to Tonson with a scathing triplet and with the words, "Tell the dog that he who wrote these lines can write more," should have been fearful in some physical aspect or other. Yet the only remark made in his time which even indirectly associates satire with his temper is a remark that Aubrey inserted in his life of Milton: "He pronounced the letter R (littera canina) very hard—a certaine signe of a Satyricall Witt—from Jo. Dreyden." Dryden's power seems to have issued solely from his words. He had mastered the satirical kind of expression as he had mastered other kinds before, and what he was like behind his mask of phrases remained of no consequence. He bitterly hated few persons, perhaps none, but he was capable of a sublime contempt, and it was contempt that he knew perfectly how to put into meter. At Shadwell he never did anything but laugh. He was never stupefied with rage as the average man is stupefied in the face of idiocy or infamy. He never forgot that he would be effective only as he remembered to be an artist. "There is a pride of doing more than is expected from us," he said, "and more than others would have done." "There's a sweetness in good verse," ran the preface to *Absalom and Achitophel*, "which tickles even while it hurts, and no man can be heartily angry with him who pleases him against his will."

Tradition distinguishes between satirists who are mild and well-mannered, like Varro, Horace, and Cowper, and those who are angry and rough, like Lucilius, Juvenal, Persius, Hall, Marston, and Churchill. Dryden belongs with Juvenal, but not in the sense that he is angry or rough. His animus is controlled, his satirical surface as smooth as worn stone. What he has in common with Juvenal is a huge thoroughness, a quality he himself attributes to the Roman in the *Discourse Concerning Satire:* "He fully satisfies my expectation, he treats his subject home . . . he drives his reader along with him. . . . When he gives over, it is a sign the subject is exhausted." This largeness and this completeness have seldom come together in a satirical poet. Juvenal alone among the Romans had the combination in a notable degree. Medieval satire lacked distinction if it had thoroughness. The so-called classical satirists at the end of Elizabeth's reign in England were angry and rough, but they were neither exalted nor exhaustive. Cleveland, Denham, and Marvell, the first English party satirists, were at best ragged and hasty, however earnest. Butler cannot be compared to anyone, least of all to Dryden, whose laughter never went off into chuckles.

John Oldham gave the most promise before Dryden of becoming the English Juvenal. With "satire in his very eye," as a contemporary put it, he went to Boileau for form and appropriated current passions for material. His *Satires upon the Jesuits,* written in 1679, first in England treated specific contemporary affairs with dramatic grandeur and swelling dignity. The Elizabethans had not been specific; Cleveland, Denham, and Marvell had not been grand. Oldham, who still seems fresh, must have struck his first readers with remarkable force. His solid, angry lines gave warning of an original and impetuous spirit. Dryden, as the poem which he wrote in 1684 certifies, was vividly impressed by his junior. It was from the *Satires upon the Jesuits,* particularly from Loyola's speech in the third part, as well as from *Paradise Lost* that he drew the stateliness of *Absalom and Achitophel.* He added humor to Oldham's preponderating gloom, he modified Oldham's abruptness

to directness, and he avoided the infelicities of rhyme and meter
with which Oldham had thought to approximate the fervor of
Juvenal. But the great original force of the man Dryden did not
pretend or wish to modulate. Oldham on his own side had
learned much from the elder poet, as numerous passages in
his works discover. It is a question whether a couplet that
appears in Oldham's *Letter from the Country to a Friend in
Town* (1678),

> That, like a powerful cordial, did infuse
> New life into his speechless, gaping Muse,

can be a paraphrase of the conclusion of Dryden's epistle to
Lady Castlemaine; * Dryden's poem seems never to have been
printed before the third *Miscellany* in 1693, and it is possible
that in preparing it for that volume Dryden borrowed the
couplet from Oldham to reinforce his ending. But there are
sixteen lines near the end of the *Letter* which certainly "trans-
verse," as the saying then was, the opening of the dedication
of *The Rival Ladies,* published fourteen years before: †

> 'Tis endless, Sir, to tell the many ways
> Wherein my poor deluded self I please:
> How, when the Fancy lab'ring for a birth,
> With unfelt throes brings its rude issue forth:
> How after, when imperfect shapeless thought
> Is by the judgment into fashion wrought;
> When at first search I traverse o'er my mind,
> None but a dark and empty void I find;
> Some little hints at length, like sparks, break thence,
> And glimm'ring thoughts just dawning into sense;
> Confused awhile the mixt ideas lie,
> With naught of mark to be discovered by,
> Like colours undistinguished in the night,
> Till the dusk Images, moved to the light,

* See page 115.
† See page 106.

> Teach the discerning faculty to choose
> Which it had best adopt, and which refuse.

What might be called the satirical accent in Dryden is noticeable from the beginning. The Juvenalian portions of the *Hastings* have already been remarked. Shadwell, in his *Medal of John Bayes*, with what foundation is unknown, declares:

> At Cambridge first your scurrilous vein began,
> When saucily you traduced a nobleman.

The *Astraea Redux* is not without strains of sarcasm, as here:

> Thus banished David spent abroad his time,
> When to be God's anointed was his crime.

The *Annus Mirabilis* comes perilously near to disrespect of Charles when it says of him that he

> Outweeps an hermit, and out-prays a saint.

And so on through the prologues and epilogues, Dryden all the while adding steadily to his stock of satirical devices. He learns that Alexandrines are of little value in a form where the motion must be swift and regular; his major satires have seven altogether. He learns that the medial pause is the most telling in the long run; he perfects himself in antithesis and balance. He discovers that alliteration gives emphasis and helps to set the meter rocking. He sees that pyrrhic feet give speed and assist in making the transitions natural. He finds that the stressing of penultimates stamps out lines which are unforgettable:

> He curses God, but God before *cursed him.*

> The midwife laid her hand on his *thick skull*
> With this prophetic blessing: Be *thou dull.*

> I will not rake the dung-hill of *thy crimes,*
> For who would read thy life that reads *thy rhymes?*

> To talk like Do-eg and to write *like thee.*

And gradually he secures full possession of the secret which is to aid him in becoming the most famous of English satirists, the secret of the contemptuous "character."

"Characters" are as old as literature, as old as human life itself. The summing up of traits was an instinct before it was an art. With Theophrastus it was a moral exercise. As a branch of the satiric art it was elaborated first by Horace and Juvenal, who by this and other means gave tones to satire which at all its high points it has never lacked. The two Romans went about in different ways, of course, to sketch personalities. Horace worked with a smile, delighting most in scraps of action and dialogue which revealed the fools he knew in Rome. The bore who joined him along the Via Sacra (Sat. I, 9) and Tigellius the Sardinian singer (Sat. I, 3) were laughably real. Tigellius was like Dryden's Zimri:

> This man never did anything of a piece. One while he would run as if he were flying from an enemy; at other times he would walk with as solemn a pace as he who carries a sacrifice to Juno. Sometimes he had two hundred servants, sometimes only ten. Now he would talk of kings and tetrarchs, and everything great; now he would say, I desire no more than a three-footed table, a little clean salt, and a gown (I do not care how coarse), to defend me from the cold. Had you given this fine manager a thousand sesterces, who was as well satisfied with a few, in five days his pockets would be empty. He would frequently sit up all night, to the very morning, and would snore in bed all day. There never was anything so inconsistent with itself.

Dryden knew this Tigellius; and once he took occasion to praise the Rupilius and the Persius who are presented by Horace in a somewhat different manner in the seventh satire of the first book. They too are shown in action, but Rupilius is introduced by a series of epithets which anticipates Juvenal.

> Durus homo, atque odio qui posset vincere Regem;
> Confidens, tumidusque; adeo sermonis amari,
> Sisennos, Barros ut equis praecurreret albis.

Juvenal invented the chain of scornful epithets and was partial to it in his satiric practice. If he resorted to action at all he made it swift and savage, like that of Messalina going to the stews. His fourth satire is a gallery of portraits, in the manner of *Absalom and Achitophel;* the various councilors who come to advise the emperor what he shall do with his monstrous turbot are seized by a firm hand and dressed in sinister new robes. The Greek parasite described in the third satire is even more of a Zimri than Tigellius was:

> Ingenium velox, audacia perdita, sermo
> Promptus et Isaeo torrentior. Ede quid illum
> Esse putes. Quemvis hominem secum attulit ad nos:
> Grammaticus rhetor geometres pictor aliptes
> Augur schoenobates medicus magus, omnia novit
> Graeculus esuriens.

Dryden has translated the passage thus:

> Quick-witted, brazen-faced, with fluent tongues,
> Patient of labours, and dissembling wrongs.
> Riddle me this, and guess him if you can,
> Who bears a nation in a single man?
> A cook, a conjurer, a rhetorician,
> A painter, pedant, a geometrician,
> A dancer on the ropes, and a physician.
> All things the hungry Greek exactly knows.

The Middle Ages and the Renaissance were rich in "characters" of types and individuals. Clerics and laymen, allegorists and chroniclers were busy at portraiture. No one has disposed of individuals in more cursory, stinging phrases than those which Dante used; no one has drawn types better than Chaucer. Barclay's Ship of Fools was full to sinking. Awdeley's *Fraternity of Vagabonds* (1565) was a populous gallery of English rogues. In Elizabeth's reign men like Greene and Nash brought forward other rascals to the light; and formal satirists like Hall and Donne gave a general flaying to the London coxcombs.

Donne was a four-dimensional Horace; the fop who adorns his first satire deserves to be one of the most famous of all literary effigies.

The seventeenth century, in England and elsewhere, saw an extraordinary development in the art of portraying personages both generalized and real. The abstract Theophrastian "character" is now a well-known form of Jacobean and Caroline prose. The "humours" of Ben Jonson were almost its starting-point; Sir Thomas Overbury, Joseph Hall, John Stevens, John Earle, Nicholas Breton, Geoffrey Minshull, Wye Saltonstall, Donald Lupton, Richard Flecknoe, and Samuel Butler handed it along, enriching it all the time with observation and humor, until Addison and Steele, who also knew La Bruyère and the French type, appropriated it for their Sir Roger de Coverley papers, and Fielding grafted on its stem his own Squire Western.

Dryden was well acquainted with this body of prose. But his especial contribution was to be made in the field of personal portraiture, a field which began to be cultivated in prose and verse somewhat later than the other. The Civil War had created a new public interest in public men, and during the Restoration it had rapidly become profitable for political writers to indulge at considerable length in personalities. The Theophrastian essay modified itself to suit this tendency, admitting each year a more direct observation and a greater proportion of particular and satiric details. But the tendency was best served by another form of prose "character" altogether, the historical-biographical, a form which was evolved simultaneously in France and in England. The models were furnished by the classical historians, chiefly Plutarch, Tacitus, and Suetonius, and by such modern writers of history as the Italian Davila, who treated the Civil Wars of France. In France the development proceeded through the historians, the writers of *Mémoires* like Richelieu and Cardinal de Retz, the romancers like Magdeleine de Scudéry, and the composers of *portraits* like Mademoiselle de Montpensier. In England the Earl of Clarendon was the master of the his-

torical "character," with a not very close second in Bishop Burnet. George Savile, Marquis of Halifax, wrote brilliant political
estimates of Charles II and others; Walton, Aubrey, and Sprat
made some of the earliest attempts at careful biographical de-
lineation; and in many cases remarkable traits were observed
by keen eyes and set down on paper from no other motive than
pure private delight.

The first Earl of Shaftesbury, Dryden's Achitophel, and
therefore an important name in the history of caricature, has
left in his fragmentary autobiography a portrait which for richness and clarity of detail ought to have a place among the best-
known passages of seventeenth-century prose. It is given here
in full because it illustrates better than any Theophrastian piece
or any historian's draft the gift possessed by Dryden's contemporaries of representing flesh and blood in graphic sentences.
The subject is Shaftesbury's neighbor Henry Hastings, of
Woodlands, Dorsetshire, a country gentleman of the old school
who was born in 1551 and who died in 1650.

Mr. Hastings, by his quality, being the son, brother and uncle
to the Earls of Huntingdon, and his way of living, had the first
place amongst us. He was peradventure an original in our age, or
rather the copy of our nobility in ancient days in hunting and not
warlike times: he was low, very strong and very active, of a red-
dish flaxen hair, his clothes always green cloth, and never all worth
when new five pounds. His house was perfectly of the old fashion,
in the midst of a large park well stocked with deer, and near the
house rabbits to serve his kitchen, many fish-ponds, and great store
of wood and timber; a bowling-green in it, long but narrow, full of
high ridges, it being never levelled since it was ploughed; they used
round sand bowls, and it had a banqueting-house like a stand, a
large one built in a tree. He kept all manner of sport-hounds that
ran buck, fox, hare, otter, and badger, and hawks long and short
winged; he had all sorts of nets for fishing; he had a walk in the
New Forest and the manor of Christ Church. This last supplied him
with red deer, sea and river fish; and indeed all his neighbours'
grounds and royalties were free to him, who bestowed all his time

in such sports, but what he borrowed to caress his neighbours' wives and daughters, there being not a woman in all his walks of the degree of a yeoman's wife or under, and under the age of forty, but it was extremely her fault if he were not intimately acquainted with her. This made him very popular, always speaking kindly to the husband, brother, or father, who was to boot very welcome to his house whenever he came; there he found beef pudding and small beer in great plenty, a house not so neatly kept as to shame him or his dirty shoes, the great hall strewed with marrow bones, full of hawks' perches, hounds, spaniels, and terriers, the upper sides of the hall hung with the fox-skins of this and the last year's skinning, here and there a polecat intermixed, guns and keepers' and huntsmen's poles in abundance. The parlour was a large long room, as properly furnished; in a great hearth paved with brick lay some terriers and the choicest hounds and spaniels; seldom but two of the great chairs had litters of young cats in them, which were not to be disturbed, he having always three or four attending him at dinner, and a little white round stick of fourteen inches long lying by his trencher that he might defend such meat as he had no mind to part with to them. The windows, which were very large, served for places to lay his arrows, crossbows, stonebows, and other such like accoutrements; the corners of the room full of the best chose hunting and hawking poles; an oyster-table at the lower end, which was of constant use twice a day all the year round, for he never failed to eat oysters before dinner and supper through all seasons: the neighbouring town of Poole supplied him with them. The upper part of this room had two small tables and a desk, on the one side of which was a church Bible, on the other the Book of Martyrs; on the tables were hawks' hoods, bells, and such like, two or three old green hats with their crowns thrust in so as to hold ten or a dozen eggs, which were of a pheasant kind of poultry he took much care of and fed himself; tables, dice, cards, and boxes were not wanting. In the hole of the desk were store of tobacco-pipes that had been used. On one side of this end of the room was the door of a closet, wherein stood the strong beer and the wine, which never came thence but in single glasses, that being the rule of the house exactly observed, for he never exceeded in drink or permitted it. On the other side was a door into an old chapel not used

for devotion; the pulpit, as the safest place, was never wanting of
a cold chine of beef, pasty of venison, gammon of bacon, or great
apple-pie with thick crust extremely baked. His table cost him not
much, though it was very good to eat at, his sports supplying all
but beef and mutton, except Friday, when he had the best sea-fish
he could get, and was the day that his neighbours of best quality
most visited him. He never wanted a London pudding, and always
sung it in with "my part lies therein-a." He drank a glass of wine
or two at meals, very often syrrup of gilliflower in his sack, and
had always a tun glass without feet stood by him holding a pint of
small beer, which he often stirred with a great sprig of rosemary.
He was well natured, but soon angry, calling his servants bastard
and cuckoldy knaves, in one of which he often spoke truth to his
own knowledge, and sometimes in both, though of the same man.
He lived to a hundred, never lost his eyesight, but always writ
and read without spectacles, and got to horse without help. Until past
fourscore he rode to the death of a stag as well as any.*

Defoe or Fielding or Scott might have done a series of novels
on Achitophel's Henry Hastings; the seventeenth century, so
prodigal of its human material, used him neither for that nor
for any other purpose.

The type of verse "character" which Dryden found at hand
in 1681 was already of a good many years' standing. In the
course of its evolution it had drawn upon each of the prose
types, the categorical and the individual, for certain of its qualities. From the Theophrastian sketch it had derived a Euphuis-
tic, antithetical niceness of phrasing which tended to resolve it
into a pleasant dance of categories. From the historical or biographical or political sketch it had derived its allusiveness, its
concreteness, and its pungency. Ever since the days of the Short
Parliament there had been Clevelands, Marvells, and nameless
writers who achieved concreteness and pungency, but rarely or
never had a note of niceness been heard. Satirists had balanced

---

* A full-length portrait of Mr. Hastings is reproduced in John Hutchin's
History and Antiquities of the County of Dorset, 3d ed., London, 1868,
vol. III, p. 155.

their epithets, but only roughly; the movement of their verse had been spasmodic rather than fleet. The Earl of Mulgrave's *Essay upon Satire*, which was circulated in manuscript in 1679 and 1680 and thought by many, because of its slashing directness, to be Dryden's, had shown great improvement in the form of its "characters"; that of Tropos (Lord Chief Justice Scroggs),

> At bar abusive, on the bench unable,
> Knave on the woolsack, fop at council table,

and that of Rochester, for which Dryden was beaten in Rose Alley, Covent Garden, because he was supposed to be its author,

> Mean in each action, lewd in every limb,
> Manners themselves are mischievous in him,

had been powerful and swift of dispatch.

Now Dryden came with his contribution, which to begin with was metrical. His Achitophel and his Zimri captivated the town first of all by virtue of their felicity and finish. Without being in the least labored they were felt at once to be important; they had the accent of authority. The "characters" of Arod and Malchus in the anonymous Roman Catholic poem, *Naboth's Vineyard*, which had been printed in 1679 as a protest against the condemnation of Lord Strafford under cover of the Popish Plot, and which more than any other verse pamphlet, by virtue of its epic solemnity, its Biblical tissue, and its general plan, gave Dryden the cue for his own masterpiece, had failed to make a great impression, possibly because Oldham's more striking *Satires* had circulated the same year. In *Naboth's Vineyard*, Jezabel, King Achab's malicious queen and counselor, had leagued herself with Arod, a kind of Achitophel:

> She summons then her chosen instruments,
> Always prepared to serve her black intents;
> The chief was Arod, whose corrupted youth
> Had made his soul an enemy to truth;

But nature furnished him with parts and wit,
For bold attempts, and deep intriguing fit.
Small was his learning; and his eloquence
Did please the rabble, nauseate men of sense.
Bold was his spirit, nimble and loud his tongue,
Which more than law, or reason, takes the throng.

Arod, in turn, had had for his tool a kind of Oates:

Malchus, a puny Levite, void of sense,
And grace, but stuffed with voice and impudence,
Was his prime tool; so venomous a brute,
That every place he lived in spued him out;
Lies in his mouth, and malice in his heart,
By nature grew, and were improved by art.
Mischief his pleasure was; and all his joy
To see his thriving calumny destroy
Those, whom his double heart and forkéd tongue
Surer than vipers' teeth to death had stung.

Arod had been invoked at another point in the poem exactly as
Zimri was to be introduced on Dryden's stage:

In the first rank of Levites Arod stood,
Court-favour placed him there, not worth or blood.

The "characters" in *Naboth's Vineyard* had been interesting,
but they had made no hit; whereas Achitophel and Zimri,
who derived directly from them, within the first month after
their appearance were known to every literate Londoner.

Of these the false Achitophel was first,
A name to all succeeding ages curst:
For close designs and crooked counsels fit,
Sagacious, bold, and turbulent of wit.
Restless, unfixed in principles and place;
In power unpleased, impatient of disgrace:
A fiery soul, which, working out its way,
Fretted the pigmy body to decay,

And o'er-informed the tenement of clay.
A daring pilot in extremity;
Pleased with the danger, when the waves went high
He sought the storms; but, for a calm unfit,
Would steer too nigh the sands to boast his wit.
Great wits are sure to madness near allied,
And thin partitions do their bounds divide;
Else why should he, with wealth and honour blest,
Refuse his age the needful hours of rest?
Punish a body which he could not please;
Bankrupt of life, yet prodigal of ease?
And all to leave what with his toil he won,
To that unfeathered two-legg'd thing, a son;
Got, while his soul did huddled notions try;
And born a shapeless lump, like anarchy.
In friendship false, implacable in hate;
Resolved to ruin or to rule the State.
To compass this the triple bond he broke;
The pillars of the public safety shook,
And fitted Israel for a foreign yoke:
Then seized with fear, yet still affecting fame,
Usurped a patriot's all-atoning name.
So easy still it proves in factious times,
With public zeal to cancel private crimes.
How safe is treason and how sacred ill,
When none can sin against the people's will!
Where crowds can wink, and no offense be known,
Since in another's guilt they find their own.
Yet fame deserved no enemy can grudge;
The statesman we abhor, but praise the judge.
In Israel's courts ne'er sat an Abbethdin
With more discerning eyes, or hands more clean;
Unbribed, unsought, the wretched to redress;
Swift of dispatch, and easy of access.

Some of their chiefs were princes of the land;
In the first rank of these did Zimri stand;

A man so various that he seemed to be
Not one, but all mankind's epitome:
Stiff in opinions, always in the wrong,
Was everything by starts, and nothing long;
But, in the course of one revolving moon,
Was chymist, fiddler, statesman, and buffoon:
Then all for women, painting, rhyming, drinking,
Besides ten thousand freaks that died in thinking.
Blest madman, who could every hour employ,
With something new to wish, or to enjoy!
Railing and praising were his usual themes;
And both (to shew his judgment) in extremes:
So over-violent, or over-civil,
That every man, with him, was God or Devil.
In squandering wealth was his peculiar art;
Nothing went unrewarded but desert.
Beggared by fools, whom still he found too late,
He had his jest, and they had his estate.
He laughed himself from court; then sought relief
By forming parties, but could ne'er be chief;
For, spite of him, the weight of business fell
On Absalom and wise Achitophel.
Thus, wicked but in will, of means bereft,
He left not faction, but of that was left.

Dryden continued throughout his career to exercise a dictatorship in the world of "characters." Often he seemed to be saying the last word about a man when actually he said almost nothing; he seemed to weave a close garment about his subject when in truth he only latticed him over with antitheses. He became the acknowledged master of melodic epithet. Yet it would be absurd to imply that his success was merely technical. His authority was that of a knowing and a smiling man as well as that of a virtuoso; humor, imagination, wisdom, and thoroughly competent scepticism were also his contributions. He testified in the *Discourse of Satire* that the fine etching of characters was not a simple trick. " 'Tis not reading, 'tis not imitation of an author, which can produce this fineness; it must be inborn; it must proceed from a genius, and particular way of thinking, which is not to be taught. . . . How easy is it to call rogue and villain, and that wittily! But how hard to make a man appear a fool, a blockhead, or a knave, without using any of those opprobrious terms! . . . there is still a vast difference betwixt the slovenly butchering of a man, and the fineness of a stroke that separates the head from the body, and leaves it standing in its place. . . . The character of Zimri in my *Absalom* is, in my opinion, worth the whole poem: it is not bloody, but it is ridiculous enough; and he, for whom it was intended, was too witty to resent it as an injury. If I had railed, I might have suffered for it justly; but I managed my own work more happily, perhaps more dexterously. I avoided the mention of great crimes, and applied myself to the representing of blindsides, and little extravagancies; to which, the wittier a man is, he is generally the more obnoxious. It succeeded as I wished; the jest went round, and he was laughed at in his turn who began the frolic." No one will deny that Dryden's pictures of men and parties between the Exclusion Bill and the Declaration of Indulgence are works of genius. Historians agree that his comments, if not always fair, still throw a brighter light upon those six years than do all other contemporary records combined; subsequent research has only increased their respect for the man who left his studies on love and honor and fell into such a distraction as to walk through the thorns and briars of controversy. Nor can anyone fail to pay tribute to a mind so various that it could proceed from Achitophel and Zimri to Jotham, from Jotham to the rollicking Og and Doeg, from them to the sects in *The Hind and the Panther*, and from the sects to Bishop Burnet, the Buzzard. Only Pope in the next generation, with his Atticus, his Sporus, and his Wharton, succeeded in carving images as rare as Dryden's. The Queen Anne poetasters as a rule lacked the necessary intellectual resources. As the author of *Uzziah and Jotham* had rather mournfully remarked in his preface in 1690, "*Absalom and Achitophel* was a masterpiece" beyond which none might expect to go. But the cadences of the Drydenian "character," if nothing more, sounded distinctly and constantly through all Augustan verse. The poems that answered the *Absalom* fell into its rhythms, and there were complete copyists like Duke in his *Review* or Mainwaring in his *Tarquin and Tullia* and his *Suum Cuiusque*. After Pope the music was less plainly heard. Churchill went out of his way to recall it; but neither Goldsmith in his *Retaliation* nor Cowper in his *Conversation* found it indispensable.

Dryden's experience before *Absalom and Achitophel* gave him many contacts with the stuff of human nature. The writing of twenty plays, for instance, afforded him an acquaintance with postures, figures, and mental complexions. He was not brilliant in dramatic characterization; his men and women are seldom easy to visualize; but he grew adept in the specification of traits, he mastered the phraseology of description. His great example was Shakespeare, whom he approached in gusto though not in penetration. He has a number of energetic Beatrices, although he has said of none of them,

> Disdain and Scorn ride sparkling in her eyes.

The heroic plays abound in creatures who are garnished with symmetrical, balanced hyperbole but who have no significance as beings. The comedies are much happier. In the writing of his prose comedies Dryden touched upon such stock types as the spendthrift, the rake, the witty mistress, the scold, the affected woman, the swashbuckler. English dramatists from Jonson on had left him a rich legacy of language with which to treat such figures, and he managed his inheritance with dexterity. The French comic writers, particularly Molière, furnished him at the same time with admirable models and brilliant materials. The outcome was that he acquired a turn for hitting off the blind sides and extravagancies of his people not so much through action, though he does that brilliantly in *Marriage à la Mode*, as through elaborate comments by other participants in the scene. His Sir Martin Mar-All, originally a creation of Molière's, becomes in his hands a really integral clown. "I never laughed so in all my life," said Pepys, who went to see him. The writing of critical essays and prefaces gave Dryden another kind of acquaintance with the outlines of character. His estimates in the *Essay of Dramatic Poesy* of authors past and present—Wild, Cleveland, Shakespeare, Jonson, and Beaumont and Fletcher—together with the frequent contrasts and parallels which he drew between famous poets, taught him discrimination in praise and opprobrium; the critical prologues and epilogues encouraged pertinency and concentration. The writing of complimentary prose and verse did not make for discrimination in the distribution of excellences, but it added to Dryden's stock of attributes and it involved important exercise in the grouping of them.

The specialized character-cadences which jolted Achitophel and Zimri into fame were by no means new to Dryden in 1681, although they had not been exactly prominent in his verse before. They had appeared as early as the *Annus Mirabilis*, when it was said of the "Belgian" admirals:

> Designing, subtile, diligent, and close,
> They knew to manage war with wise delay.

They had been heard in *The State of Innocence*, when Adam declared against woman,

> Add that she's proud, fantastic, apt to change,
> Fond without art, and kind without deceit.

Often, as in *The Spanish Friar*, blank verse characters had been sketched in the later Caroline cadences rather than in those which were to become known as Dryden's and Pope's. Pedro had spoken thus of Dominick:

> I met a reverend, fat, old gouty friar,—
> With a paunch swoll'n so high, his double chin

Might rest upon it; a true son of the church;
Fresh-coloured, and well thriven on his trade,—
Come puffing with his greasy bald-pate choir,
And fumbling o'er his beads in such an agony,
He told them false, for fear. About his neck
There hung a wench, the label of his function,
Whom he shook off, i' faith, methought, unkindly.
It-seems the holy stallion durst not score
Another sin, before he left the world.

Restoration blank verse, it will be seen, encouraged a bound-less extravagance in portraiture rather than a Gallic justness, or appearance of justness.

Absalom and Achitophel, then, like Waller's poetry, came out forty thousand strong before the wits were aware. Its impression on Dryden himself was fully as remarkable as its impression on its readers or on the other poets of London. Dryden realized at once that he had woven patches of verse which would wear like iron, and proceeded to acquaint himself with all the varieties of texture which the new weave would admit. From 1681 to 1700 he wrote scarcely a poem which he did not enrich with "characters" or the cadences of "characters." *The Medal* was one long likeness of Shaftesbury, with a few concentrated passages like the following, which showed that gifted Whig sitting for the engraver:

Five days he sate for every cast and look;
Four more than God to finish Adam took.
But who can tell what essence angels are,
Or how long Heaven was making Lucifer?
O could the style that copied every grace,
And plowed such furrows for an eunuch face,
Could it have formed his ever-changing will,
The various piece had tired the graver's skill!
A martial hero first, with early care
Blown, like a pigmy by the winds, to war.

> A beardless chief, a rebel, ere a man.
> (So young his hatred to his prince began.)
> Next this, (how wildly will ambition steer!)
> A vermin wriggling in the usurper's ear.
> Bartering his venal wit for sums of gold,
> He cast himself into the saintlike mold;
> Groaned, sighed, and prayed, while godliness was gain,
> The loudest bagpipe of the squeaking train.

Mac Flecknoe, whenever it may have been composed, began with a "character" which for sheer cumulative destructiveness has no equal in satire. Says Flecknoe:

> Shadwell alone my perfect image bears,
> Mature in dulness from his tender years;
> Shadwell alone of all my sons is he
> Who stands confirmed in full stupidity.
> The rest to some faint meaning make pretense,
> But Shadwell never deviates into sense.
> Some beams of wit on other souls may fall,
> Strike through and make a lucid interval;
> But Shadwell's genuine night admits no ray,
> His rising fogs prevail upon the day.
> Besides, his goodly fabrick fills the eye
> And seems designed for thoughtless majesty:
> Thoughtless as monarch oaks that shade the plain,
> And, spread in solemn state, supinely reign.

The second part of *Absalom and Achitophel*, with its Ben-Jochanan, its Og and its Doeg, opened a new world of broad comedy; for once Dryden frolicked like Rabelais. Doeg, or Settle, and Og, or Shadwell, are irresistible. Merriment elbows resentment aside in lines like these:

> Doeg, though without knowing how or why,
> Made still a blundering kind of melody;
> Spurred boldly on, and dashed through thick and thin,
> Through sense and nonsense, never out nor in;

Free from all meaning, whether good or bad,
And in one word, heroically mad;
He was too warm on picking-work to dwell,
But fagotted his notions as they fell,
And if they rhymed and rattled, all was well.
Spiteful he is not, though he wrote a Satyr,
For still there goes some thinking to ill-nature;
He needs no more than birds and beasts to think,
All his occasions are to eat and drink.
If he call rogue and rascal from a garret,
He means you no more mischief than a parrot;
The words for friend and foe alike were made,
To fetter 'em in verse is all his trade.

Now stop your noses, readers, all and some,
For here's a tun of midnight work to come,
Og from a treason tavern rolling home.
Round as a globe, and liquored every chink,
Goodly and great he sails behind his link;
With all his bulk there's nothing lost in Og,
For every inch that is not fool is rogue:
A monstrous mass of foul corrupted matter,
As all the Devils had spewed to make the batter.
When wine has given him courage to blaspheme,
He curses God, but God before cursed him;
And if man could have reason, none has more,
That made his paunch so rich and him so poor. . . .
But though Heaven made him poor, (with reverence
    speaking,)
He never was a poet of God's making;
The midwife laid her hand on his thick skull,
With this prophetic blessing—Be thou dull;
Drink, swear and roar, forbear no lewd delight,
Fit for thy bulk, do anything but write.
Thou art of lasting make, like thoughtless men,
A strong nativity—but for the pen;
Eat opium, mingle arsenick in thy drink,
Still thou mayst live, avoiding pen and ink.

I see, I see, 'tis counsel given in vain,
For treason botched in rhyme will be thy bane;
Rhyme is the rock on which thou art to wreck,
'Tis fatal to thy fame and to thy neck.
Why should thy meter good King David blast?
A psalm of his will surely be thy last.
Dar'st thou presume in verse to meet thy foes,
Thou whom the penny pamphlet foiled in prose?
Doeg, whom God for mankind's mirth has made,
O'ertops thy talent in thy very trade;
Doeg to thee, thy paintings are so coarse,
A poet is, though he's the poet's horse.
A double noose thou on thy neck does pull,
For writing treason and for writing dull;
To die for faction is a common evil,
But to be hanged for nonsense is the Devil.
Hadst thou the glories of thy king expressed,
Thy praises had been satire at the best;
But thou in clumsy verse, unlicked, unpointed,
Hast shamefully defiled the Lord's anointed:
I will not rake the dung-hill of thy crimes,
For who would read thy life that reads thy rhymes?
But of King David's foes be this the doom,
May all be like the young man Absalom;
And for my foes may this their blessing be,
To talk like Doeg and to write like thee.

Dryden had not stopped laughing a year later when in *The Vindication of the Duke of Guise* he answered three pamphleteering adversaries, one of whom he believed to be Shadwell. "Og may write against the King if he pleases, so long as he drinks for him," he observed; "and his writings will never do the Government so much harm, as his drinking does it good; for true subjects will not be much perverted by his libels, but the wine duties rise considerably by his claret. He has often called me an atheist in print; I would believe more charitably of him, and that he only goes the broad way because the other

is too narrow for him. He may see by this, I do not delight to
meddle with his course of life, and his immoralities, though
I have a long bead-roll of them. I have hitherto contented myself with the ridiculous part of him, which is enough in all
conscience to employ one man: even without the story of his
late fall at the Old Devil, where he broke no ribs, because the
hardness of the stairs could reach no bones; and for my part, I
do not wonder how he came to fall, for I have always known
him heavy; the miracle is, how he got up again. . . . But to
leave him, who is not worth any further consideration, now I
have done laughing at him. Would every man knew his own
talent, and that they who are only born for drinking, would let
both poetry and prose alone." So cheerfully it was that Mr.
Bayes shed the venom of his assailants.

The *Religio Laici* indulged in a more subdued kind of caricature when it summed up the accomplishments of the private
spirit in theology. *The Hind and the Panther* was crowded with
mature and calm though none the less vivid pictures of persons
and sects: the Roman Catholic milk-white Hind herself (I,
1-8); the Independents, the Quakers, the Freethinkers, the
Anabaptists, and the Arians (I, 35-61); the Presbyterians (I,
160-189); the Brownists (I, 310-326); the noble Anglican
Panther (I, 327-510); the mind of the Anglican establishment
(III, 70-79):

> Disdain, with gnawing envy, fell despite,
> And cankered malice stood in open sight;
> Ambition, interest, pride without control,
> And jealousy, the jaundice of the soul;
> Revenge, the bloody minister of ill,
> With all the lean tormentors of the will;

the Latitudinarians (III, 160-172); the Huguenot exiles (III,
173-190); the Anglican tradition (III, 400-409):

> Add long prescription of established laws,
> And pique of honour to maintain a cause,

And shame of change, and fear of future ill,
And zeal, the blind conductor of the will;
And chief among the still-mistaking crowd,
The fame of teachers obstinate and proud,
And, more than all, the private judge allowed;
Disdain of Fathers which the dance began,
And last, uncertain whose the narrower span,
The clown unread, and half-read gentleman;

the Martin, or Father Petre (III, 461-468); James II, "a plain good man" (III, 906-937); the Anglican clergy (III, 944-954); and finally the Buzzard, or Bishop Burnet (III, 1141-1191):

More learn'd than honest, more a wit than learn'd. . . .
Prompt to assail, and careless of defense,
Invulnerable in his impudence,
He dares the world and, eager of a name,
He thrusts about and jostles into fame.
Frontless and satire-proof, he scours the streets,
And runs an Indian muck at all he meets.
So fond of loud report, that not to miss
Of being known, (his last and utmost bliss,)
He rather would be known for what he is.

The blank-verse tragedies which Dryden wrote after the Revolution were gorgeously hung with portraits. Shakespearean cadences prevailed in them; yet now and then the old lilt would insist upon a hearing, as in the second act of *Don Sebastian:*

What honour is there in a woman's death!
Wronged, as she says, but helpless to revenge,
Strong in her passion, impotent of reason,
Too weak to hurt, too fair to be destroyed.
Mark her majestic fabric; she's a temple
Sacred by birth, and built by hands divine;

or in the third act of the same play:

> The genius of your Moors is mutiny;
> They scarcely want a guide to move their madness;
> Prompt to rebel on every weak pretense;
> Blustering when courted, crouching when oppressed;
> Wise to themselves, and fools to all the world;
> Restless in change, and perjured to a proverb.
> They love religion sweetened to the sense;
> A·good, luxurious, palatable faith.

The *Juvenal* and the *Persius,* as might be expected, contain a number of ruthlessly consummate delineations; the Vectidius of Persius (IV, 50-73) is one of Dryden's most mocking. As Dryden proceeded with his translations and his narratives he came more and more to rely upon the antithetical paragraph as a device for introductions, transitions, and summaries. It proved useful not only for analyzing the natures of men but for sketching scenes and stating situations. Almost every page of the *Virgil* and the *Fables* rang with the familiar tones. Chaucer himself had not been without his rocking rhythms; so when Dryden found lines in the *Canterbury Tales* that were suited to his purpose he brought them straight over. Such a line as this in *The Knight's Tale,*

> Blak was his berd, and manly was his face,

was no way altered except in spelling. More of Chaucer yet would have been appropriated without change had his syllabication possessed utility for Dryden. The "Character of a Good Parson" in the *Fables,* elaborated from Chaucer's Prologue at the request of Samuel Pepys, was like most of Dryden's Christian poems, tame. The last "character" of all was one of the best. The ten lines on the Rhodian militia in *Cymon and Iphigenia* have as much satiric meat in them as have any ten lines in Dryden or in English. Their cadences, which are well under the poet's control, convey a burly, amused contempt:

> The country rings around with loud alarms,
> And raw in fields the rude militia swarms;

Mouths without hands; maintained at vast expense;
In peace a charge, in war a weak defence;
Stout once a month they march, a blustering band,
And ever, but in times of need, at hand.
This was the morn when, issuing on the guard,
Drawn up in rank and file they stood prepared
Of seeming arms to make a short essay,
Then hasten to be drunk, the business of the day.

Dryden's ratiocinative pulse beats with a longer, slower stroke, but it is never feeble. "Reasoning!" exclaimed Bayes in *The Rehearsal*, "I gad; I love reasoning in verse." Tom Brown, offering once to explain who Dryden was at all, said: "He is that accomplished person, who loves reasoning so much in verse, and hath got a knack of writing it smoothly." "The favourite exercise of his mind was ratiocination," thought Dr. Johnson. "When once he had engaged himself in disputation, thoughts flowed in on either side; he was now no longer at a loss; he had always objections and solutions at command." That is to say, Dr. Johnson implied, Dryden may often have looked about him for images which he could not find, but he never needed to scour for reasons or inferences. "They cannot be good poets," said Dryden himself, "who are not accustomed to argue well." Dryden was fascinated by the technical problems involved in making rhyme and reason lie down together. He was a versifier of propositions rather than a philosopher resorting to poetry, or even a poet speculating. No mind mastered him as Epicurus mastered Lucretius, or even, to come much farther down, as Bolingbroke mastered Pope. His imagination did not explore as Dante's and Milton's did. He was not curious, and absorbed, and quaintly condensed, like Sir John Davies, nor had he a trace of Cowper's neighborly discursiveness. His two chief ratiocinative poems dealt with the most transitory of topics, creeds and ecclesiastical expedients. The *Religio Laici* and *The Hind and the Panther* never have been and never will be read by many persons. The first attracted only slight attention even

when it was timely; the second was never timely, for it had
its thunder stolen by James's Declaration of Indulgence before
it was printed, and within a year it was nullified in most respects
by the Revolution. Here, as elsewhere in Dryden, it is not his
ideas but his way of thinking that is important. From such a
point of view the *Religio Laici* is a truly engaging poem; *The
Hind and the Panther* is a great representative work; and
Gray's "thoughts that breathe and words that burn" is not an
impossible phrase.

It is hardly worth while to become exercised over the question whether Dryden's ratiocinative poems are really poems.
It has been denied that argument has any place in poetry.
Whatever the truth may be, it remains that Dryden has
achieved an effect of his own which has been achieved by no
other writer, in prose or in verse. Congreve was off the scent
when he wrote: "Take his verses and divest them of their
rhyme, disjoint them in their numbers, transpose their expressions, make what arrangement and disposition you please of
his words, yet shall there eternally be poetry, and something
which will be found incapable of being resolved into absolute
prose." Horace's test is not to be applied to Dryden. It is precisely in his rhymes, his numbers, his expressions, his arrange-
ments, and his dispositions that Dryden has been an artist.
The triumph is a fragile one; the spell would be broken by
translation; *The Hind and the Panther* in French would almost
certainly be dull; but while the spell lasts it is real.

Dryden's devices were numerous, his ratiocinative technique
was complex. Tom Brown thought arguing in verse to be a
simple matter. "To do this," he said, "there is no need of brain,
'tis but scanning right; the labor is in the finger, not in the
head." Brown, quite naturally, was not interested in the subtle-
ties which labor of this kind involves. It may not be too fantastic to say that Dryden's brains were in his fingers, that he
thought in meter. Alliteration in him binds words, phrases,
lines, couplets, paragraphs together. Rhyme, by holding the

reader's mind, as Taine says, "on the stretch," gives to the poet's statements a strange factitious potency, so that they satisfy the curiosity of the ear rather than that of the mind. Alexandrines close discussions as if forever. *Enjambement* allows the imagination leisure to thread its way through meditative passages. Series of well-chosen adjectives advance a proposition with steady strides:

> Not that tradition's parts are useless here,
> When general, old, disinterested and clear.

Metaphors unobtrusively employed clinch a point before the reader is aware of the advantage which is being taken of him:

> This was the fruit the private spirit brought,
> Occasioned by great zeal and little thought.
> While crowds unlearned, with rude devotion warm,
> About the sacred viands buzz and swarm.

Exclamations draw many meanings briskly together. Queries serve for transitions. Catchwords and connectives like "then," "granting that," "True, but—," "thus far," " 'tis true," keep the game of ratiocination animated and going. Aphorisms set off arguments. Repetition and refrain speak proselyting sincerity or else confessional ecstasy. Abrupt apostrophes seem to denote overwhelming convictions suddenly arrived at. Passages of limpid and beautiful statement appear the issues of a serenely composed conscience. Angry, headlong digressions subside into mellow confessions of faith.

Neither the *Religio Laici* nor *The Hind and the Panther* can be exhibited with success in fragments. The strength of the two lies in what De Quincey called their "sequaciousness." They must be known in all their ins and outs before they can begin to impress a stranger with the variety yet continuity of their pattern. If some passage must be quoted, one should be lifted from a section lying somewhere between those extremes which are "nearest prose" and those which are most impassioned. This

extract from the Hind's address to the Panther on the subject
of the Apostolic Succession displays a proper share of Dryden's
ratiocinative talent.

> 'Tis said with ease, but never can be proved,
> The Church her old foundations has removed,
> And built new doctrines on unstable sands:
> Judge that, ye winds and rains; you proved her, yet she
>   stands.
> Those ancient doctrines, charged on her for new,
> Shew when, and how, and from what hands they grew.
> We claim no power, when heresies grow bold,
> To coin new faith, but still declare the old.
> How else could that obscene disease be purged,
> When controverted texts are vainly urged?
> To prove tradition new, there's somewhat more
> Required than saying: " 'Twas not used before."
> Those monumental arms are never stirred,
> Till schism or heresy call down Goliah's sword.
>
>   Thus what you call corruptions are in truth
> The first plantations of the gospel's youth;
> Old standard faith; but cast your eyes again,
> And view those errors which new sects maintain,
> Or which of old disturbed the Church's peaceful reign:
> And we can point each period of the time,
> When they began, and who begot the crime;
> Can calculate how long the eclipse endured,
> Who interposed, what digits were obscured:
> Of all which are already passed away,
> We know the rise, the progress and decay.
>
>   Despair at our foundations then to strike,
> Till you can prove your faith apostolic;
> A limpid stream drawn from the native source;
> Succession lawful in a lineal course.
> Prove any Church, opposed to this our head,
> So one, so pure, so unconfinedly spread,
> Under one chief of the spiritual State,
> The members all combined, and all subordinate.

Shew such a seamless coat, from schism so free,
In no communion joined with heresy.
If such a one you find, let truth prevail;
Till when, your weights will in the balance fail;
A Church unprincipled kicks up the scale.

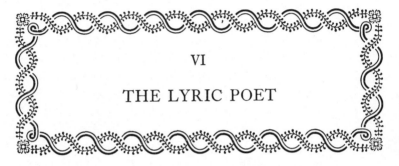

VI

THE LYRIC POET

DRYDEN owes his excellence as a lyric poet to his abounding metrical energy. The impetuous mind and the scrupulous ear which Wordsworth admired nourished a singing voice that always was powerful and sometimes was mellow or sweet. The songs, the operas, and the odes of Dryden are remarkable first of all for their musical excitement.

The seventeenth century was an age of song. Composers like John Dowland, Thomas Campion, William and Henry Lawes, Nicholas Laniere, John Wilson, Charles Coleman, William Webb, John Gamble, and the Purcells, together with publishers like John and Henry Playford, to mingle great with small, maintained a long and beautiful tradition of "ayres"; miscellanies and "drolleries," with their fondness for tavern tunes, urged on a swelling stream of popular melody; while poets, from Ben Jonson to Tom D'Urfey, never left off trifling with measured catches high or low. But there were changes from generation to generation. The poets of the Restoration sang in a different key from that of the Jacobeans; and it was generally believed that there had been a falling off.

"Soft words, with nothing in them, make a song,"

wrote Waller to Creech. It was charged that France had corrupted English song with her Damons and Strephons, her
"Chlorisses and Phyllisses," and that the dances with which she
was supposed to have vulgarized the drama and the opera
had introduced notes of triviality and irresponsibility into all
lyric poetry. Dryden for one was fond of dances, and ran them
into his plays whenever there was an excuse. In *Marriage à la
Mode* Melantha and Palamede quote two pieces from Molière's
ballet in *Le Bourgeois Gentilhomme*. Voiture's airy nothings
also had their day in England. The second song in Dryden's
Sir Martin Mar-All, beginning,

> Blind love, to this hour,
> Had never, like me, a slave under his power.
> Then blest be the dart
> That he threw at my heart,
> For nothing can prove
> A joy so great as to be wounded with love,

was adapted from Voiture:

> L'Amour sous sa loy
> N'a jamais eu d'amant plus heureux que moy;
> Benit soit son flambeau,
> Son carquois, son bandeau,
> Je suis amoreux,
> Et le ciel ne voit point d'amant plus heureux.

But the most serious charge against France was brought against
her music.

Music had an important place in the education of gentlemen
and poets throughout the Europe of the sixteenth and seventeenth centuries. A larger proportion of trained minds than
before or since claimed intimate acquaintance with musical technique. The studies of philosophers as well as poets included
ecclesiastical and secular song, the uses made of it being vari-

ous, of course. Hobbes, says Aubrey, "had alwayes bookes of prick-song lyeing on his Table:—e. g. of H. Lawes &c. *Songs*— which at night, when he was abed, and the dores made fast, & was sure nobody heard him, he sang aloud, (not that he had a very good voice) but to cleare his pipes: he did beleeve it did his Lunges good, and conduced much to prolong his life." Poets drew much of their best knowledge and inspiration from musicians, so that any alteration in musical modes was certain to affect the styles of verse.

The seventeenth century in England was a century of secularization, first under Italian and then under French influences. In former times, when music had been bound to the service of the church, clear-cut rhythms had been avoided as recalling too much the motions of the body in the dance, and composers of madrigals had been confined to the learned contrivances of counterpoint. John Dowland, the Oxford and Cambridge lutanist, Thomas Campion, magical both as poet and as composer, and Henry Lawes, the friend of all good versifiers, three seventeenth-century native geniuses who were also disciples of Italy, introduced in succession new and individual song rhythms which were so compelling that by the time of the Restoration there had come into being an excellent body of sweet and simple secular airs with just enough strains of the older, more intricate harmonies lingering in them to remind of the golden age. Even in church and chamber music there had been a tendency to substitute songs for madrigals and dance-tunes for choral measures.

The Restoration saw complete and rapid changes. Charles II, who insisted on easy rhythms at his devotions to which he could beat time with his hand, sent his choir-boys to France to school, and encouraged his musicians to replace the lute and the viol with the guitar and the violin. The violin or fiddle, which John Playford called "a cheerful and sprightly instrument," was as old as the Anglo-Saxons, but it had been used before only for dancing, not in the church or the chamber. It was the rhythm of the dance that now pervaded theater and chapel and all the world of lyric poetry. There was hearty objection to the new mode. Playford began the preface to his *Musick's Delight on the Cithera* (1666) with the remark: "It is observed that of late years all solemn and grave musick is much laid aside, being esteemed too heavy and dull for the light heels and brains of this nimble and wanton age." The preface to the sixth edition of the same author's *Skill of Musick* in 1672 continued the complaint: "Musick in this age . . . is in low esteem with the generality of people. Our late and solemn Musick, both Vocal and Instrumental, is now justled out of Esteem by the new Corants and Jigs of Foreigners, to the Grief of all sober and judicious understanders of that formerly solid and good Musick." John Norris of Bemerton, in the preface to his *Poems* (1678), declared that music like poetry had degenerated "from grave, majestic, solemn strains . . . where beauty and strength go hand in hand. 'Tis now for the most part dwindled down to light, frothy stuff." Henry Purcell objected on the whole with greater effect than the others against what he called "the levity and balladry of our neighbours"; for his attack upon French opera in favor of Italian opera was in the end entirely successful. Yet even Purcell was well aware that French music had "somewhat more of gayety and Fashion" than any other, and he was not so insensible to current demands as to compose songs for the stage that were lacking in vivacity.

Dryden, who had secured the services of a French musician, Grabut, for his opera *Albion and Albanius* in 1685, was considered in 1690 a convert to "the English school" when in the dedication of *Amphitryon* he wrote of "Mr. Purcell, in whose person we have at length found an Englishman, equal with the best abroad. At least my opinion of him has been such, since his happy and judicious performances in the late opera (*The Prophetess*), and the experience I have had of him in the setting my three songs for this 'Amphitryon.' " Before Purcell died in 1695 he had not only written the accompaniment for an opera of Dryden's, *King Arthur,* but set to music the songs from *Cleomenes, The Indian Emperor,* an adaptation of *The Indian Queen, Aureng-Zebe, Oedipus, The Spanish Friar, Tyrannic Love,* and *The Tempest;* so that Dryden had the full advantage of an association with this powerful composer who, as Motteux put it in the first number of his *Gentleman's Journal* in 1692, joined "to the delicacy and beauty of the Italian way, the graces and gayety of the French."

It is debatable whether the musical personalities of Purcell and other contemporary composers were in general a good or a bad influence on Restoration lyric style. It is at least thinkable that as the new rhythms asserted themselves more powerfully the writers who supplied words for songs were somehow the losers in independence and originality. There was complaint at the end of the century that jingling music from France had won the field and was domineering over poetry. Charles Gildon in his *Laws of Poetry* (1721) pointed to a degeneration in song, attributing it to "the slavish care or complaisance of the writers, to make their words to the goust of the composer, or musician: being obliged often to sacrifice their sense to certain sounding words, and feminine rhymes, and the like; because they seem most adapted to furnish the composer with such cadences which most easily slide into their modern way of composition." Others besides Gildon felt with justice that genius was being ironed out of lyric verse; song was becoming singsong. Relations between poets and composers were now the reverse of what they had been in the time of Henry Lawes. Lawes had been content to subordinate his music to the words; for him the poetry was the thing. If it seemed difficult at first glance to adapt a given passage to music, the difficulty was after all the composer's, and the blame for infelicities must accrue to him. "Our English seems a little clogged with consonants," he wrote in the preface to the first book of *Ayres and Dialogues* (1653), "but that's much the composer's fault, who, by judicious setting, and right tuning the words, may make it smooth enough." Milton was acknowledging the generous, pliant technique of his friend in the sonnet of 1646:

> Harry, whose tuneful and well-measured song
> First taught our English music how to span
> Words with just note and accent, not to scan
> With Midas' ears, committing short and long;
> Thy worth and skill exempts thee from the throng,
> With praise enough for Envy to look wan;
> To after age thou shalt be writ the man
> That with smooth air could humour best our tongue.

It was the delicacy and justness of Lawes that won him the affection of the most gifted lyrists of the mid-century; it will always be remembered of him that he loved poetry too well to profane the intricate tendernesses of songs like Herrick's to the daffodils.

Whatever conditions imposed themselves upon English song in the Restoration, Dryden for his own part was inclined to welcome swift, simple, straight-on rhythms, and he was destined to become master of the lyric field solely by virtue of his speed. His range of vowels was narrow; his voice was seldom round or deep, limiting itself rather monotonously to soprano sounds. Nor was the scope of his sympathies wide; a number of contemporaries sang more human songs. Rochester's drinking-pieces, like that which begins,

> Vulcan, contrive me such a cup
> As Nestor used of old,

Sedley's love-lines,

> Not, Celia, that I juster am,
> Or better than the rest,

And Dorset's playful flatteries,

> To all you ladies now at land,
> We men at sea indite,

are likely to touch nerves which Dryden leaves quiet. Congreve's diamond-bright cynicism and Prior's ultimate social grace exist in worlds far removed from his own. It was sheer lyrical gusto and momentum that carried Dryden forward, that drew to him the attention of the Playfords as they published their new collections, that made the editor of the *Westminster Drolleries* of 1671 and 1672 hasten to include his six best songs to date in those "choice" volumes.

Dryden's first song had something of the older Caroline manner in that its stanzas were tangled and reflective. It was sung in *The Indian Emperor,* and began:

> Ah fading joy, how quickly art thou past!
>> Yet we thy ruin haste.
> As if the cares of human life were few,
> > We seek out new:
> And follow fate that does too fast pursue.

Dryden passed swiftly from this to a more modern, more breathless world of song, a world where he fell at once, in *An Evening's Love,* into the dactylic swing that was to win him his way into the irrepressible *Drolleries:*

> After the pangs of a desperate lover,
> > When day and night I have sighed all in vain,
> Ah what a pleasure it is to discover,
> > In her eyes pity, who causes my pain.

Another song in *An Evening's Love* ran more lightly yet; it was marked by the anapestic lilt which on the whole is Dryden's happiest discovery:

> Calm was the even, and clear was the sky,
> > And the new-budding flowers did spring,
> When all alone went Amyntas and I
> > To hear the sweet nightingale sing.
> I sate, and he laid him down by me,
> > But scarcely his breath he could draw;

> For when with a fear, he began to draw near,
> He was dashed with "A ha ha ha ha!"

This lilt is heard in Dryden as many as fifteen times, being at its best in *Marriage à la Mode:*

> Why should a foolish marriage vow,
>   Which long ago was made,
> Oblige us to each other now,
>   When passion is decayed?
> We loved, and we loved, as long as we could,
>   Till our love was loved out in us both;
> But our marriage is dead, when the pleasure is fled;
>   'Twas pleasure first made it an oath.
>
> If I have pleasures for a friend,
>   And farther love in store,
> What wrong has he whose joys did end,
>   And who could give no more?
> 'Tis a madness that he should be jealous of me,
>   Or that I should bar him of another;
> For all we can gain is to give ourselves pain,
>   When neither can hinder the other;

in *Amphitryon,* where Dryden for once is very much like Prior:

> Fair Iris I love, and hourly I die,
> But not for a lip nor a languishing eye:
> She's fickle and false, and there we agree,
> For I am as false and as fickle as she.
> We neither believe what either can say;
> And, neither believing, we neither betray.
>
> 'Tis civil to swear, and say things of course;
> We mean not the taking for better or worse.
> When present, we love; when absent, agree;
> I think not of Iris, nor Iris of me.
> The legend of love no couple can find,
> So easy to part, or so equally joined;

and in *The Lady's Song*, a piece of Jacobite propaganda which
represents Dryden's long, loping jingle in its most gracious and
mellow aspects:

> A choir of bright beauties in spring did appear,
> To choose a May-lady to govern the year;
> All the nymphs were in white, and the shepherds in green;
> The garland was given, and Phyllis was queen;
> But Phyllis refused it, and sighing did say:
> "I'll not wear a garland while Pan is away."
>
> While Pan and fair Syrinx are fled from our shore,
> The Graces are banished, and Love is no more;
> The soft god of pleasure, that warmed our desires,
> Has broken his bow, and extinguished his fires;
> And vows that himself and his mother will mourn,
> Till Pan and fair Syrinx in triumph return.
>
> Forbear your addresses, and court us no more,
> For we will perform what the deity swore;
> But if you dare think of deserving our charms,
> Away with your sheephooks, and take to your arms:
> Then laurels and myrtles your brows shall adorn,
> When Pan, and his son, and fair Syrinx return.

The Lady's Song calls to mind two iambic pieces of a graver
sort. The song from *The Maiden Queen* is subdued to a plane
of elegy which Dryden seldom visited:

> I feed a flame within, which so torments me,
> That it both pains my heart, and yet contents me;
> 'Tis such a pleasing smart, and I so love it,
> That I had rather die than once remove it.
>
> Yet he for whom I grieve shall never know it;
> My tongue does not betray, nor my eyes show it:
> Not a sigh, nor a tear, my pain discloses,
> But they fall silently, like dew on roses.

Thus to prevent my love from being cruel,
My heart's the sacrifice, as 'tis the fuel;
And while I suffer this, to give him quiet,
My faith rewards my love, tho' he deny it.

On his eyes will I gaze, and there delight me;
Where I conceal my love, no frown can fright me;
To be more happy, I dare not aspire;
Nor can I fall more low, mounting no higher.

The "Zambra Dance" from the first part of *The Conquest of Granada* begins with two stately stanzas that shed a soft Pindaric splendor:

Beneath a myrtle shade,
Which love for none but happy lovers made,
I slept; and straight my love before me brought
Phyllis, the object of my waking thought.
Undressed she came my flames to meet,
While love strewed flowers beneath her feet;
Flowers which, so pressed by her, became more sweet.

From the bright vision's head
A careless veil of lawn was loosely spread:
From her white temples fell her shaded hair,
Like cloudy sunshine, not too brown nor fair;
Her hands, her lips, did love inspire;
Her every grace my heart did fire;
But most her eyes, which languished with desire.

Dryden has used the iambic measure only slightly more often than the anapestic, but he has used it more variously. The two poems just quoted are far removed from the Cavalier conciseness of these lines in *An Evening's Love:*

You charmed me not with that fair face,
Tho' it was all divine:
To be another's is the grace
That makes me wish you mine;

or from the lively languor of these in *The Spanish Friar:*

> Farewell, ungrateful traitor!
>   Farewell, my perjured swain!
> Let never injured creature
>   Believe a man again.
>
> The pleasure of possessing
> Surpasses all expressing,
> But 'tis too short a blessing,
>   And love too long a pain;

or from a pretty, rocking conceit like this in the *Song to a Fair Young Lady Going Out of Town in the Spring:*

> Ask not the cause, why sullen Spring
>   So long delays her flowers to bear;
> Why warbling birds forget to sing,
>   And winter storms invert the year.
> Chloris is gone, and fate provides
> To make it Spring where she resides.

The trochaic pieces, such as that in *Tyrannic Love,*

> Ah how sweet it is to love!
> Ah how gay is young desire!

and that in *King Arthur,* sung in honor of Britannia,

> Fairest isle, all isles excelling,
>   Seat of pleasures and of loves;
> Venus here will choose her dwelling,
>   And forsake her Cyprian groves,

attack the ear with characteristic spirit.

The songs of Dryden never go deeper than the painted fires of conventional Petrarchan love, but in a few cases they go wider. The "Sea-Fight" from *Amboyna,* the incantation of Tiresias in the third act of *Oedipus,* the Song of Triumph of the Britons and the Harvest Song from *King Arthur* are ro-

bust departures in theme from the pains and desires of Alexis
and Damon. The incantation from *Oedipus* brings substantial
relief, promising cool retreats:

> Choose the darkest part o' the grove,
> Such as ghosts at noon-day love.
> Dig a trench, and dig it nigh
> Where the bones of Laius lie.

The one hymn known to be Dryden's, the translation of
Veni, Creator Spiritus which appeared under his name in the
third *Miscellany* of 1693, is in a certain sense a rounder and
deeper utterance than any of the songs. The vowels are more
varied and the melody has a more solid core to it; the bass of
a cathedral organ rumbles under the rhythms. Scott on poor
authority printed two other hymns as Dryden's, the *Te Deum*
and what he called the *Hymn for St. John's Eve;* but it has
been convincingly denied that, with the exception of *Veni, Creator Spiritus,* any of the hundred and twelve hymns which
made up the Catholic *Primer* of 1706 had been translated from
the Latin by the great convert between 1685 and 1700.* Dryden was a born writer of hymns, though the hymns he wrote
were never, save in this one case, labeled as such. Praise with
him was as instinctive as satire; he delighted as much in glorious openings and upgathered invocations as in contemptuous
"characters." The King's prayer in *Annus Mirabilis,* Achitophel's first words to Absalom, the beginning of the *Lucretius,*
the beginning of the *Georgics,* and the prayers in *Palamon and
Arcite* are his most godlike pleas. "Landor once said to me,"
wrote Henry Crabb Robinson in his *Diary* for January 6, 1842,
"Nothing was ever written in hymn equal to the beginning of
Dryden's *Religio Laici,*—the first eleven lines."

---

* *Hymns Attributed to John Dryden.* Edited with an Introduction and Notes
by George Rapall Noyes and George Reuben Potter. University of California
Press, Berkeley, California, 1937.

Dim as the borrowed beams of moon and stars
To lonely, weary, wandering travellers,
Is Reason to the soul; and, as on high
Those rolling fires discover but the sky,
Not light us here, so Reason's glimmering ray
Was lent, not to assure our doubtful way,
But guide us upward to a better day.
And as those nightly tapers disappear
When day's bright lord ascends our hemisphere;
So pale grows Reason at Religion's sight;
So dies, and so dissolves in supernatural light.

Dryden's operas, as poetry, are unfortunate. Here for once, partly from apathy towards a form of writing which the prologues and epilogues show did not command his respect, partly from a sense of obligation or dependence, he capitulated to the composer; thinking to produce new musical effects with his pen, he succeeded in bringing forth what was neither poetry nor music. The result in each of two cases, at least, was what St. Evremond defined any opera to be, "an odd medley of poetry and music wherein the poet and the musician, equally confined one by the other, take a world of pain to compose a wretched performance." *The State of Innocence,* which was never performed but which was first published as "an opera" probably in 1677, is not one of the two cases. It is an independent poem of some originality and splendor. *Albion and Albanius* (1685), however, and its sequel *King Arthur* (1691) deserve a fair share of St. Evremond's disdain. Dryden has taken the trouble in connection with them to describe his labors as a poet-musician. In the preface to *Albion and Albanius* he says he has been at pains to "make words so smooth, and numbers so harmonious, that they shall almost set themselves." In writing an opera a poet must have so sensitive an ear "that the discord of sounds in words shall as much offend him as a seventh in music would a good composer." "The chief secret is the choice of words"; the words are "to be varied according to the nature of the subject." The "songish part" and the chorus call for "harmonious sweetness," with "softness and variety of numbers," but the recitative demands "a more masculine beauty." The superiority of Italian over French or English as a musical language is heavily stressed; and it is plain that throughout the opera Dryden has aimed at an Italian "softness" through the use of feminine rhymes and dissyllabic coinages similar to those which were to mark the *Virgil*. The work as a whole is inane, and often it is doggerel; it is at best a welter of jingling trimeters and tetrameters, tail-rhyme stanzas, heroic couplets, and tawdry Pindaric passages. One song by the Nereids in Act III begins better than it ends:

> From the low palace of old father Ocean,
> Come we in pity your cares to deplore;
> Sea-racing dolphins are trained for our motion,
> Moony tides swelling to roll us ashore.
>
> Every nymph of the flood, her tresses rending,
> Throws off her armlet of pearl in the main;
> Neptune in anguish his charge unattending,
> Vessels are foundering, and vows are in vain.

King Arthur is in blank verse, with many departures into song and dance. The dedication praises Purcell and admits that the verse has in certain cases been allowed to suffer for the composer's sake. "My art on this occasion," says Dryden, "ought to be subservient to his." "A judicious audience will easily distinguish betwixt the songs wherein I have complied with him, and those in which I have followed the rules of poetry, in the sound and cadence of the words." The "freezing scene" in the third act does neither the poet nor the composer any credit; the effect of shivering, even if legitimate, is not exactly happy. The best songs are those in which, as Dryden says, he has "followed the rules of poetry": those like "Fairest isle, all isles excelling," the "Harvest Home," and the song of the nymphs before Arthur:

> In vain are our graces,
>   In vain are our eyes,
>   If love you despise;
> When age furrows faces,
>   'Tis time to be wise.
> Then use the short blessing,
> That flies in possessing:
>   No joys are above
>   The pleasures of love.

The short *Secular Masque* which Dryden wrote for a re-
vival of Fletcher's *Pilgrim* in 1700 is the least objectionable
of the pieces which he designed to accompany stage music. The
masque celebrates the opening of a new century. Janus, Chronos,
and Momus hold a sprightly review of the century just past
and come to the conclusion that the times have been bad.
Diana, representing the court of James I, is the first to pass in
review, singing as she goes a hunting song which long remained
popular:

> With horns and with hounds I waken the day,
> And hie to my woodland walks away;
> I tuck up my robe, and am buskined soon,
> And tie to my forehead a wexing moon.
> I course the fleet stag, unkennel the fox,
> And chase the wild goats o'er summits of rocks;
> With shouting and hooting we pierce thro' the sky,
> And Echo turns hunter, and doubles the cry.

The three gods agree with her of the silver bow that

> Then our age was in its prime,
> Free from rage, and free from crime;
> A very merry, dancing, drinking,
> Laughing, quaffing, and unthinking time.

Mars next thunders in and recalls the wars of Charles I. But
Momus is a pacifist:

> Thy sword within the scabbard keep,
>   And let mankind agree;
> Better the world were fast asleep,
>   Than kept awake by thee.
> The fools are only thinner,
>   With all our cost and care;
> But neither side a winner,
>   For things are as they were.

Venus now appears to celebrate the softer conquests of Charles II and James II. But she also is found wanting, and so Dryden's poem ends with a sweeping dismissal of three Stuart generations:

> All, all of a piece throughout;
>   Thy chase had a beast in view;
>   Thy wars brought nothing about;
>   Thy lovers were all untrue.
> 'Tis well an old age is out,
>   And time to begin a new.

The force which drove Dryden forward through the somewhat foreign waters of song plunged him into a native ocean in the ode. His greatest lyrics are odes. He was constitutionally adapted to a form of exalted utterance which progressed by the alternate accumulation and discharge of metrical energy. The study of his utterances in this kind begins not with his first formal ode, but with the first appearance of swells in the stream of his heroic verse. That first appearance, as has been suggested before, is in the heroic plays, where the thump and rattle of the couplets is relieved from time to time by towering speeches like that of Almanzor to Lyndaraxa.* *The State of Innocence* is virtually one protracted ode. Partly in consequence of a new and close acquaintance with Milton's blank verse, partly as the fruit of his experience among rhythms, Dryden here has swollen his stream and learned to compose with a powerful, steady

* See page 88.

pulse. Milton's paragraphing, whether or not it has been an important inspiration, is after all Dryden's greatest example in this instance, though Milton's metrical progression is little like that of his junior. Milton relies chiefly upon *enjambement* to give roll to his verse; as can best be seen for the present purpose in the *Vacation Exercise* of 1628, which is in heroic couplets. The bond of the couplets is broken only once, and then by drawing the sense variously from one line into another. The poet is addressing his native language:

> Yet I had rather, if I were to choose,
> Thy service in some graver subject use,
> Such as may make thee search thy coffers round,
> Before thou clothe my fancy in fit sound.
> Such where the deep transported mind may soar
> Above the wheeling poles, and at Heaven's door
> Look in, and see each blissful Deity
> How he before the thunderous throne doth lie,
> Listening to what unshorn Apollo sings
> To the touch of golden wires, while Hebe brings
> Immortal nectar to her kingly sire;
> Then, passing through the spheres of watchful fire,
> And misty regions of wide air next under,
> And hills of snow and lofts of piléd thunder,
> May tell at length how green-eyed Neptune raves,
> In heaven's defiance mustering all his waves;
> Then sing of secret things that came to pass
> When beldam Nature in her cradle was;
> And last of Kings and Queens and Heroes old,
> Such as the wise Demodocus once told
> In solemn songs at King Alcinous' feast,
> While sad Ulysses' soul and all the rest
> Are held, with his melodious harmony
> In willing chains and sweet captivity.

Dryden relies less on *enjambement*, though occasionally he relies on that too, than on sheer rhythmical enthusiasm, an enthusiasm that expresses itself first through a series of rapidly advancing couplets and last in a flourish of triplets or Alexandrines. One example has been given from *The State of Innocence*.* Another is the speech of Lucifer at the end of the first scene:

> On this foundation I erect my throne;
> Through brazen gates, vast chaos, and old night,
> I'll force my way, and upwards steer my flight;
> Discover this new world, and newer Man;
> Make him my footstep to mount heaven again:
> Then in the clemency of upward air,
> We'll scour our spots, and the dire thunder scar,
> With all the remnants of the unlucky war,
> And once again grow bright, and once again grow fair.

Eve's account of Paradise in the third act is more elaborately heaped:

> Above our shady bowers
> The creeping jessamin thrusts her fragrant flowers;
> The myrtle, orange, and the blushing rose,
> With bending heaps so nigh their blooms disclose,
> Each seems to swell the flavor which the other blows;
> By these the peach, the guava and the pine,
> And, creeping 'twixt them all, the mantling vine
> Does round their trunks her purple clusters twine.

The State of Innocence was only a beginning. Dryden's proclivity towards the ode grew stronger each year. His addresses, his invocations, his hymns were only odes imbedded in heroic verse. Even a prologue might end with a lyrical rush, as for instance that "To the Duchess on Her Return from Scotland" (1682):

> Distempered Zeal, Sedition, cankered Hate,
> No more shall vex the Church, and tear the State:
> No more shall Faction civil discords move,
> Or only discords of too tender love;

---

* See page 89.

> Discord like that of Music's various parts;
> Discord that makes the harmony of hearts;
> Discord that only this dispute shall bring,
> Who best shall love the Duke and serve the King.

It is perhaps a question whether the poem on Oldham is an elegy or an ode. The "epiphonema" of the *Eleonora* is surely an ode of a kind; and the *Virgil* is one long Pindaric narrative.

Dryden's habit of dilating his heroic verse with Alexandrines not only grew upon him so that he indulged in flourishes when flourishes were not required, but it became contagious. Poetasters like John Hughes who lacked the impetus of Dryden learned his tricks and abused his liberties. There was something tawdry, in fact, about all but the very best of even Dryden's enthusiastic rhythms. It seemed necessary at least to Edward Bysshe in 1702, when he was compiling some "Rules for making English Verse" for his *Art of English Poetry*, to warn against license and to place restrictions on the use of long lines, allowing them only in the following cases:

1. "When they conclude an episode in an Heroic poem."
2. "When they conclude a triplet and full sense together."
3. "When they conclude the stanzas of Lyrick or Pindaric odes; Examples of which are frequently seen in Dryden and others."

Regardless of form, there always have been two distinct modes of utterance in the ode, two prevailing tempers. The Horatian temper is Attic, choice, perhaps didactic, and is stimulated by observation of human nature. The Pindaric temper is impassioned and superlative, and is inspired by the spectacle of human glory. In English poetry the Horatians have been Ben Jonson, Thomas Randolph, Marvell, Collins, Akenside, Cowper, Landor, and Wordsworth in the *Ode to Duty*; the Pindars have been Spenser, Milton, Cowley, Dryden, Gray, Wordsworth in the *Intimations*, Coleridge, Byron, Shelley, Keats, Tennyson, and Swinburne. Cowley is included among Pindaric

writers of odes more by courtesy than from desert, for he was
mortally deficient in afflatus; his importance is that of a pre-
ceptor and experimentalist, not that of a creator. His *Pindaric
Odes* of 1656, with the preface and the explanatory notes that
accompanied them, constituted a kind of charter for a whole
century of English *vers librists* who sought in the name of
Pindar to become grand and free. A parallel movement in
France involved a gradual departure from the rigors of Malherbe and enlisted such men as Corneille, La Fontaine, Molière, and Racine; Boileau making himself the spokesman in
1693 when in his *Discours sur l'Ode* he defended Pindar
against the current charges of extravagance and declared for
the principle of enthusiasm in lyric poetry. Cowley considered
that he was restoring one of the "lost inventions of antiquity,"
restoring, that is, what he believed was Pindar's art of infinitely
varying his meter to correspond to the involutions of his theme.
It was his notion that Pindar had been lawless in his splendor,
or at the most only a law to himself; that he had proceeded
without a method, now swelling, now subsiding according as
his verse was moved to embrace great things or small. Cowley's
Praise of Pindar began:

> Pindar is imitable by none,
>   The Phoenix Pindar is a vast species alone;
> Whoe'er but Daedalus with waxen wings could fly
>   And neither sink too low, nor soar too high?
>   What could he who followed claim,
> But of vain boldness the unhappy fame,
>   And by his fall a sea to name?
> Pindar's unnavigable song
> Like a swoln flood from some steep mountain pours along;
> The ocean meets with such a voice
> From his enlargéd mouth, as drowns the ocean's noise.
>
> So Pindar does new words and figures roll
> Down his impetuous dithyrambic tide,
>   Which in no channel deigns to abide,
>   Which neither banks nor dykes control;

> Whether the immortal gods he sings
> In a no less immortal strain,
> Or the great acts of God-descended kings,
> Who in his numbers still survive and reign;
> Each rich embroidered line
> Which their triumphant brows around
> By his sacred hand is bound,
> Does all their starry diadems outshine.

Cowley had an interesting theory that the Hebrew poets were sharers with Pindar of the great secret. In his preface he remarked: "The Psalms of David (which I believe to have been in their original, to the Hebrews of his time . . . the most exalted pieces of poesy) are a great example of what I have said." And one of his *Pindaric Odes* was a version of Isaiah xxxiv. "The manner of the Prophets' writing," he observed in a note, "especially of Isaiah, seems to me very like that of Pindar; they pass from one thing to another with almost Invisible connections, and are full of words and expressions of the highest and boldest flights of Poetry." Gildon followed Cowley in his *Laws of Poetry* (1721) when he cited among the great odes of the world the psalm that begins: "By the waters of Babylon we sat down and wept, when we remembered thee, O Sion."

Congreve wrote a *Discourse on the Pindarique Ode* in 1706 to prove that Cowley had violated the first law of Pindar when he discarded shape; he explained the rigid strophic structure of the Greek ode and deplored the "rumbling and grating" papers of verses with which Cowley's loose example had loaded the England of the past half century. He was not the first to make this point; Edward Phillips in the preface to his *Theatrum Poetarum* (1675) had observed that English Pindaric writers seemed ignorant of the strophe, antistrophe, and epode, and that their work seemed rather on the order of the choruses of Aeschylus; while Ben Jonson had left in his ode on Cary and Morison a perfect specimen of Pindar's form. But Con-

greve was the first conspicuous critic of Cowleian *vers libre*, and
it was not until after him that Akenside and Gray and Gilbert
West demonstrated on an extensive scale what could be done
with strophe and antistrophe in a Northern tongue. Yet the
difference between Cowley and Gray was far more than the difference between lawless verse and strophic verse. Cowley's
crime had been not so much against Pindar as against poetry:
he had written and taught others to write what metrically was
nonsense. The alternation of long with short lines in itself does
not of necessity make for grandeur; often, as Scott suggests,
the effect of a Restoration ode was no different rhythmically
from that of the inscription on a tombstone. Cowley was out
of his depth in the company of Pindar; he was constituted for
wit, for "the familiar and the festive," as Dr. Johnson said,
but not for magnificence. The passage which has been quoted
from the *Praise of Pindar* is not equaled by him elsewhere;
most of the time he is writing like this, at the conclusion of
The Muse:

> And sure we may
> The same too of the present say,
> If past and future times do thee obey.
> Thou stop'st this current, and does make
> This running river settle like a lake;
> Thy certain hand holds fast this slippery snake;
> The fruit which does so quickly waste,
> Man scarce can see it, much less taste,
> Thou comfitest in sweets to make it last.
> This shining piece of ice,
> Which melts so soon away
> With the sun's ray,
> Thy verse does solidate and crystallize,
> Till it a lasting mirror be!
> Nay, thy immortal rhyme
> Makes this one short point of time
> To fill up half the orb of round eternity.

The trouble here is simply that there are no "numbers"; the stanza is not organic; there are no involutions which the ear follows with the kind of suspense with which it follows, for instance, an intricate passage in good music. Cowley has thought to forestall such an objection in the general preface to his folio of 1656. "The numbers are various and irregular," he says, "and sometimes (especially some of the long ones) seem harsh and uncouth, if the just measures and cadences be not observed in the pronunciation. So that almost all their sweetness and numerosity (which is to be found, if I mistake not, in the roughest, if rightly repeated) lies in a manner wholly at the mercy of the reader." But the most merciful and best of readers must fail to make certain of the odes of Cowley sound like poetry. Cowley had not a dependable ear.

It was Dryden's "excellent ear" which saved the Pindaric ode for Gray. Dryden diagnosed the ills of contemporary Pindarism with lofty precision in the preface to *Sylvae* in 1685. "Somewhat of the purity of English, somewhat of more equal thoughts, somewhat of sweetness in the numbers, in one word, somewhat of a finer turn and more lyrical verse is yet wanting. . . . In imitating [Pindar] our numbers should, for the most part, be lyrical . . . the ear must preside, and direct the judgement to the choice of numbers: without the nicety of this, the harmony of Pindaric verse can never be complete; the cadency of one line must be a rule to that of the next; and the sound of the former must slide gently into that which follows, without leaping from one extreme into another. It must be done like the shadowings of a picture, which fall by degrees into a darker colour." This is by far his most significant statement on the ode: it is not only an accurate analysis of the errors of others; it is an intimation of his own ideal, and incidentally it embodied a forecast of his best accomplishment. For his peculiar contribution was none other than the shading and the "finer turn" of which he speaks here. He let his ear preside; he let his cadences rule and determine one another in the interests of an integral harmony. He placed his words where they would neither jar nor remain inert, but flow. His best Pindaric passages are streams of words delicately and musically disposed.

The earliest instance of all, the "Zambra Dance" * from *The Conquest of Granada,* is fine but slight. The first ambitious effort is the translation of the twenty-ninth ode of the third book of Horace in *Sylvae.* "One ode," explains Dryden in the preface, "which infinitely pleased me in the reading, I have attempted to translate in Pindaric verse. . . . I have taken some pains to make it my master-piece in English: for which reason I took this kind of verse, which allows more latitude than any other." The combination of Horatian felicity with Pindaric latitude is the happier for Dryden's excellent understanding of the bearings of each. Creech's *Horace,* published the previous year with a dedication to Dryden, had shown, as certain pieces from Horace in the first *Miscellany* (1684) had shown, what might be done in the way of running the Stoic odes into elaborate stanzaic molds; but Creech was most of the time perilously near prose. His version of the present poem, not particularly spirited but solid and just, may have suggested further possibilities to Dryden, who indeed did appropriate his predecessor's best phrases. As for the language of Horace, says Dryden, "there is nothing so delicately turned in all the Roman language. There appears in every part of his diction . . . a kind of noble and bold purity. . . . There is a secret happiness which attends his choice, which in Petronius is called *curiosa felicitas.*" As for his own versification, which of course is anarchy compared with Horace, he hopes that it will help to convey the Roman's "briskness, his jollity, and his good humour." The result is as nice as anything in Dryden. The ear has presided, and the shading is almost without flaw. Only five lines disappoint; four of these are Alexandrines (lines 33, 38, 59, 64) and one is a fourteener (line 39). Dryden has not learned as yet in this least rigid of all forms to dispose his long lines so

* See page 183.

well that none of them will halt the movement and kill the stanza; in the present instance it is significant that all of the five dead lines are attempts at reproducing effects of Nature. The first, second, third, fourth, sixth, eighth, ninth, and tenth stanzas are unexceptionable. The poem begins with a passage of remarkable carrying power; something somewhere seems to be beating excellent time:

> Descended of an acient line,
>   That long the Tuscan scepter swayed,
> Make haste to meet the generous wine,
>   Whose piercing is for thee delayed:
> The rosy wreath is ready made,
>   And artful hands prepare
> The fragrant Syrian oil, that shall perfume thy hair.

The eighth stanza is in a way the most distinct and final writing that Dryden did:

> Happy the man, and happy he alone,
>   He, who can call today his own;
>   He who, secure within, can say:
> "Tomorrow, do thy worst, for I have lived today.
>   Be fair, or foul, or rain, or shine,
> The joys I have possessed, in spite of fate, are mine.
>   Not Heav'n itself upon the past has power;
> But what has been has been, and I have had my hour."

This is brisk yet liquid. The current of the stream widens and accelerates swiftly, but there is no leaping or foaming. The "cadency" of each line noiselessly transmits energy to the next. Alliteration helps to preserve an equable flow, while varied vowels heighten the murmur. And the monosyllables now have their revenge; for fifty-nine words of the sixty-eight are monosyllables.

The next Pindaric ode of Dryden's, the *Threnodia Augustalis,* is rambling and arbitrary in its rhythms; there is little or no momentum. A few passages, however, shine in isolation. At the news that Charles had rallied and might live, says Dryden,

> Men met each other with erected look,
> The steps were higher that they took,
> Friends to congratulate their friends made haste,
> And long-inveterate foes saluted as they passed.

There is a pride of pace in these lines that suits the sense. When Charles was restored from France, continues Dryden,

> The officious Muses came along,
> A gay harmonious choir, like angels ever young;
> (The Muse that mourns him now his happy triumph sung.)
> Even they could thrive in his auspicious reign;
> And such a plenteous crop they bore
> Of purest and well-winnowed grain
> As Britain never knew before.
> Though little was their hire, and light their gain,
> Yet somewhat to their share he threw;
> Fed from his hand, they sung and flew,
> Like birds of Paradise, that lived on morning dew.

The ode *To the Pious Memory of the Accomplished Young Lady, Mrs. Anne Killigrew*, written in the same year with the *Horace* and the *Threnodia*, while it is sadly uneven is yet the most triumphant of the three. For although its second, third, fifth, sixth, seventh, eighth, and ninth stanzas are equal at the most only to Cowley and are indeed a good deal like him, the first, fourth, and tenth are emancipated and impetuous. The first stanza, which Dr. Johnson considered the highest point in English lyric poetry, rolls its majestic length without discord or hitch; its music is the profoundest and longest-sustained in Dryden, and its grammar is regal. The fourth stanza hurls itself with violent alliteration down the steep channel which it describes:

O gracious God! how far have we
Profaned thy heavenly gift of poesy!
Made prostitute and profligate the Muse,
Debased to each obscene and impious use,
Whose harmony was first ordained above
For tongues of angels and for hymns of love!
O wretched we! why were we hurried down
    This lubric and adulterate age,
(Nay, added fat pollutions of our own,)
    To increase the steaming ordures of the stage?
What can we say to excuse our second fall?
Let this thy vestal, Heaven, atone for all.
Her Arethusian stream remains unsoiled,
Unmixed with foreign filth, and undefiled;
Her wit was more than man, her innocence a child!

The last stanza is a musical and grammatical triumph like the first, but one of a lesser magnitude. The triplet in the middle of it is something of an obstruction, and three near-conceits give the effect of a melody scraped thin. The *Ode on the Death of Mr. Henry Purcell* (1696) also suffers from conceits, being nowhere remarkable save perhaps in the first stanza, which aims at prettiness:

Mark how the lark and linnet sing;
    With rival notes
They strain their warbling throats
    To welcome in the spring.
    But in the close of night,
When Philomel begins her heavenly lay,
    They cease their mutual spite,
    Drink in her music with delight,
And listening and silent, and silent and listening,
    and listening and silent obey.

It seems now to have been almost inevitable that there should grow up at the end of the seventeenth century a custom of celebrating St. Cecilia's Day with poems set to music; so close were

poets and musicians together, and so worshipful of music in
that age were men as different from one another as Milton,
Cowley, Waller, Marvell, and Dryden. During half a century before 1683, when the first Feast was celebrated, Orpheus
and Amphion had been among the mythological personages
most affectionately cultivated in English verse; and a whole
splendid language had been constructed for the praise of the
powers of harmony. Dryden's *Song for St. Cecilia's Day* in
1687 and his *Alexander's Feast* in 1697 were the most distinguished performances of the century, each making fashionable
a new and sensational method. There was something sensational
and monstrous, it must be admitted, about the whole series of
music odes from Fishburn, Tate, Fletcher, and Oldham before
Dryden to Bonnell Thornton in the eighteenth century, whose
burlesque ode called into service of sound and fury such im-
plements as salt-boxes, marrow-bones, and hurdy-gurdies.
There was very little excellent poetry on the whole laid at the
feet of St. Cecilia, and there was a deal of cheap program-
music offered to her ears, even by Purcell and Handel. But the
music had always a saving vigor; sixty voices and twenty-five
instruments, including violins, trumpets, drums, hautboys, flutes,
and bassoons, could make amends of a kind for the paltriest
verse. Dryden's odes, if artificial and sensational, were the last
thing from paltry; they are among the most amazing *tours de
force* in English poetry.

The *Song* of 1687 established a new kind of imitative harmony in which verse became for practical purposes an orchestra,
the poet drawing upon his vowels and his phrases as a conductor draws upon his players. Dryden had toyed with somewhat similar devices before. The song from *The Indian Emperor*
had ended with the noise, he thought, of gently falling water:

> Hark, hark, the waters fall, fall, fall
> And with a murmuring sound
> Dash, dash upon the ground,
>   To gentle slumbers call.

Oldham in his Cecilia Ode of 1684 had employed some such scheme as Dryden was soon to make famous. And of course it had been almost a century since Spenser had performed his miracles of sound with verse. But Dryden now was the first to declare a wholly orchestral purpose and to rely upon a purely instrumental technique. The first stanza is a rapid overture which by a deft, tumbling kind of repetition summons and subdues to the poet's hand all the wide powers of harmony. The second stanza slips through liquid cadences and dissolves among the sweet sounds of a harp:

> What passion cannot Music raise and quell!
> When Jubal struck the corded shell,
> His listening brethren stood around,
> And, wondering, on their faces fell
> To worship that celestial sound.
> Less than a god they thought there could not dwell
> Within the hollow of that shell
> That spoke so sweetly and so well.
> What passion cannot Music raise and quell!

A suggestion for this may have come from Marvell's *Music's Empire:*

> Jubal first made the wilder notes agree
> And Jubal tunèd Music's Jubilee;
> He called the echoes from their sullen cell,
> And built the organ's city, where they dwell;

although Marvell has only hinted of the possibilities that lie in the figure of Jubal and in the "-ell" rhymes; while Dryden has extracted the utmost, whether of drama or of sound, from both. The third, fourth, and fifth stanzas secure by obvious but admirable means the effects of trumpets, drums, flutes, and violins. From the sixth there ascend the softly rushing notes of the organ. The "Grand Chorus" which closes the poem is cosmically pitched:

As from the power of sacred lays
    The spheres began to move
And sung the great Creator's praise
    To all the blest above;
So, when the last and dreadful hour
This crumbling pageant shall devour,
The Trumpet shall be heard on high,
The dead shall live, the living die,
And Music shall untune the sky.

Dryden, as has been said, seems always to have been moved by the idea of universal dissolution. The Hebrew notion of the Day of Judgment had reached him through the Bible and Joshua Sylvester. The Lucretian theory of disintegration had fascinated him when he was at the university if not before. He must have long been acquainted with Lucan's rehearsal of the final crumbling in the first book of the *Pharsalia*. His concern was with the physics rather than the metaphysics of a disappearing world. Milton's *Solemn Musick* and *Comus* spoke of a mortal mold which original sin had cursed with discord but which on the last day would melt into the great harmony of the invisible spheres. Dryden is not theological; his finale is the blare of a trumpet, and his last glimpse is of painted scenery crashing down on a darkened stage. His ode on Anne Killigrew and his *Song* of 1687 end hugely and picturesquely, like Cowley's ode on *The Resurrection*, where Dryden had read:

Till all gentle Notes be drowned
In the last Trumpet's dreadful sound
That to the spheres themselves shall silence bring,
Untune the universal string. . . .
Then shall the scattered atoms crowding come
Back to their ancient Home.

On the third of September, 1697, Dryden informed his sons at Rome: "I am writing a song for St. Cecilia's Feast, who, you know, is the patroness of music. This is troublesome, and no way beneficial; but I could not deny the stewards of the feast, who came in a body to me to desire that kindness." There is a tradition that he became agitated during the composition of this song, which was to be the *Alexander's Feast*, and that Henry St. John, afterwards Lord Bolingbroke, found him one morning in a great tremble over it. It is likely that he worked coolly enough at all times; yet he may well have exulted when the idea for this most famous of his lyrics first took shape in his mind. The idea of casting a music ode into narrative or dramatic form was itself a new and happy one. The materials for the story of Alexander probably came harder and were only gradually pieced together in Dryden's imagination. It had been a commonplace among classical, post-classical, and Renaissance writers that ancient Greek music, especially "the lost symphonies," had strangely affected the spirits of men; Pythagoras had cured distempers and passions by the application of appropriate harmonies. Longinus had written (xxxiv): "Do not we observe that the sound of wind-instruments moves the souls of those that hear them, throws them into an ecstasy, and hurries them sometimes into a kind of fury?" Athenaeus had cited Clitarchus as authority for the statement that Thais was the cause of the burning of the palace in Persepolis. Suidas, quoted by John Playford in his *Skill of Musick,* had related that Timotheus moved Alexander to arms. "But the story of Ericus musician," added Playford, "passes all, who had given forth, that by his musick he could drive men into what affections he listed; being required by Bonus King of Denmark to put his skill in practice, he with his harp or polycord lyra expressed such effectual melody and harmony in the variety of changes in several keyes, and in such excellent Fugg's and sprightly ayres, that his auditors began first to be moved with some strange passions, but ending his excellent voluntary with some choice fancy upon this Phrygian mood, the king's passions were altered, and excited to that height, that he fell upon his most trusty friends which were near him, and slew some of them with his fist for lack of another weapon; which our musician perceiving, ended with the sober Dorick; the King came to himself, and much lamented what he had done." Burton, after Cardan the mathematician, had said in *The Anatomy of Melancholy* that "Timotheus the musician compelled Alexander to skip up and down and leave his dinner." Cowley's thirty-second note to the first book of the *Davideis,* a veritable discourse on the powers of harmony, had contained the remark: "Timotheus by Musick enflamed and appeased Alexander to what degrees he pleased." Tom D'Urfey's ode for St. Cecilia's Day in 1691 had run merrily on through change after change of tempo, somewhat in the manner which Dryden was to employ:

> And first the trumpet's part
> Inflames the hero's heart; . . .
> And now he thinks he's in the field,
> And now he makes the foe to yield, . . .
> The battle done, all loud alarms do cease,
> Hark, how the charming flutes conclude the peace . . .
> Excesses of pleasure now crowd on apace.
> How sweetly the violins sound to each bass,
> The ravishing trebles delight every ear,
> And mirth in a scene of true joy does appear. . . .
> Now beauty's power inflames my breast again,
> I sigh and languish with a pleasing pain.
> > The notes so soft, so sweet the air,
> > The soul of love must sure be there,
> That mine in rapture charms, and drives away despair.

In Motteux's *Gentleman's Journal* for January, 1691-2, was written: "That admirable musician, who could raise a noble fury in Alexander, and lay it as easily, and make him put on the Hero, or the Lover, when he pleased, is too great an Instance of the power of Music to be forgotten." And only three months before Dryden was writing to his sons at Rome, Jeremy Collier, who is seldom thought to have been a benefactor of Restoration poets, had published in the second part of his *Es-*

says upon Several Moral Subjects an essay *Of Musick* wherein
it was told how "Timotheus, a Grecian, was so great a Master,
that he could make a man storm and swagger like a Tempest,
and then, by altering the Notes, and the Time, he would take
him down again, and sweeten his humour in a trice. One time,
when Alexander was at Dinner, this Man played him a Phrygian Air: the Prince immediately rises, snatches up his Lance,
and puts himself into a Posture of Fighting. And the Retreat
was no sooner sounded by the Change of Harmony, but his
Arms were Grounded, and his Fire extinct; and he sate down
as orderly as if he had come from one of Aristotle's Lectures."
Such were the scraps that lay at Dryden's disposal in September of 1697.

"I am glad to hear from all hands," he wrote to Tonson in
December, "that my Ode is esteemed the best of all my poetry,
by all the town: I thought so myself when I writ it; but being
old I mistrusted my own judgment." It is a question whether
Absalom and Achitophel and the *Oldham* are not better poetry
than *Alexander's Feast*, which perhaps is only immortal rag-
time. Some of the cadences are disappointing; lines 128, 139,
140, and 145 puzzle and lower the voice of the reader. Yet
few poems of equal length anywhere have been brought to a
finish on so consistently proud a level and in such bounding
spirits. Here is brilliant panorama; here are responsive, ringing
rhythms; here is good-nature on the grand scale.

And thrice he routed all his foes, and thrice he slew the slain.

The enormous vitality of this ode not only has insured its own
long life; for a century it inspired ambitious imitators and
nameless parodists. John Wilkes in 1774 * and the Prince of
Wales in 1795 † found themselves hoisted in mockery to the
highest throne that pamphleteers could conceive, the imperial
throne of Philip's warlike son.

* W—s's Feast, or Dryden Travesti: A Mock Pindaric Inscribed to His
Most Incorruptible Highness Prince Patriotism. London. 1774.
† Marriage Ode Royal After the Manner of Dryden. 1795.

VII

THE NARRATIVE POET

THE GREATEST of all poems have been narrative, for the highest function of poetry is to tell a story. The conquest which prose fiction has made in the world of story since Dryden's day may or may not signify that poetry is beaten; whether the withdrawal by poets into special corners where they cultivate temperament instead of understanding denotes that the poetry of the future will not be important like the poetry of the past, only time will tell. Certain it is that the idea of narration in verse is often now discredited. At any time in the seventeenth century this would have been heresy. Among theorists at least, occasional, journalistic, or lyric verse was seldom if ever taken seriously; the epic was undisputed king. Yet out of the quantities of narrative verse which that age produced little had much or any meaning. The decay of the heroic tradition was already well-nigh complete. Even Milton's triumph, to modern secular minds, is one chiefly of style and mood; his supreme moments are moments of gorgeous reminiscence, when in his imagination the regions and the deeds made famous centuries before *illustrium poetarum fabulis* come sweeping by.

There is no reason to feel sorry with Scott that Dryden never
got around to writing his projected epic on Arthur or the Black
Prince. It would most likely have been a disappointment; much
as Dryden revered the institution of the heroic poem, he had
not the power to illuminate and interpret heroic motives. His
contribution was critical. His *Essay of Heroic Plays*, his
Apology for Heroic Poetry, his *Discourse of Satire*, and the
dedication of his *Aeneis* summed up contemporary tastes and
theories in this department as no other group of essays did; he
was the sponsor but not the chief performer. His tributes to
the epic, "the most noble, the most pleasant, and the most
instructive way of writing in verse," as well as "the greatest
work of human nature," were many and resounding. His re-
quirements for the writer of an epic, as set forth in the *Discourse
of Satire*, were many and rigorous; a heroic poet, he said, is
one "who, to his natural endowments, of a large invention, a
ripe judgment, and a strong memory, has joined the knowledge
of the liberal arts and sciences, and particularly moral philosophy, the mathematics, geography, and history, and with all
these qualifications is born a poet; knows, and can practice the
variety of numbers, and is master of the language in which he
writes." Dryden's narrative sphere was a slighter one than this;
it was the sphere of the episode or the tale. He is even said to
have been capable of taking delight in the humblest ballads.
Addison wrote in the eighty-fifth *Spectator*, "I have heard that
the late Lord Dorset . . . had a numerous collection of old
English ballads, and took a particular pleasure in the reading
of them. I can affirm the same of Mr. Dryden"; and Gildon,
in *A New Rehearsal* (1714), declared his victim Rowe another
Mr. Bayes in "his admiration of some odd books, as 'Reynard
the Fox,' and the old ballads of 'Jane Shore.'" Dryden's spe-
cialty was the short story; he belongs in the company not of
Homer, Virgil, Dante, Spenser, and Milton, but of Ovid,
Chaucer, Crabbe, Scott, Macaulay, Byron, Keats, Tennyson,
Longfellow, Arnold, Morris, and Masefield.

Dryden was neither an original nor a skillful weaver of plots. He did not tell a story particularly well. Yet he always had the air of telling a story well; he was master of a swift and plausible manner. He was not adept in psychological research, or refined, or especially true; he could be slovenly and gross; but he was never limp or lame. His verse was as strong as the English mastiff and as fleet as the Frenchman's greyhound; and like a good hound it never tired. "I must confess," said Daniel in his *Defence of Rime*, "that to mine own ear those continual cadences of couplets used in long and continued poems are very tiresome and unpleasing, by reason that still methinks they run on with a sound of one nature, and a kind of certainty which stuffs the delight rather than entertains it." Dryden was not without monotony and stiffness; yet the last analysis must find him fresh and various as few other poets have been. There was always his capacious skepticism to keep him sensible; there was always his speed to dissolve his blemishes and lend a vividness to his materials good and bad. "The wheels take fire from the mere rapidity of their motion," observed Coleridge in the *Biographia Literaria*. Dryden paused only to gather momentum. There was pulse in his narrative medium as there had been pulse in his occasional, satirical, and lyrical mediums; his settings, his addresses, his descriptions of persons, his exposition of emotional cause and effect, were never dead; they were magazines of narrative energy. There can hardly be said to exist in English a perfect verse instrument for narrative; continuous couplets give too little pause, while stanzas halt too often. Dryden has come as near as any poet to a durable compromise. He can run straight on as far as he likes; then when he likes he can bring himself up sharply, and go on by leisurely stages. He can hesitate and exclaim, he can stop and wonder, he can meditate and meander.

Dryden's first narrative poem was not a tale but a chronicle. The *Annus Mirabilis* was almost the last echo of Lucan in English. Warner, Daniel, and Drayton had been the Elizabethan "historians in verse"; Dryden in 1666 constituted himself the chronicler of Charles's war with the Dutch and of the Great Fire of London. He was hardly geared, like old Nestor in Shakespeare's *Troilus and Cressida*, for walking hand in hand with Time; his gait was better suited to breathless, bizarre romance. His heroic stanzas stalk along with a quaint, spectral dignity, while no great amount of history gets told, though more perhaps than got told in the elaborately embroidered stanzas of the Elizabethans. The couplet, not the quatrain, was to be his vehicle.

The writing of plays gave Dryden's hand valuable practice in the quick sketching of action. There was an audience in this case which needed to know briefly what had happened off the stage. The necessity was for being straightforward, not for wandering among rare similes and precious allusions. A fair example is the speech of the Duke of Arcos to King Ferdinand in the second part of *The Conquest of Granada*, recounting the death of the master of Alcantara:

> Our soldiers marched together on the plain;
> We two rode on, and left them far behind,
> Till coming where we found the valley wind,
> We saw these Moors; who, swiftly as they could,
> Ran on to gain the covert of a wood.
> This we observed; and, having crossed their way,
> The lady, out of breath, was forced to stay;
> The man then stood, and straight his faulchion drew;
> Then told us, we in vain did those pursue,
> Whom their ill fortune to despair did drive,
> And yet, whom we should never take alive.
> Neglecting this, the master straight spurred on;
> But the active Moor his horse's shock did shun,
> And, ere his rider from his reach could go,
> Finished the combat with one deadly blow.
> I, to revenge my friend, prepared to fight;
> But now our foremost men were come in sight,
> Who soon would have dispatched him on the place,

> Had I not saved him from a death so base,
> And brought him to attend your royal doom.

This is far from Dryden's maturest narrative writing; the inversions are stilted, and the movement is somewhat mechanical. Its only significance lies in its directness and its clarity. The rhymes are less relied on to accentuate the movement than is usually to be the case hereafter. Dryden at his best did not smother his rhymes, but propelled himself by them and by the steady forward stroke of the end-stopped couplet.

Three of the satires gained by being cast in a narrative mold. *Absalom and Achitophel,* which took its tone from *Paradise Lost* and Cowley's *Davideis,* was an epic situation overlaid with humor and huge scorn. *Mac Flecknoe* was a full-blown mock-heroic incident. *The Hind and the Panther* began and ended on a note that was neither heroic nor familiar, but was well adjusted to Dryden's complicated motive. Near the close of the second part there is this passage:

> By this the Hind had reached her lonely cell,
> And vapours rose, and dews unwholesome fell.
> When she, by frequent observation wise,
> As one who long on Heaven had fixed her eyes,
> Discerned a change of weather in the skies.
> The western borders were with crimson spread,
> The moon descending looked all flaming red;
> She thought good manners bound her to invite
> The stranger dame to be her guest that night.
> 'Tis true, coarse diet, and a short repast,
> (She said,) were weak inducements to the taste
> Of one so nicely bred, and so unused to fast;
> But what plain fare her cottage could afford,
> A hearty welcome at a homely board,
> Was freely hers; and, to supply the rest,
> An honest meaning, and an open breast.

No portion of the poem is more charged with irony; almost every line here fires a political shot. At the same time Dryden

has capitulated to the genius of story-telling. He has fallen into
his most engaging narrative style purely for the pleasure of
doing so. The two fables of the swallows and the doves in the
third part are justly famous. The emphasis there is on situation
rather than on action, as befits the poet's satiric and didactic
purpose; yet flourishes are added that evince real relish in the
tale that is being told. In the fable of the swallows, for instance, there is a triplet that Dryden remembered twelve years
later when he was giving his account of Iphigenia asleep:

> Night came, but unattended with repose;
> Alone she came, no sleep their eyes to close;
> Alone and black she came; no friendly stars arose.

The great bulk of Dryden's narrative verse consists of
episodes translated or adapted from other poets. The habit of
versifying events out of Ovid and Virgil was an old one at the
Restoration, but it grew upon English poets rather more rapidly
after 1660, leaving its deepest mark on the *Miscellanies* which
Dryden himself began to edit in 1684. Dryden's first examples
are the *Nisus and Euryalus* and the *Mezentius and Lausus*
which he brought over from Virgil for the second *Miscellany* in
1685 and which he incorporated with slight changes in the folio
of 1697.* He was particularly fond of the Nisus stories, as the
poem on Oldham shows and as is even more clearly seen in a
letter to Tonson concerning the make-up of the volume in which
they first appeared: "I care not who translates them besides me,
for let him be friend or foe, I will please myself, and not give
off in consideration of any man." The poems, both as they were
then printed and as they now stand, are marred by hasty lines
and latinisms, but taken as wholes they are manly narratives,
rich, passionate, flushed with friendly warmth, and reinforced
by strong intelligence. They are profusely colored throughout
and in places they are highly spiced with alliteration. They

* See his *Aeneis*, V, 373-475 and IX, 221-600, for the first episode, and X,
1071-1313 for the second.

glorify a reckless personal loyalty and a shouting defiance of fate, the qualities which Dryden in his less critical moments delighted most to treat, the qualities which moved Byron at nineteen to try his own hand with Nisus and Euryalus. The deaths of Nisus and his friend in Dryden are brutish but effective. *Enjambement* is used to smooth transitions, as here:

> Thus armed they went. The noble Trojans wait
> Their issuing forth, and follow to the gate
> With prayers and vows. Above the rest appears
> Ascanius, manly far beyond his years.

But at the more critical stages of the action and in the speeches the couplets are conventionally definitive. Mezentius addresses his horse before he mounts to ride to his death:

> O Rhoebus, we have lived too long for me,
> (If life and long were terms that could agree).
> This day thou either shalt bring back the head
> And bloody trophies of the Trojan dead;
> This day thou either shalt revenge my woe,
> For murdered Lausus, on his cruel foe;
> Or, if inexorable fate deny
> Our conquest, with thy conquered master die.
> For, after such a lord, I rest secure,
> Thou wilt no foreign reins, or Trojan load endure.

The episodes from Ovid and Homer in the third *Miscellany* of 1693 are not remarkable, in spite of Dryden's statement in the preface that those from Ovid "appear to me the best of all my endeavours in this kind. Perhaps this poet is more easy to be translated than some others whom I have lately attempted; perhaps, too, he was more according to my genius. . . . I have attempted to restore Ovid to his native sweetness, easiness, and smoothness; and to give my poetry a kind of cadence, and, as we call it, a run of verse, as like the original, as the English can come up to the Latin." The first book of the *Metamorphoses* as here given is swift and smooth, and the other pieces

are picturesque and copious, but it must always be clear to anyone that Dryden was more at home among the warriors of the
Aeneid. Ovid was attractive mainly because of his enameled
extravagance; he wrote with license yet with elegance; poetically he was a finished rogue.

Dryden's career ended as it began, in a triumph of the will.
His probable resolution at twenty-three or twenty-four to proceed to London and become a poet is matched only by the fire
and perseverance which drove him at the end of his life through
pain and sickness to the conclusion of his *Fables.* An old man
divorced from the Court and vilely lampooned by Whigs each
year that he lived, he might have raged or snarled or complained or degenerated. He settled down instead to the telling
of stories. "The tattling quality of age," he had written in the
Discourse of Satire, "as Sir William Davenant says, is always
narrative." He kept his gracious grandniece, Mrs. Steward of
Cotterstock Hall, well informed concerning the progress of his
volume. "Between my intervals of physic," he wrote to her
on Candlemas-Day, 1698, "I am still drudging on: always a
poet, and never a good one. I pass my time sometimes with
Ovid, and sometimes with our old English poet Chaucer; translating such stories as best please my fancy; and intend besides
them to add somewhat of my own; so that it is not impossible,
but ere the summer be passed, I may come down to you with
a volume in my hand, like a dog out of the water, with a duck
in his mouth." On the fourth of March he continued: "I am
still drudging at a book of Miscellanies, which I hope will be
well enough; if otherwise, threescore and seven may be pardoned." Twenty days before his death, on the eleventh of April,
1700, he could write her with some pride: "The ladies of the
town . . . are all of your opinion, and like my last book of
Poems better than anything they have formerly seen of mine."
The work was certainly drudgery, and it was done as rapidly
as possible for money; but it is clear that Dryden grew fonder
of his occupation as he proceeded. The golden *Preface* describes

his delighted progress from Homer to Ovid, from Ovid to Chaucer, and from Chaucer to Boccaccio, the volume constantly swelling in his hands; "I have built a house," he concludes, "where I intended but a lodge." If he had thought of the lodge as a green retreat for a fading muse, he found the house a bustling hall built for the entertainment of his ripest powers; there had been no fading. At no time after the Revolution did he need to say like Virgil's Moeris:

> Cares and time
> Change all things, and untune my soul to rhyme.
> I could have once sung down a summer's sun,
> But now the chime of poetry is done.
> My voice grows hoarse.

The chime of Dryden's verse was never done.

There is no fine bloom of romance about the *Fables*. The generation for which they were produced was not possessed of delicate ideals; Spenser's vision of the virtues of man was as remote as Wordsworth's vision of Nature's quiet powers. "Dryden had neither a tender heart, nor a lofty sense of moral dignity," wrote Wordsworth to Scott in 1805. "Whenever his language is poetically impassioned, it is mostly upon unpleasing subjects, such as the follies, vices, and crimes of classes of men, or of individuals." The *Fables*, with certain notable exceptions, catered to a jaded taste that craved the strong meat of incest, murder, flowing blood, cruel and sensual unrealities, or else the biting acid of satire. Dryden's search for materials was far and wide. He did not confine himself to what Cowley in 1656 had contemptuously dismissed as "the obsolete threadbare tales of Thebes and Troy." He plundered medieval as well as ancient story; he went to the greatest tellers of tales wherever they were, whether they were Greek, Roman, Italian, or English. In a different sense from Walt Whitman's he decided:

> Come, Muse, migrate from Greece and Ionia.
> Cross out, please, those immensely overpaid accounts;
> That matter of Troy and Achilles' wrath, and Aeneas',
>   Odysseus' wanderings. . . .
> For know a better, fresher, busier sphere, a wider,
>   untried domain awaits and demands you.

Whatever the reason, Homer and Ovid do not show quite so well in the *Fables* as do Chaucer and Boccaccio. "That matter of Troy" and those "confused antiquated dreams of senseless . . . Metamorphoses," to quote Cowley once again, only occasionally ring familiar and true. *The First Book of Homer's Ilias*, in translating which Dryden did not use the original Greek, is striking only in its passages of invocation and abuse. The closing scene with Vulcan is grandiosely convivial:

> At Vulcan's homely mirth his mother smiled,
> And smiling took the cup the clown had filled.
> The reconciler bowl went round the board,
> Which, emptied, the rude skinker still restored.
> Loud fits of laughter seized the guests, to see
> The limping god so deft at his new ministry.
> The feast continued till declining light;
> They drank, they laughed, they loved, and then
>   'twas night.
> Nor wanted tuneful harp, nor vocal choir;
> The muses sung; Apollo touched the lyre.
> Drunken at last, and drowsy they depart,
> Each to his house, adorned with labored art
> Of the lame architect.

Pope's rendering of the same scene is not half so lively; the laughter of his gods is imitation laughter, this is real. It is thinkable that a complete *Iliad* by the author of these lines would be, even now, the most Homeric thing in English.

From Homer, says Dryden, "I proceeded to the translation of the Twelfth Book of Ovid's *Metamorphoses,* because it con-

tains, among other things, the causes, the beginning, and ending, of the Trojan war. Here I ought in reason to have
stopped." But he went on, so that almost a third of the *Fables*
derives from the *Metamorphoses*. The *Meleager and Atalanta*
from the eighth book is a hectic recital of a bloody boar-hunt
and a triple murder. Ovid has been lavish and audacious
enough, but Dryden goes him one better; he is facetious when
Ovid is sober, and he plays with words when Ovid speaks
plainly. Ovid's Althea, when the corpses of her brothers are
brought in, cries out merely and goes into mourning. In Dryden it is written:

> Pale at the sudden sight, she changed her cheer,
> And with her cheer her robes.

Ovid's Meleager, as soon as his image has been thrown to the
fire by his mother, writhes and laments the bloodless death
that he must die. Dryden says:

> Just then the hero cast a doleful cry,
> And in those absent flames began to fry;
> The blind contagion raged within his veins,
> But he with manly patience bore his pains;
> He feared not fate, but only grieved to die
> Without an honest wound, and by a death so dry.

Dryden has a pretty "turn" where Ovid has none; it occurs in
the account of the grief felt by the sisters of the Calydonian
hero:

> Had I a hundred tongues, a wit so large
> As could their hundred offices discharge;
> Had Phoebus all his Helicon bestowed,
> In all the streams inspiring all the god;
> Those tongues, that wit, those streams, that god in vain
> Would offer to describe his sisters' pain.

Baucis and Philemon, from the eighth book, is by far the
best of the Ovidian pieces. Dryden praises this "good-natured

story" in the *Preface*. "I see Baucis and Philemon as perfectly
before me," he declares, "as if some ancient painter had drawn
them." It had always pleased him to write of homely hospitality and rustic honesty. In the prologue to *All for Love* he had
remarked how those in high places liked at times to descend
among the low and

> Drink hearty draughts of ale from plain brown bowls,
> And snatch the homely rasher from the coals.

The household cheer of his Hind had been of this sort, as has
been seen. Some of his most genial letters were those he wrote
in old age to Mrs. Steward thanking her for gifts of venison
and marrow pudding. "As for the rarities you promise," he
protested on one occasion, "if beggars might be choosers, a
part of a chine of honest bacon would please my appetite more
than all the marrow puddings; for I like them better plain;
having a very vulgar stomach." He reveled among Ovid's details and added others of his own, stirring all in to make his
poem rich. Jove and Hermes fared like this:

> High o'er the hearth a chine of bacon hung;
> Good old Philemon seized it with a prong,
> And from the sooty rafter drew it down;
> Then cut a slice, but scarce enough for one;
> Yet a large portion of a little store,
> Which for their sakes alone he wished were more;
> This in the pot he plunged without delay,
> To tame the flesh and drain the salt away.
> The time between, before the fire they sat,
> And shortened the delay with pleasing chat. . . .
> Pallas began the feast, where first were seen
> The party-colored olive, black and green;
> Autumnal cornels next in order served,
> In lees of wine well pickled and preserved;
> A garden salad was the third supply,
> Of endive, radishes, and succory;

Then curds and cream, the flower of country fare,
And new-laid eggs, which Baucis' busy care
Turned by a gentle fire and roasted rare. . . .
The wine itself was suiting to the rest,
Still working in the must, and lately pressed.
The second course succeeds like that before;
Plums, apples, nuts, and, of their wintry store,
Dry figs and grapes, and wrinkled dates were set
In canisters.

There is no padding here, no clutter of circumlocutions. Dryden feels at home, which means that he is rapid, vivid, and concrete, and therefore for once a good story-teller.

Pygmalion and the Statue, from the tenth book, had a good Restoration theme which lent itself to vulgarization; it was so treated by Dryden, who could rarely be trusted with lovers. The *Cinyras and Myrrha*, from the same book, a tale of incest, was likewise handled without restraint. The *Ceyx and Alcyone*, from the eleventh book, the history of a shipwreck, a drowning, and a body washed ashore, is extremely fantastic in Ovid; in Dryden, who now is plainly tired, it is grotesque and literal. Ovid's two lines on King Ceyx in the water,

Dum natet, absentem, quotiens sinit hiscere fluctus,
Nominat Alcyonen ipsisque inmurmurat undis,

become four in the *Fables:*

As oft as he can catch a gulp of air,
And peep above the seas, he names the fair;
And even when plunged beneath, on her he raves,
Murmuring Alcyone below the waves.

The twelfth book, which is "wholly translated," recounts the famous fight in the cave, Dryden being fully as graphic and gory as the original. *The Speeches of Ajax and Ulysses*, from the thirteenth book, find him once more in his element. A forensic contest is on between brain and brawn, and the trans-

lator of Lucretius is in his best argumentative trim. The verse
is strong, intelligent and swift. Ulysses concludes, speaking to
Ajax:

> Brawn without brain is thine; my prudent care
> Foresees, provides, administers the war.
> Thy province is to fight; but when shall be
> The time to fight, the king consults with me.
> No dram of judgment with thy force is joined.
> Thy body is of profit, and my mind.
> By how much more the ship her safety owes
> To him who steers, than him that only rows;
> By how much more the captain merits praise
> Than he who fights, and fighting but obeys;
> By so much greater is my worth than thine,
> Who canst but execute what I design.

When Dryden in the preface to his *Fables* elaborately declared the superiority of Chaucer to Ovid in sanity and truth
to nature he revived the sunken reputation of one of the greatest
English poets much as in the *Essay of Dramatic Poesy* he had
established for all Augustan generations the tone of evaluation
of the greatest, and he reared himself head and shoulders above
contemporary criticism. Perhaps the most saving thing about
him as a poet is the fact that he championed and gave vogue
to the *Canterbury Tales*. The reputation of Chaucer was lower
in the seventeenth century than it had been before or has been
since. No edition of his works was issued between the two
reprints of Speght in 1602 and 1687. He was seldom read,
though he was often mentioned as a difficult old author who
had a remarkable but obscure vein of gaiety. Spenser's tribute
was forgotten, and Milton's went unobserved. "Mr. Cowley
despised him," according to Dryden, and Addison, in the *Account of the Greatest English Poets* which he contributed
to the fourth *Miscellany* in 1694, pronounced what seemed a
final benediction over the skeleton of his fame:

In vain he jests in his unpolished strain
And tries to make his readers laugh in vain. . . .
But now the mystic tale that pleased of yore
Can charm an understanding age no more.

Now Dryden, in an age when "nature" was more talked about than explored, took pains to deny that Chaucer was "a dry, old-fashioned wit, not worth reviving," proving rather that he had "followed Nature everywhere," and had written for all time. "We have our forefathers and great-grand-dames all before us, as they were in Chaucer's days; their general characters are still remaining in mankind, and even in England, though they are called by other names . . . for mankind is ever the same, and nothing lost out of Nature, though everything is altered." The humanity of Chaucer had its effect on the *Fables,* where *The Cock and the Fox,* for instance, is bubbling and droll like nothing else in Dryden. It is a pleasure to behold the old poet who has dealt so exclusively throughout his career in the styles and accidents of utterance expand and ripen under the influence of a richly human writer. "In sum, I seriously protest," he concluded, "that no man ever had, or can have, a greater veneration for Chaucer than myself. I have translated some part of his works, only that I might perpetuate his memory, or at least refresh it, amongst my countrymen."

In modernizing Chaucer Dryden had to overcome two current prejudices concerning his language. On the one hand there was a majority who considered that language too stale to be worth restoring; on the other there was a minority consisting of certain "old Saxon friends" like the late Earl of Leicester who supposed, according to Dryden, "that it is little less than profanation and sacrilege to alter it. They are farther of opinion, that somewhat of his good sense will suffer in this transfusion, and much of the beauty of his thoughts will infallibly be lost, which appear with more grace in the old habit." His answer to the first was that now they might see for themselves

whether Chaucer was worth knowing, and his answer to the
second was that he worked in the interest not of scholars but of
those "who understand sense and poetry as well as they, when
that poetry and sense is put into words which they understand."
A more serious problem that had to be met in the process of
modernization was the problem of versification. Dryden's
dilemma at this point has not been sufficiently appreciated. He
has been smiled at, to begin with, for his ignorance of Chaucer's
metrical scheme; and by those who do not mind that, he has
been condemned for his obliteration of Chaucer's exquisite
metrical personality. His ignorance, which was real, he shared
with most of his contemporaries; and he cannot be blamed because the text he used was so mangled that no uniform meter
emerged. It was literally true for him that not all lines had the
full ten syllables; Speght had not guarded his final *e*'s as must
a modern editor. The passage in which Dryden surveys the
field is too important not to be quoted: "The verse of Chaucer,
I confess, is not harmonious to us; . . . they who lived with
him, and some time after him, thought it musical; and it continues so, even in our judgment, if compared with the numbers
of Lidgate and Gower, his contemporaries: there is the rude
sweetness of a Scotch tune in it, which is natural and pleasing,
though not perfect. 'Tis true, I cannot go so far as he who
published the last edition of him; for he would make us believe
the fault is in our ears, and that there were really ten syllables
in a verse where we find but nine: but this opinion is not worth
confuting; 'tis so gross and obvious an error, that common sense
(which is a rule in everything but matters of Faith and Revelation) must convince the reader, that equality of numbers, in
every verse which we call heroic, was either not known, or not
always practiced, in Chaucer's age. It were an easy matter to
produce some thousands of his verses, which are lame for want
of half a foot, and sometimes a whole one, and which no
pronunciation can make otherwise." But even if Dryden had
known all that was to be known about the verse of Chaucer, it

still would have been impossible for him, as it must be always for anyone, to modernize that verse and preserve its flavor. To use Dryden's own word, its most precious qualities "evaporate" when exposed to another air. The crux is in the weak final syllables, which have a caressing sound never heard in the necessarily brisker verse of modern times. Since it seemed especially important in Dryden's day to throw the full weight of each line into the last syllable or the last word, and since Dryden himself had a dislike for feminine rhymes and indecisive endings, it is not to be wondered that he sharpened and hardened his fourteenth-century master.

"I have not tied myself to a literal translation," he says in the *Preface:* "but have often omitted what I judged unnecessary, or not of dignity enough to appear in the company of better thoughts. I have presumed further, in some places, and added somewhat of my own where I thought my author was deficient, and had not given his thoughts their true lustre, for want of words in the beginning of our language." That is to say, his aim has been to round out Chaucer and give him an even, enameled surface; he has wished to remove all traces of the Gothic. He has had in mind a kind of fourth "unity," the unity of effect, to secure which it has been necessary to employ different means in different poems.

In *Palamon and Arcite* he has applied the seventeenth-century heroic formulas to Chaucer's *Knight's Tale,* which he says he prefers "far above all his other stories" because of its epic possibilities. The result is a sometimes stilted poem, one of the least interesting for its length in the *Fables.* Surrendering to the Restoration heroic tradition, Dryden has drawn the sting of Chaucer's colloquial charm and injected with a blunt needle the false dignity of Almanzor and Aureng-Zebe. Neither the jovial satire nor the purple melodrama of the other tales is here. Epithets, circumlocutions, latinisms, grave conceits, and standard allusions are run profusely in to thicken but not ennoble the

original texture. The verse is uniform and handsome, but the
psychology is almost everywhere gross. For Chaucer's lines,

> The quene anon, for verray wommanhede,
> Gan for to wepe, and so did Emeleye,
> And alle the ladies in the companye,

Dryden has substituted:

> The queen, above the rest, by nature good,
> (The pattern formed of perfect womanhood,)
> For tender pity wept: when she began,
> Through the bright choir the infectious virtue ran.
> All dropped their tears, even the contented maid.

And Chaucer's simile,

> As wilde bores gonne they to smyte,
> That frothen whyte as foom for ire wood,

becomes:

> Or, as two boars whom love to battle draws,
> With rising bristles, and with frothy jaws,
> Their adverse breasts with tusks oblique they wound;
> With grunts and groans the forest rings around.

The poem is partially redeemed on one side by the regal "characters" of Lycurgus and Emetrius, the prayers of Palamon,
Emily, and Arcite to Venus, Cynthia, and Mars, the splendid
settings which are given for martial actions, and on the other
side by occasional couplets in which Dryden's mind has slashed
with a shining malice through the tissue of knightly palaver.
His knowingness now is not ugly, not smart. He never looks
greedily out of the corner of his eye to see how you take it; it
is too native with him for him to be concerned about that, and
he himself is too humane. At the end of Aegeus' consolatory
speech on the death of Arcite, Dryden, not Chaucer, observes
somewhat enigmatically:

With words like these the crowd was satisfied,
And so they would have been, had Theseus died.

Both poets like to describe groups of men conversing; but when Chaucer was only amused, Dryden became contemptuous. Chaucer's delicious account in the Squire's tale of the loquacious courtiers who gathered around the steed of brass that stood before the throne of Cambinskan and speculated upon its origin is perhaps matched here in the Knight's Tale by a few lines hitting off the throng that forecast the outcome of tomorrow's tournament:

> The paleys ful of peples up and doun,
> Heer three, ther ten, holding hir questioun,
> Divyninge of thise Theban knightes two.
> Somme seyden thus, somme seyde it shal be so;
> Somme helden with him with the blake berd,
> Somme with the balled, somme with the thikke-berd;
> Somme seyde, he looked grim and he wolde fighte;
> He hath a sparth of twenty pound of wighte.
> Thus was the halle ful of divyninge,
> Longe after that the sonne gan to springe.

Dryden is more graphic in this case, and more caustic:

> In knots they stand, or in a rank they walk,
> Serious in aspect, earnest in their talk;
> Factious, and favoring this or t' other side,
> As their strong fancies and weak reason guide.
> Their wagers back their wishes; numbers hold
> With the fair freckled king, and beard of gold;
> So vigorous are his eyes, such rays they cast,
> So prominent his eagle's beak is placed.
> But most their looks on the black monarch bend,
> His rising muscles and his brawn commend;
> His double-biting ax, and beamy spear,
> Each asking a gigantic force to rear.
> All spoke as partial favor moved the mind;
> And, safe themselves, at others' cost divined.

The Cock and the Fox is another story; it is one of the best and most original of the *Fables*. It must be sheer affectation to insist that Chaucer's *Nun's Priest's Tale* has suffered in the hands of Dryden. Chaucer's poem is surpassingly human, concrete, and sly; but Dryden's is no less so, though its pitch is altered. The opening account of the poor old widow in her cottage and of the amorous Chanticleer among his dames is superior comedy; Dryden has tactfully elaborated such facetious hints as are given from time to time by the original. The disputation between Dame Partlet and the Cock on the subject of dreams offers an opportunity which is both welcome and improved. And the merchant's simple gibe at his friend,

> I sette not a straw by thy dreminges,
> For swevenes been but vanitees and japes.
> Men dreme al-day of owles or of apes,
> And eke of many a mase therewithal;
> Men dreme of thing that nevere was ne shal,

becomes in Dryden's hands a piece of Lucretian exposition:

> Dreams are but interludes which fancy makes;
> When monarch Reason sleeps, this mimic wakes;
> Compounds a medley of disjointed things,
> A court of cobblers, and a mob of kings.
> Light fumes are merry, grosser fumes are sad;
> Both are the reasonable soul run mad:
> And many monstrous forms in sleep we see,
> That neither were, nor are, nor e'er can be.
> Sometimes forgotten things long cast behind
> Rush forward in the brain, and come to mind.
> The muse's legends are for truth received,
> And the man dreams but what the boy believed.
> Sometimes we but rehearse a former play;
> The night restores our actions done by day,
> As hounds in sleep will open for their prey.
> In short the farce of dreams is of a piece,
> Chimeras all.

The episode of the brother murdered at the inn is excellently and swiftly told. The digression on freewill gives Dryden a ratiocinative cue which he takes half in the spirit of *Religio Laici* and half in the spirit of the Nun's Priest's Tale itself.

The Flower and the Leaf and *The Wife of Bath, Her Tale* are extraordinary in Dryden for their luxuriant, spirited representation of fairy worlds. *The Flower and the Leaf,* a poem not by Chaucer, is a singularly pure and magical piece of pageantry in rhyme-royal. Dryden has flushed and accelerated it; its wheels have caught fire, and glowing masses of fresh detail are swept into the race. The splendor is mostly genuine; few of Dryden's descriptions are less prolix. The genius of Spenser has rushed to reinforce the old Augustan in this couplet on the nightingale:

> So sweet, so shrill, so variously she sung,
> That the grove echoed, and the valleys rung.

And in the passage on the jousting knights Dryden has remembered the metrical pattern which he used some years before to describe the Trojan boys as they wheeled and met in warlike play on the plains of Sicily: *

> Thus marching to the trumpets' lofty sound,
> Drawn in two lines adverse they wheeled around,
> And in the middle meadow took their ground.
> Among themselves the turney they divide,
> In equal squadrons ranged on either side;
> Then turned their horses' heads, and man to man,
> And steed to steed opposed, the justs began,
> They lightly set their lances in the rest,
> And, at the sign, against each other pressed;
> They met; I sitting at my ease beheld
> The mixed events, and fortunes of the field.
> Some broke their spears, some tumbled horse and man,
> And round the field the lightened coursers ran.

* See page 64.

> An hour and more, like tides, in equal sway
> They rushed, and won by turns and lost the day.

The twenty-five lines with which Chaucer began the story of the
Wife of Bath have grown into forty-five in the *Fables*. Dryden
has drawn upon Shakespeare's *Romeo and Juliet* and *Midsum-
mer Night's Dream*, Spenser's *Faerie Queene*, and Milton's
L'Allegro to enrich the text of the *Canterbury Tales:*

> I speak of ancient times, for now the swain
> Returning late may pass the woods in vain,
> And never hope to see the nightly train;
> In vain the dairy now with mints is dressed,
> The dairymaid expects no fairy guest,
> To skim the bowls, and after pay the feast.
> She sighs, and shakes her empty shoes in vain,
> No silver penny to reward her pain;
> For priests with prayers, and other godly gear,
> Have made the merry goblins disappear;
> And where they played their merry pranks before,
> Have sprinkled holy water on the floor. . . .
> The maids and women need no danger fear
> To walk by night, and sanctity so near;
> For by some haycock, or some shady thorn,
> He bids his beads both even song and morn.
> It so befell in this King Arthur's reign,
> A lusty knight was pricking o'er the plain. . . .

An open attack on the court follows soon after, commencing:

> Then courts of kings were held in high renown,
> Ere made the common brothels of the town.

The tale proceeds without especial distinction; the long speech
at the end by the loathly lady is expanded from Chaucer with
the aid of Lucretius.

"I think his translations from Boccaccio are the best, at least
the most poetical, of his poems," wrote Wordsworth to Scott.
They are among the best known of the *Fables*; and they are

the most successful of all Dryden's poems as narratives. It must be admitted that in general his stories in verse are interesting not so much for their action as for something by the way: the meter, the speeches, the settings, the "characters," the satiric interpolations, the semblance of action. With the exception perhaps of *Palamon and Arcite,* none of the pieces from Chaucer or Ovid is remembered wholly for what happens in it; Dryden's narrative surface is more animated than moving. But in those from Boccaccio the story is everything; these poems burn with narrative energy. It was not for nothing that Dryden turned at last to a prince of storytellers and went in heartily for melodrama. *Sigismonda and Guiscardo* is a blazing tale of lovers' lust and murder. We see a secret bride and groom somewhat brutally enjoy each other until the father discovers them and orders the husband put to death. Wordsworth's criticism can hardly be improved upon. "It is many years since I saw Boccaccio," he said, "but I remember that Sigismunda is not married by him to Guiscard. . . . I think Dryden has much injured the story by the marriage, and degraded Sigismunda's character by it. He has also, to the best of my remembrance, degraded her still more, by making her love absolute sensuality and appetite; Dryden had no other notion of the passion. With all these defects, and they are very gross ones, it is a noble poem." The narrative on the whole is economical, though there are some wide wastes of verbiage. Sigismonda's address to Tancred defending Guiscardo and vindicating virtuous poverty is sound oratory but it is too long and too formal. Dryden in the *Preface* invites comparison between it and the speech of the hag at the end of *The Wife of Bath.* Neither speech as it is written belongs exactly where it is placed.

Theodore and Honoria is a haunting tale of terror, long popular and the only one of Dryden's narratives with an atmosphere that is sustained. The forests of old Ravenna cast a deep romantic shade over the knights and ladies, real and visionary, who play their grisly parts. Dryden has opened both eyes wide upon a dark fantastic world; and his ear was never fitter. The poem makes a rousing start:

> Of all the cities in Romanian lands,
> The chief, and most renowned, Ravenna stands,
> Adorned in ancient times with arms and arts,
> And rich inhabitants, with generous hearts.
> But Theodore the brave, above the rest,
> With gifts of fortune and of nature blest,
> The foremost place for wealth and honour held,
> And all in feats of chivalry excelled.
>   This noble youth to madness loved a dame,
> Of high degree, Honoria was her name;
> Fair as the fairest, but of haughty mind,
> And fiercer than became so soft a kind.

The setting for the apparition of the hunted maid owes its success to a group of ominous cadences which reproduce the terror and suspense of Nature herself:

> It happened one morning, as his fancy led,
> Before his usual hour he left his bed,
> To walk within a lonely lawn, that stood
> On every side surrounded by the wood.
> Alone he walked, to please his pensive mind,
> And sought the deepest solitude to find. . . .
> While listening to the murmuring leaves he stood,
> More than a mile immersed within the wood,
> At once the wind was laid; the whispering sound
> Was dumb; a rising earthquake rocked the ground;
> With deeper brown the grove was overspread:
> A sudden horror seized his giddy head,
> And his ears tinkled, and his color fled.
> Nature was in alarm; some danger nigh
> Seemed threatened, though unseen to mortal eye.
> Unused to fear, he summoned all his soul,
> And stood collected in himself, and whole;
> Not long: for soon a whirlwind rose around,
> And from afar he heard a screaming sound,

> As of a dame distressed, who cried for aid,
> And filled with loud laments the secret shade.

The story whirls on without an interruption or a couplet out of place. The effect is single; Dryden nowhere stops merely to heap up words or to paint an impossible, unnecessary scene.

Cymon and Iphigenia, the last of all the *Fables,* is less of a piece than the *Theodore.* It is famous not for its plot but for its by-play. No one remembers the last two-thirds of the poem; but the first hundred and fifty-seven lines are classic. Dryden has conceived simple Cymon and the most desirable Iphigenia with infinite zest. The hero is removed by his father to the farm:

> Thus to the wilds the sturdy Cymon went,
> A squire among the swains, and pleased with banishment.
> His corn and cattle were his only care,
> And his supreme delight a country fair.
>   It happened on a summer's holiday,
> That to the greenwood shade he took his way;
> For Cymon shunned the church, and used not much to pray.
> His quarterstaff, which he could ne'er forsake,
> Hung half before, and half behind his back.
> He trudged along, unknowing what he sought,
> And whistled as he went, for want of thought.

He comes upon Iphigenia asleep much as Thomson's Damon in *Summer* comes upon Musidora, and after a spell of staring he is inspired to analyze his first love's charms:

> Thus our man-beast, advancing by degrees,
> First likes the whole, then separates by degrees,
> On several parts a several praise bestows,
> The ruby lips, the well-proportioned nose,
> The snowy skin, the raven-glossy hair,
> The dimpled cheek, the forehead rising fair,
> And even in sleep itself a smiling air.

This is romance, but romance sunned and dried in the smiling mind of a massive old satirist. Here in this legend of two preposterous lovers and afterwards in the "character" of the raw militia swarming on the fields of Rhodes are exhibited most of the traits of Dryden. One will observe the absence of wonder, and the powerful presence of hard, substantial laughter.

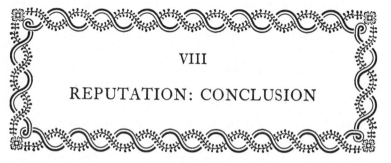

VIII

REPUTATION: CONCLUSION

THE REPUTATION of Dryden as a poet is scarcely international. Where English is not spoken his name may be respected, but his poetry is seldom read. It is only a few poets who can be or need be translated. Dryden, in whom style was paramount, and whose manner proved generally incommunicable even to native successors, can hardly have expected to prevail in other tongues. Thackeray asserted in his essay on Congreve and Addison that Dryden died "the marked man of all Europe," but that is an exaggeration. Naturally enough, he was heard more of in France than elsewhere on the continent; yet he was never famous there. At no time before 1700 were the French much interested in England's *belles lettres;* it did not much matter to Boileau whether Dryden or Blackmore was best among the poets across the Channel. Boileau, indeed, when told of Dryden's death is said to have affected never to have heard his name. Rapin on the other hand may have learned English merely to read him.

At all events it was not until the next century, when everything English suddenly became of enormous concern to Frenchmen, that Voltaire celebrated and gave some little vogue to

"l'inégal et impétueux Dryden," "un très-grand génie," as he
called him in the dedication of *Zaïre* in 1736. He had introduced the author of *Aureng-Zebe* to the French public in 1734,
in his letter on English tragedy: "C'est Dryden Poète du tems
de Charles second, Auteur plus fécond que judicieux, qui aurait
une réputation sans mélange, s'il n'avait fait que la dixième
partie de ses Ouvrages, et dont le grand deffaut est d'avoir
voulu être universel." In 1752, in the thirty-fourth chapter of
his *Siècle de Louis XIV*, he announced of Dryden's works that
they were "pleins de détails naturels à la fois et brillants,
animés, vigoureux, hardis, passionés, mérite qu'aucun ancien n'a
surpassé." He drew upon *The Wife of Bath* in 1764 for the
idea of his tale in verse, *Ce Que Plaît aux Dames*. *Alexander's
Feast* was always for him a *point de repère* in English poetry.
In his article on Enthusiasm in the Dictionary he showed an
excellent understanding of the conventional English judgments
upon it: "De toutes les odes modernes, celle où il règne le
plus grand enthousiasme qui ne s'affaiblit jamais, et qui ne
tombe ni dans le faux ni dans l'ampulé, est le *Timothée*, ou la
fête d'Alexandre, par Dryden; elle est encore regardée en
Angleterre comme un chef-d'œuvre inimitable, dont Pope n'a
pu approcher quand il a voulu s'exercer dans le même genre.
Cette ode fût chantée; et si on avait eu un musicien digne du
poète, ce serait le chef-d'œuvre de la poésie lyrique." To M.
de Chabanon, who had just published a translation of Pindar
with an essay on the Pindaric *genre*, he wrote from Ferney on
the 9th of March, 1772: "Vous appelez Cowley le Pindare
anglais . . . c'était un poète sans harmonie. . . . Le vrai Pindare est Dryden, auteur de cette belle ode intitulée *la Fête
d'Alexandre, ou Alexandre et Timothée*. Cette ode . . . passe
en Angleterre pour le chef-d'œuvre de la poésie la plus sublime et la plus variée; et je vous avoue que, comme je sais
mieux l'anglais que le grec, j'aime cent fois mieux cette ode
que tout Pindare." Boswell told Johnson "that Voltaire, in a
conversation with me, had distinguished Pope and Dryden thus:

'Pope drives a handsome chariot, with a couple of neat trim nags; Dryden a coach, and six stately horses.'" It will be seen that Voltaire had not listened for nothing to the wits and savants of London. And he must have known that he was safer in extolling *Alexander's Feast* than he would have been on any other ground. Dryden's last ode has penetrated where none of the other poems will ever go. Handel's music kept it long familiar to Germans who had no taste for the other lyrics. Henry Crabb Robinson wrote in his diary in 1803, after a visit to Voss, the German translator of Homer: "I was quite unable to make him see the beauty of Dryden's translations from Horace,—such as the 'Ode on Fortune.'" A. W. Schlegel was at a loss to understand what he considered the inflated reputation at home of the plays, the translations, and the "political allegories." It is in England, and incidentally in America, that one must remain if one would find what eminence Dryden has enjoyed.

"I loved Mr. Dryden," said Congreve with a simplicity that was rare with him and his generation. The stout old poet with his cherry cheeks, his heavy eyes, his long gray hair, and his snuff-soiled waistcoat was not in want of affectionate as well as valuable friends after the Revolution. He kept company not only with poets but with important laymen. He was a believer in conversation, though he may not have been an adept himself. "Great contemporaries whet and cultivate each other," he wrote in 1693 in the *Discourse of Satire*. Back in the time of Charles he had been intimate with the wits and poets of the court. "We have . . . our genial nights," he reminded Sedley in the dedication of *The Assignation* in 1673, "where our discourse is neither too serious nor too light, but always pleasant, and, for the most part, instructive; the raillery neither too sharp upon the present, nor too censorious on the absent; and the cups only such as will raise the conversation of the night, without disturbing the business of the morrow." In his last decade he was welcome in the houses of his relations, Mrs. Steward of Cotterstock Hall, near Oundle, Northamptonshire, and John Driden of Chesterton, in Huntingdonshire, and in that of the really noble Duke of Ormond. Thomas Carte, who wrote a life of the Duke in 1736, said that "once in a quarter of a year he used to have the Marquis of Halifax, the earls of Mulgrave, Dorset, and Danby, Mr. Dryden, and others of that set of men at supper, and then they were merry and drank hard." *

His position among the poets of that decade is too well known to require an elaborate account. Pope told Spence that "Dryden employed his mornings in writing; dined, *en famille;* and then went to Will's." His coffee-house dictatorship has long been proverbial in English literary history; "the great patriarch of Parnassus" who ruled by the fire in winter and out on the balcony in summer is the most striking figure between the blind Milton and the rolling Johnson. His prologues and epilogues, and later his satires, made him respected, feared, and sought as a judge of verse. There has come down from about 1682 a decision which he wrote for an unknown company concerning a disputed passage in Creech's *Lucretius*. The dispute was as to

* John Caryll of Lady Holt, Sussex, who formed the amiable habit late in the century of inviting celebrities to his house and accompanying his invitations with gifts of venison, transcribed for Pope or himself about 1729 a letter from Dryden, dated July 21, 1698, sent in answer to one of his hospitable notes. The copy may be found among the Additional MSS. at the British Museum (28, 618, f. 84). It runs as follows:

Sir

'T is the part of an honest Man to be as good as his Word, butt you have been better: I expected but halfe of what I had, and that halfe, not halfe so Good. Your Vaneson had three of the best Qualities, for it was both fatt, large & sweet. To add to this you have been pleased to invite me to Ladyholt, and if I could promise myself a year's Life, I might hope to be happy in so sweet a Place, & in the Enjoyment of your good Company. How God will dispose of me, I know not: but I am apt to flatter myself with the thoughts of itt, because I very much desire itt, and am Sr with all manner of Acknowledgement,

Yr most Obliged and most
faith full Servant
John Dryden.

July 21, 1698.

whether the passage made sense. Dryden reported: "I have considered the verses, and find the author of them to have notoriously bungled; that he has placed the words as confusedly as if he had studied to do so." He proceeded to analyze the error and to suggest an amendment of it, concluding: "The company having done me so great an honour as to make me their judge, I desire . . . the favour of making my acknowledgements to them; and should be proud to hear . . . whether they rest satisfied in my opinion." By 1685 his authority at Will's already was established, if Spence's story of how young Lockier won his approbation there may be trusted. Robert Wolseley the same year, in his preface to Rochester's play *Valentinian,* referred a quarrel with Mulgrave in all confidence to "Mr. Dryden, . . . whose judgment in anything that relates to Poetry, I suppose, he will not dispute." There was little disposition among the younger followers of literature like Walsh and Dennis to contest a definition or a preference of Mr. Dryden's.

Nor was there serious doubt in the minds of beginning poets as to what was the best in matter, form, and style; Dryden had stamped an image of himself on every world of verse, and few could refrain from falling in some measure into the cadences of his prologues, his epistles, his satires, his discourses, his songs, his odes, his narratives. Publicly also it was understood that Dryden represented the taste of the nation in poetry. The man who once had subsisted by panegyrizing the Crown, by propitiating the coxcombs of the theaters, and later by being a partisan in verse, was now more honorably engaged in selling his verses to the readers of England generally. The two folios of 1697 and 1700, the *Virgil* and the *Fables,* are memorials not only of an aged poet's power but of an awakening audience's temper. The bookseller with his subscription editions was now in a position to guarantee a kind of independence and professional prosperity to men of gifts; there was coming into existence a reading public. Long before the first of the two folios appeared it was a prevailing wish that Dryden might build an English monument in meter. "We hope that Mr. Dryden will undertake to give us a Translation of Virgil," wrote Motteux in his "News of Learning from Several Parts" in the *Gentleman's Journal* for March, 1694; " 'tis indeed a most difficult work, but if anyone can assure himself of success in attempting so bold a task, 'tis doubtless the Virgil of our age, for whose noble Pen that best of Latin Poets seems reserved." The *Virgil* and the *Fables* seem today to stand astride of the interval between *Paradise Lost* and Pope's *Homer*. For a generation at least, anyone who pretended to be a reader read them, as one who expected to be a poet studied them. Dryden himself, complacently enough, was the first to admit his own supremacy; knowing that no man wrote better poetry, he said as much, and so infuriated for a new reason such rivals in trade as grudged him his eminence, such enemies in politics as still remembered his ill-timed conversion to Roman Catholicism, and such desperate wits as subsisted at the fringe of literary society by making sport of the famous. "More libels have been written against me, than almost any man now living," he could say in 1693. He suffered both the advantages and the disadvantages of having no real rival to draw a portion of the fire.

An investigator of the reputation of a poet seeks to answer three questions. As for his vogue, what poems have continued to be read? As for his standing, how has he been criticized and where has he been ranked? And as for his influence, what poets have been governed or at any rate touched by his power? It seems advisable in the case of Dryden to pursue each of these inquiries through three periods since his death: the eighteenth century, or such portions of it as preserved fairly uniform Augustan standards; the late eighteenth and early nineteenth centuries, when there was a more or less abrupt break with those standards; and subsequent time.

Dryden's vogue as a poet in any one period cannot be determined with exactness by counting collected editions. Taken in proportion to the whole of the literary public the readers of Dryden's poems in the nineteenth century were scarcely one-fourth as numerous as they had been in the eighteenth; yet the nineteenth century saw four times as many editions. Tonson printed a very imperfect folio in 1701 consisting chiefly of *Poems on Various Occasions and Translations from Several Authors* extracted from the *Miscellanies,* binding it with two volumes of the plays and the 1700 issue of the *Fables.* No other collection appeared until forty-two years later, when the house of Tonson and the Rev. Thomas Broughton brought out in two compact volumes the *Occasional Poems and Translations;* although Congreve's edition of the plays in six volumes in 1717 was popular, furnishing the material for new editions in 1725, 1735, 1760, and 1762. Two volumes of *Poems and Fables* appeared in Dublin in 1741 and 1753, while Glasgow supported two volumes of *Original Poems* in 1756, 1770, 1773, 1775, and 1776, the last time in company with the *Fables.* Samuel Derrick in 1760 and 1767 produced for the Tonsons again what he claimed was a complete set of the miscellaneous poems and translations in four beautiful octavo volumes, adding an ambitious *Life* and some elaborate notes, the first of their kind upon the subject. This work probably forestalled a somewhat more bulky edition of both the prose and the verse projected by James Ralph in 1758. Two volumes of *Original Poems and Translations* (1777) were followed in rapid succession during the next three-quarters of a century by the famous series of reprints of British poets, a series more bought than read. The collections of Bell in 1777 and 1782, those called Johnson's in 1779, 1790, and 1822, and those of Anderson in 1793, Park in 1806 and 1808, Chalmers in 1810, Sandford in 1819, the Aldine Poets in 1832-33, 1834, 1843, 1844, 1852, 1854, 1865, 1866, 1871, and 1891, the Cabinet Poets in 1851, Routledge in 1853, Robert Bell in 1854, 1862, and 1870, and Gilfillan in 1855, 1874, and 1894, to name no others, did not succeed in bringing great bodies of eager new readers to Dryden. Scott's exhaustive

edition of 1808, reissued in 1821 and revised by Professor Saintsbury in 1882-1893, was unfortunately as well as fortunately a
monument; it never has lent itself to familiar handling. The
four volumes edited from the notes of the Wartons in 1811,
intended to complement Malone's four volumes of the prose
(1800), were printed again in 1851 and 1861. W. D. Christie's
Globe *Dryden* of 1870, since republished many times, has furnished the model for editions of the poems in a single volume.
Its successors have made the poet easily accessible and in matters
of textual accuracy and bibliography have done him justice. The
Cambridge *Dryden* is an American masterpiece. Most of these
many editions have indicated little more than that the English-
reading world has expanded and that new libraries have called
for new sets of standard works. It is elsewhere that one must
go to find what poems of Dryden in particular and in truth
have lived to please.

The eighteenth century, being interested mostly in Dryden's
style, was much devoted to his translations, in which it was
considered, not very accurately, that his style showed fullest and
best. The *Virgil* was reprinted in 1698, 1709, 1716, 1721, 1730,
1748, 1763, 1769, 1772, 1773, 1782, 1792, and 1793, the excep-
tional interval between 1730 and 1763 being partly explainable
by the appearance of Christopher Pitt's translation of the *Aeneid*
in 1740. Pitt was a better scholar than Dryden, and for a time
he stood more in favor. But Dr. Johnson was of the opinion
"that Pitt pleases the critic, and Dryden the people; that Pitt
is quoted, and Dryden read." Neither is read often or carefully
now, but it is plain that if Dryden lost by departing from Virgil,
Pitt gained nothing by staying close. The *Juvenal* and *Persius*
were published in 1697, 1702, 1711, 1713, 1726, 1732, and
1735. Various portions of the *Ovid* appeared in 1701, 1705,
1709, and 1712. Sir Samuel Garth's composite *Metamorphoses*
gave due prominence to Dryden's pieces both in the first edition
of 1717 and in the later editions of 1751 and 1794; but these
came out separately again in 1719, 1720, 1725, 1729, 1735,

1761, 1776, 1782, 1791, and 1795. The *Fables* were well known to the writers of the *Spectator* and *Tatler*, and even Swift permitted himself to quote them. They were freshly issued in 1713, 1721, 1734, 1737, 1741, 1742, 1745, 1755, 1771, 1773, 1774, and with sumptuous engravings in 1797. "It is to his Fables," predicted Joseph Warton in the *Essay on Pope*, "that Dryden will owe his immortality." The most famous single poem of Dryden's throughout the century seems to have been *Alexander's Feast*. Performed by musicians, quoted by aestheticians and essayists, printed in anthologies, translated into Greek and Latin, and parodied, it had every reason to be known; published for the second time by Tonson in the *Fables* of 1700, it was republished in other forms in 1738, 1740, 1743, 1751, 1756, 1758, 1760, 1773, 1778, 1779, and 1780. The *Song for St. Cecilia's Day* (1687) was less in vogue, but it found its way into type in 1754, 1760, 1764, and 1778. The ode on Anne Killigrew seems never to have commanded serious attention until Dr. Johnson's bold praise of it in the *Life,* praise which shocked certain readers of the *Gentleman's Magazine* into sober protest. In general the miscellaneous non-dramatic verse had to live by anthologies and pirations. As has been observed before, Tonson's imperfect edition of 1701 had no successor until 1743; and neither Broughton's volumes then nor those of Derrick later were notably popular. Yet during the interval between Tonson and Broughton it was never difficult to become acquainted with Dryden the occasional and lyric poet. The earlier editions of *Poems on Affairs of State* virtually excluded him on the ground of his politics, but into the later volumes of that series and into most other repositories he had easy entry. From the *Westminster Drolleries* in 1671-2 to Tom D'Urfey's *Pills to Purge Melancholy* in 1719-20, and longer, no collection of English songs omitted the most rousing of those from Dryden's plays, while broadsides flung them into rougher company. Handbooks like those of Bysshe and Gildon drew heavily upon him for examples of good verse. More than half of Bysshe's

"Collection of the most Natural, Agreeable and Noble Thoughts . . . that are to be found in the best English Poets" hails from Dryden. But Dryden's *Miscellany* itself gave him the most currency. The four *Miscellany* volumes which he had engineered for Tonson in 1684, 1685, 1693, and 1694, and which had been by no means the least sign of his leadership while he lived, were followed after his death by a fifth part in 1704 and a sixth part in 1709. In 1716 and again in 1727 all six were collected and reissued with new material, Dryden being honored by the inclusion of ninety-six of his pieces. The first volume opened with *Mac Flecknoe*, as it had at the beginning of the series, in 1684; and here or there all of the public poems found place: that is to say, the two parts of *Absalom and Achitophel*, the *Heroic Stanzas*, *Astraea Redux*, *To His Sacred Majesty*, *To My Lord Chancellor*, *The Medal*, *Annus Mirabilis*, *Threnodia Augustalis*, *The Hind and the Panther*, *Britannia Rediviva*, and *Religio Laici*. The occasional verse was represented by nineteen of the prologues and eleven of the epilogues, by the epistles to Etherege, Kneller, Howard, Lady Castlemaine, Charleton, Higden, the Duchess of York, Congreve, and Roscommon, and by the elegies, epitaphs, and epigrams on Hastings, "Amyntas," "A Very Young Gentleman," Dundee, "Young Mr. Rogers," Lady Whitmore, Sir Palmes Fairborne, "Eleonora," Anne Killigrew, and Milton. There were six songs and the *Veni Creator;* there was the *Art of Poetry;* and there were the translations from Theocritus, Lucretius, and Horace, with the *Hector and Andromache* from Homer, and the fourth and ninth *Eclogues* together with the episodes of Nisus, Mezentius, and Vulcan from Virgil. Here was the body, certainly, of Dryden's verse. Yet it is a question whether he gained by being shuffled so recklessly between Tonson's covers among dozens of other poets living and dead, good and indifferent, like and unlike him. It was Broughton's aim, at least, in 1743, to separate him from the mass and give him the dignity of two pleasant duodecimo volumes that could be set alongside the small editions already current of the *Fables*, the *Virgil*, the *Juvenal*, and the dramatic works. The collectors throughout the century of fugitive and minor poetry, like Dodsley, Pearch, and Nichols, were inclined to pass Dryden by as already standard. A. F. Griffith's *Collection . . . of English Prologues and Epilogues Commencing with Shakespeare and Concluding with Garrick*, in four volumes, 1779, the completest thing of its kind in the language, gave him the first place with eighty prologues and epilogues. It may safely be concluded of Dryden in the eighteenth century that although he was never contagious except as a songster, or much on the lips of society, he yet was steadily current. Lady Mary Wortley Montagu carried his best couplets in her mind to Constantinople. Upon the occasion of Thornhill's first visit to the Vicar of Wakefield's daughters, music was proposed and "a favourite song of Dryden's" was sung. For the most part Dryden continued to keep the company of literary men. The *Spectator* and *Tatler* made frequent use of the translations and of the "characters" from the satires; Dr. Johnson, virtually every page of whose Dictionary gleamed with lines from Dryden as well as Pope and Shakespeare, was fond of quoting him in his own letters; Gibbon, who said he had grown up on the *Virgil* and Pope's *Homer*, knew the *Fables* and the satires well; and Burke and Charles James Fox were deeply indebted to the prose.

As the eighteenth century wore away it was increasingly difficult to be interested in much of Dryden's political and occasional verse or in many of his translations from the classics. Editions of the *Juvenal* and *Persius* in 1810, 1813, and 1822, of the *Virgil* in 1802, 1803, 1806, 1807, 1811, 1812, 1813, 1819, 1820, 1822, 1823, 1824, 1825, and 1830, and of the *Ovid* in 1804, 1807, 1812, 1815, 1824, 1826, 1833, and 1850, to come no further down, signified ambition in publishers or the survival of old-fashioned tastes in readers, rather than a live vogue. Scott's efforts in behalf of a Dryden tradition included an attractive picture of "Glorious John" in the fourteenth chap-

ter of *The Pirate*, a picture which appealed at least to anti-
quarian and tory minds. "I wish I could believe," wrote Lockhart in the *Life*, "that Scott's labours had been sufficient to
recall Dryden to his rightful station, not in the opinion of those
who make literature the business or chief solace of their lives—
for with them he had never forfeited it—but in the general
favour of the intelligent public. That such has been the case,
however, the not rapid sale of two editions, aided as they were
by the greatest of living names, can be no proof; nor have I
observed among the numberless recent publication of the English booksellers a single reprint of even those tales, satires and
critical essays, not to be familiar with which would, in the last
age, have been considered as disgraceful in any one making the
least pretension to letters." Lockhart was perhaps too pessimistic. The *Fables* had found publishers in 1806 and 1822; the
anthologists of the time were paying due attention both to them
and to the satires, the best of the occasional poems, and the odes.
Campbell's *Specimens of the British Poets* (1819) included the
"characters" of Achitophel, Zimri, Og, and Doeg, the *Killigrew*, the descriptions of Lycurgus and Emetrius and of the
preparation for the tournament in *Palamon and Arcite*, all of
Cymon and Iphigenia, and *The Flower and the Leaf*. Hazlitt's
Select British Poets (1824) offered *Absalom and Achitophel*,
Mac Flecknoe, *Religio Laici*, and *The Hind and the Panther*,
the epistles to Congreve, Kneller, and Driden of Chesterton,
the elegy on Oldham, *Alexander's Feast* and the *Secular
Masque*, *The Cock and the Fox*, *Sigismonda and Guiscardo*,
Theodore and Honoria, *Cymon and Iphigenia*, and *Baucis and
Philemon*.

The trend of the nineteenth century away from Dryden
aroused a number of genuine but ineffectual protests from professional literary men. The editor of a volume of *Selections* in
1852 began his preface thus: "The merits of Dryden are not
sufficiently acknowledged at present. Our zeal for the poets
who preceded the civil wars, like most reactions, is become too

exclusive." The reviewer of Bell's edition of 1854 in the *Edinburgh* for July, 1855, enumerated four reasons for "the oblivion into which the works of Dryden have so singularly fallen": inability to distinguish between Dryden and his unworthy imitators; failure to see that Dryden himself was not another Pope; "monstrous" ignorance on the part of Wordsworth, Keats, and the new schools; and a heretical notion generally that Dryden and Pope were not poets. There were other and better reasons. But whatever the whole cause, it was and is true regarding the bulk of Dryden's work that, as Lowell declared, "few writers are more thoroughly buried in that great cemetery of the 'British Poets.' " He has not become absorbed into English speech like Pope, nor are his longer poems read with enthusiasm as wholes. He lies about in splendid fragments: the four "characters" of Shaftesbury, Buckingham, Burnet, and Settle, and the two of Shadwell; the beginning of *Religio Laici* and the passage there on tradition; the first eighty lines of *The Hind and the Panther* and the eulogy of the Roman Catholic Church in the second part; the translations of Lucretius on death and Horace on contempt of Fortune; the epigram on Milton; the elegy on Oldham; the prologues at Oxford and before *Aureng-Zebe;* the epistles to Congreve and John Driden; the odes on Anne Killigrew and St. Cecilia's Day; and half a dozen of the songs. *Alexander's Feast* has probably never been rivaled in popularity by another of the poems. The two Cecilia Odes were all of Dryden that Palgrave printed in his *Golden Treasury,* and no anthologist since has neglected them. On the whole it may be said that Dryden's odes, "those surprising masterpieces," Robert Louis Stevenson wrote to Mr. Edmund Gosse on the sixth of December, 1880, "where there is more sustained eloquence and harmony of English numbers than in all that has been written since," seem the most indestructible portions of his verse.

No important detailed criticism of Dryden appeared in the eighteenth century outside of Dr. Johnson's *Life,* which in itself covered all the ground then visible. Remarks were made, eulogies were delivered, commonplaces were handed along, but little was said that penetrated. Swift was always contemptuous, though never long or elaborately so. Spence quotes Tonson as saying: "Addison was so eager to be the first name, that he and his friend Sir Richard Steele used to run down even Dryden's character as far as they could. Pope and Congreve used to support it." A publisher of a man's works may be pardoned some jealousy of his reputation, but it is probable that Tonson exaggerated the feuds that were waged even in the Augustan temple of fame. Addison showed himself early and late to be closely acquainted with Dryden's poetry, and usually he was judicious in his observations upon it. In his poem *To Mr. Dryden* (1693) and his *Account of the Greatest English Poets* (1694) he gave the old poet warm if vague praise. In the *Tatler*, the *Spectator*, and the *Guardian* he discounted Dryden's tragic style as bombastic, revised his definition of wit, praised his satires at the same time that he predicted short life for them because of the temporary character of their allusions, and pointed out defects in his otherwise admirable translations. Whatever may have been Addison's attempts to injure Dryden in conversation, in writing he was a fair and indeed a salutary critic.

At one time it was believed of Pope that, far from coming to Dryden's aid, he was conspiring against his remains. John Dennis, who had been born in 1657 and who consequently had been brought up on Dryden in another generation than Pope's, was moved in 1715 to defend the great poet of his choice against what he understood to be a determined conspiracy. A letter to Tonson on the fourth of June expressed his sentiments: "When I had the good fortune to meet you in the city, it was with concern that I heard from you of the attempt to lessen the reputation of Mr. Dryden; and 'tis with indignation that I have since learnt that that attempt has chiefly been carried on by small poets. . . . But when I heard that this . . . was done in favour of little Pope, that diminutive of Parnassus and of hu-

manity, 'tis impossible to express to what a height my indignation and disdain were raised. Good God!" And he went on to
justify his "zeal for the Reputation of my departed Friend,
whom I infinitely esteemed when living for the Solidity of his
Thought, for the Spring, the Warmth, and the beautiful Turn
of it; for the Power, and Variety, and Fullness of his Harmony; for the Purity, the Perspicuity, the Energy of his Expression; and (whenever the following great Qualities were
required) for the Pomp and Solemnity, and Majesty of his
Style." As a matter of fact, nothing is more familiar than the
veneration of little Pope for Dennis's hero.

Congreve's preface to Tonson's edition of the dramatic works
in 1717 pursued a lofty vein of eulogy, as did a passage in
Garth's preface to the *Metamorphoses* the same year. Thereafter, Dryden was discussed almost exclusively as a man with a
style. John Oldmixon blamed Pope for this turn of affairs. "Mr.
Dryden's genius," he observed in his *Essay on Criticism* (1728),
"did not appear [according to Pope] in anything more than
his Versification; and whether the critics will have it ennobled
for that versification only, is a question. The Translator [of
Homer] seems to make a good genius and a good ear to be the
same thing. Dryden himself was more sensible of the difference
between them, and when it was in debate at Will's Coffeehouse,
what character he would have with posterity, he said, with a
sullen modesty, 'I believe they will allow me to be a good versifier.' " But the process of ennobling Dryden for his versification only went on. It has been seen that Dennis drew or implied
a distinction between Dryden and Pope on the score of wealth
and fire of expression. This survived and became hackneyed;
men repeated it who had no other notion of it than that it justified a noble negligence in the older poet. Dryden's name seems
to have been destined to come down jointly with Pope's; if
not to support a distinction, as in the eighteenth century, at least
to imply an identity, as in the nineteenth. Pope himself, convinced as he was that Dryden had wanted "the greatest art—

the art to blot," struck the note that was to reverberate through
all the criticism of his master for a century:

> Waller was smooth; but Dryden taught to join
> The varying verse, the full resounding line,
> The long majestic march, and energy divine.

It occurred to some to couple Dryden with Milton rather than
with Pope. Gildon did so, on the score of harmony in versification, in his *Laws of Poetry* (1721). Gray seemed at least to do
so when in *The Progress of Poesy* he followed praise of Milton's epic with praise of Dryden's odes, but did not go on to
Pope:

> Behold, where Dryden's less presumptuous car,
> Wide o'er the fields of glory bear
> Two Coursers of ethereal race,
> With necks in thunder clothed, and long-resounding pace.

James Beattie, in a long footnote to his *Essay on Poetry and
Music as They Affect the Mind* (1776), objected to any identification of Pope with Dryden: "Critics have often stated a comparison between Dryden and Pope, as poets of the same order,
and who differed only in degree of merit. But, in my opinion,
the merit of the one differs considerably in kind from that of
the other"; that is to say, Dryden is more original, various, and
harmonious though less correct. Dr. Johnson in the *Life of
Pope* gave the palm for genius "with some hesitation" to Dryden. His answer to Boswell when Boswell quoted Voltaire's *mot*
concerning Pope's "neat nags" and Dryden's "stately horses"
was characteristic: "Why, Sir, the truth is, they both drive
coaches and six: but Dryden's horses are either galloping or
stumbling: Pope's go at a steady even trot." A passage in the
Life of Pope again is perhaps the classical statement of the
contrast: "Dryden's page is a natural field, rising into inequalities, and diversified by the varied exuberance of abundant
vegetation; Pope's is a velvet lawn, shaven by the scythe, and

levelled by the roller." The distinction thrived long after it ceased to be of critical value. In 1788 Joseph Weston translated a Latin poem on archery, *Philotoxi Ardenae*, by John Morfitt, into couplets "attempted in the manner of Dryden," and wrote an enthusiastic preface to demonstrate "the Superiority of Dryden's Versification over that of Pope and of the Moderns." "I cannot help thinking," he confessed, "that English Rhyme was brought by that Wonderful Man to the Acme of Perfection; and that it has been, for many years, gradually declining from good to indifferent—and from indifferent to bad." He anticipated Wordsworth's attack on "poetic diction," appealing—in Dryden—to romantic powers of speech and music. Anna Seward, defending Pope, debated with Weston at great length in the *Gentleman's Magazine* during 1789 and 1790. Half a dozen others were drawn into the controversy, which ended only when a neutral reader protested to the editor against so many stale irrelevancies. The subject was never completely dismissed. When Mrs. Barbauld edited Collins in 1797 she could still speak of "Dryden, who had a musical ear, and Pope who had none." The insistence by amateur critics upon a comparison of the two poets had even furnished material for burlesque. Dick Minim had said all that needed to be said in the sixtieth *Idler* in 1759. George Canning's critique of "The Knave of Hearts" in the *Microcosm* for February 12, 1787, did not lack a sober pronouncement that "Ovid had more genius but less judgment than Virgil; Dryden more imagination but less correctness than Pope."

In whatever relation he was kept to Pope, Dryden's position on the scale of English poets at the end of the eighteenth century was very different from that which he had enjoyed in 1700. During the first half of the eighteenth century, roughly speaking, it was customary to mention him without shame among the most famous of all poets, to set him a little lower perhaps than Shakespeare and Milton and Spenser but at least to leave him secure in their company. The "poetical scale" which Goldsmith drew up for the *Literary Magazine* in January, 1758, was standard mid-century criticism:

	Genius	Judgement	Learning	Versification
Chaucer	16	12	10	14
Spenser	18	12	14	18
Shakespeare	19	14	14	19
Jonson	16	18	17	8
Cowley	17	17	15	17
Waller	12	12	10	16
Milton	18	16	17	18
Dryden	18	16	17	18
Addison	16	18	17	17
Prior	16	16	15	17
Pope	18	18	15	19

Men like Joseph Warton changed all that. His sentimental but potent essay on Pope in 1756 placed the Elizabethans on another level from the Augustans, and refused Dryden and Pope admittance on any poetical basis to the society of Shakespeare and Spenser and Milton. Among what he called "the second class" of poets, the panegyrical, occasional, and didactic poets, he found the author of *Windsor Forest*, *The Rape of the Lock*, and *Eloisa to Abelard* first because of his perfection; but the author of *Alexander's Feast* crowded a close second by virtue of the "genius" he had shown in that "divine" poem. Dryden's ode was called on more than once to save the face of Augustan verse. "Goldsmith asserted, that there was no poetry produced in this age," wrote Boswell, referring to a conversation in 1776. "Dodsley appealed to his own *Collection*, and maintained, that though you could not find a palace like Dryden's *Ode on St. Cecilia's Day*, you had villages composed of very pretty houses. . . . *Johnson* . . . 'You may find wit and humour in verse, and yet no poetry.'" Warton's main thesis outlasted any of its qualifications. Dryden and Pope were buried by him where it seemed less and less important each year to decide which had more or any genius. The glance of the new century fell on the standard poets of England from new and dizzy altitudes. Even now, when "orders" and "classes" of poetry mean nothing, Dryden is likely to be discounted before he is read.

"He has not written one line that is pathetic, and very few that can be considered as sublime," decided Jeffreys in his review of Ford's plays for the *Edinburgh Review* in 1811. Add of Dryden that it was generally believed he had written little that was ineffably beautiful, and the central position of early nineteenth-century Dryden criticism is established. Criticism of poetry at that time usually meant the invoking and imposing of categories rather than the first-hand studying of men; the preoccupation of critics was mostly with "kinds" of writing. There were dogmas then as there had been dogmas at the beginning of the last century. New conceptions of the creative function of the imagination had led to a deep distrust of Hobbes's psychology and the poetry of the "empirical school." Admiration of Dryden had to be expressed in terms of opposition to the new creeds or in terms of Pope. A few Tories in taste fell back on the old-fashioned glories. To the editor Scott, Dryden was "our immortal bard," second only to Milton and Shakespeare; "Glorious John," even when he had said nothing, had written imperishably noble verse; *Alexander's Feast* was the best of English lyrics. George Ellis, writing to Scott about the edition he had fathered, admitted that "I ought to have considered that whatever Dryden wrote must, for some reason or other, be worth reading"; and he professed himself in particular a passionate admirer of the *Fables*, "the noblest specimen of versification . . . that is to be found in any modern language"; *Theodore and Honoria*, he said, should have "a place on the very top-most shelf of English poetry." George Canning, writing on July 26th, 1811, spoke to Scott of "the majestic march of Dryden (to my ear the perfection of harmony)." Henry Hallam's review of the *Dryden* in the *Edinburgh* deplored Scott's occupation with the rubbish of the minor works, but

agreed, while finding fault with the *Fables,* that at the best
Dryden's animation and variety were hardly surpassable.

The most important criticism of Dryden in this period, however, ranged itself about the question whether he and Pope had
been poets. "It is the cant of our day—above all, of its poetasters," said Lockhart, "that Johnson was no poet. To be sure,
they say the same of Pope—and hint it occasionally even of
Dryden." It was more than "said" of Pope, and it was more
than "hinted" of Dryden; it was solemnly asseverated of both,
one of the results being an intermittent controversy between
Bowles, Wordsworth, Keats, Southey, Coleridge, and the like
on the one hand and Byron, Campbell, Crabbe, Rogers, Gifford,
and the like on the other. The controversy started over Pope.
Bowles's edition of Pope in 1806 contained some strictures on
his character as a man and as a poet. Byron was careful to ridicule Bowles for this, among other things, in his *English Bards*
of 1809. To Campbell's championship of Pope in the preface
to his *Specimens* in 1819 Bowles replied in the same year with
a paper on the *Invariable Principles of Poetry.* In Wordsworth's *Essay Supplementary to the Preface* (1815) had appeared a few remarks derogating Dryden's treatment of Nature.
Byron broke out in the third canto of *Don Juan:*

> "Pedlars" and "Boats" and "Waggons!" Oh! Ye shades
>   Of Pope and Dryden, are we come to this?
> The "little boatman" and his Peter Bell
>   Can sneer at him who drew "Achitophel"!

And in 1821 he published a *Letter . . . on the Rev. William
L. Bowles's Strictures on the Life and Writings of Pope.* A
letter written from Ravenna on March 15th, 1820, in reply
to an article in *Blackwood's* on *Don Juan,* was devoted in the
second half to a passionate defense of Pope. Byron attributed
what he found to be a decline in English poetry to the fact
that poets could no longer appreciate the little Queen Anne
master. "Dilettanti lecturers" and reviewers were following in

the wake of the poetasters, and only a handful of men remained in England—Crabbe, Rogers, Gifford, Campbell, and himself—with liberal perspectives. As for himself he declared: "I have ever loved and honoured Pope's poetry with my whole soul, and hope to do so till my dying day." Nothing was being produced now, he swore, to match Pope's *Essay on Man*, *Eloisa to Abelard*, *The Rape of the Lock*, and "Sporus," or Dryden's *Fables*, odes, and *Absalom*. Bowles had preferred Dryden to Pope on musical grounds. Byron himself had written in the *English Bards*, after some lines on Pope:

> Like him great Dryden poured the tide of song,
> In stream less smooth, indeed, yet doubly strong.

But in general he was inclined to call Pope a better because a more perfect poet.

The tradition of Dryden's "genius" survived in one form or another throughout the discussion. Coleridge decided that "if Pope was a poet, as Lord Byron swears, then Dryden . . . was a very great poet." Hazlitt, in his essay on Dryden and Pope, was no more inclined than Coleridge to credit either with essentially poetic powers, though as he surveyed them within their class he found Pope to be a more consummate artificer; Dryden seemed largely tinsel, his odes wholly mechanical and meretricious. Yet it mortified Hazlitt, who knew that the Augustans, if they had not been great poets, had been at least great writers of some sort, to hear Wordsworth disparage Pope and Dryden, "whom, because they have been supposed to have all the possible excellences of poetry, he will allow to have none." Wordsworth's position is well known. His letter to Scott in 1805 contained all the praise that he could honestly give, which was that Dryden possessed "a certain ardour and impetuosity of mind, with an excellent ear"; while his various prefaces sternly denied both to Dryden and to Pope the highest imaginative gifts. Henry Crabb Robinson, in his diary for January 6th, 1842, recorded a walk with Wordsworth: "Today he talked of poetry. He held Pope to be a greater poet than Dryden; but Dryden to have most talent, and the strongest understanding." Landor was moderately an admirer of the great satirist of the Exclusion Bill.

> None ever crost our mystic sea
> More richly stored with thought than he;
> Though never tender nor sublime,
> He wrestles with and conquers Time,

he wrote to Wordsworth. In the second Imaginary Conversation with Southey he confined his praise to Dryden's couplet-verse, dismissing the Pindarics as vulgar. "*Alexander's Feast* smells of gin at second-hand, with true Briton fiddlers full of native *talent* in the orchestra." Its author, he answered for Southey, must be content with credit for "a facility rather than a fidelity of expression."

If Dryden's reputation left the romantic battleground in a somewhat battered condition, it has pursued a smooth course down the nineteenth-century highway. Historians of English literature have been busy establishing Dryden's importance as a representative figure and giving him his due as an innovator; aestheticians have contributed their notions of the points wherein he is entitled to please; and great cosmopolitan critics have brought to him a learning and a taste ripened through contact with many other literatures. He emerges without his old glory, perhaps, but with a respectable group of virtues which seem to be his now for all time. Discussion of him has inclined to be general, and writers have tended to grant him vaguely defined powers which they themselves have not always understood; yet a limited body of readers has continued to know him intimately and soundly. A steady succession of articles in the tory periodicals, notably in the *Quarterly Review*, perhaps the mainstay of his reputation, has kept his name fresh, while from time to time new emphasis has been laid upon the obscurer portions of his work. Robert Bell's *Life* in 1854, as well as reviews of it in

Fraser's Magazine and elsewhere, singled out the prologues and the epilogues for applause. Tennyson, Fitzgerald, Professor Conington, and others have insisted upon the original and enduring qualities of the *Virgil*, which Wordsworth gave up trying to surpass, and which still has more vitality than any other translation. The *Juvenal* and the *Lucretius* maintain a solid place among versions of the classics, both for their strength and for their beauty. Latterly there has been a tendency to emphasize the lyrics, especially the songs, those from the plays having been reprinted in the last two editions of the poems in a more complete form than that in which the Warton volumes presented them in 1811.

Macaulay's brilliant but doctrinaire essay of 1828 has made it seem necessary to most subsequent critics to discuss the character of Dryden. While Dryden the turncoat, Dryden the flatterer, Dryden the writer of indecent plays and poems has been scrupulously damned by men like Christie, numerous editors and reviewers have stepped to his defense bringing elaborate excuses. The better view seems latterly to be that there is little reason to be sorrowful over the behavior of a canny man of letters who never at any time pretended to be equipped with principles worth dying or becoming a pauper for.

As a poet his personality has often been sketched. Lowell, whose respect for Dryden was permanent and wholesome, and whose essay of 1868 contains what is still, except for that of Dr. Johnson, the most conscientious criticism of the poet in English, found, after making all the necessary deductions from his character and his fame, that something indefinably large remained. "You feel," he said, "that the whole of him is better than any random specimens, though of his best, seem to prove." "There is a singular unanimity in allowing him a certain claim to *greatness* which would be denied to men as famous and more read,—to Pope or Swift, for example." "He is a curious example of what we often remark of the living, but rarely of the dead,—that they get credit for what they might be as much as for what they are,—and posterity has applied to him one of his own rules of criticism, judging him by the best rather than the average of his achievement, a thing posterity is seldom wont to do." These were shrewd remarks; yet they were not followed by an account equally shrewd of Dryden's rhythmical genius and intellectual gathering-power, it being there that his largeness, indefinable or not, resides.

Emerson, blandly wild, threw all of Dryden overboard in the essay on *Poetry and Imagination* which he cast into final shape in 1872. "Turnpike is one thing and blue sky another. Let the poet, of all men, stop with his inspiration. The inexorable rule in the Muses' court, either inspiration or silence, compels the bard to report only his supreme moments. . . . Much that we call poetry is but polite verse." "A little more or less skill in whistling is of no account. See those weary pentameter tales of Dryden and others."

Matthew Arnold, warring against provincialism in the study of literature and bringing "touchstones" from the ends of the earth wherewith to test the poets of his own country, found, as he reported in the *Introduction* to Ward's *English Poets* (1880), that Dryden and Pope had been the inaugurators of an immensely important "age of prose and reason" but that they were insignificant as poets, perhaps not poets at all. In the essay on Gray he explained his position in greater detail, saying, "The difference between genuine poetry and the poetry of Dryden, Pope, and all their school, is briefly this: their poetry is conceived and composed in their wits, genuine poetry is conceived and composed in the soul." This proposition sounds broad enough; yet in Arnold it received a narrow handling. "Soul" in Arnold suggests stoicism; stoicism suggests philosophic melancholy; philosophic melancholy suggests sentiment; a poem "conceived in the soul" suggests a poem conceived in spiritual pain. Arnold's touchstones, if not sentimental, did deal in pain, sad old memories, and death, an atmosphere which Dryden could hardly expect to survive. If there were to be no touchstones ringing with malice, disdain, or merriment, Dryden could lay no claim to a soul. He had not written his verse to "console" or "sustain" a bewildered generation of *fin de siècle* scholars. He had written to please hard-headed men of the world; he had labored to satisfy critics of poetry, not critics of souls. He had written genuine poetry, but he was not a Dante. In the *Introduction* again Arnold thought he detected a truer note in a passage of Dryden's prose which, if the truth be known, is the least expressive possible of the indomitable Augustan: "What Virgil wrote in the vigour of his age, in plenty and at ease, I have undertaken to translate in my declining years; struggling with wants, oppressed with sickness, curbed in my genius, liable to be misconstrued in all I wrote." Arnold felt tenderly toward this; Swift had simply roared. Arnold was unjust to the odes. In the essay on Gray he placed the most miserable stanza of the *Killigrew* alongside of the best three lines in Pindar and observed that Pindar killed Dryden. It may be true that Pindar will kill Dryden under any circumstances; in the present instance Dryden died without a fighting chance. Pater agreed with Arnold that Dryden's prose was more beautiful than his verse. "Dryden," he wrote in 1888 in *Style*, "with the characteristic instinct of his age, loved to emphasize the distinction between poetry and prose, the protest against their confusion coming with somewhat diminished effect from one whose poetry was so prosaic." The influence of Arnold has been very great. In an age whose infinitely flexible prose has captured the throne of the imagination and promises to hold it while the language lasts, he has taught nine readers out of ten that Dryden is a prosaic poet. He is dogmatic and wrong; but protests are irrelevant till the whole wheel of fashion turns another round.

Dryden is nothing if not a poets' poet, which Lowell denied he was. He is not for philosophers, plainly, or for laymen; he does not move the minds of the few or the hearts of the many.

He has tempered not spirits but pens; Lowell notwithstanding, he is as much as Spenser a poet for poets. Not only in his own generation, or in the next, but in all that have succeeded he has stood on the shelves of writers and offered the stimulus of a style that is both musical and stout. Poets of widely varying complexions have made important use of him, never exactly reproducing him, for that is impossible even if desirable, but drawing from him the strength or the beauty they have seemed to need.

In the eighteenth century he shared with Milton and Pope the distinction, enviable or not, of inspiring the "poetic diction" which Wordsworth later on was to receive so coldly. Milton in blank verse and Dryden and Pope in the heroic couplet were, if Spenser and his stanza be for the moment disregarded, the great models of versification under Queen Anne and the first two Georges. On the side of the heroic couplet Dryden exercised two varieties of influence according as he was identified with Pope or distinguished from him. In a certain sense he had identified himself with Pope when he had created him; for if Dryden had not written, it is a question what Pope would be. "I learned versification wholly from Dryden's works," Pope told Spence; he has echoed Dryden everywhere, not only cadence for cadence but sometimes word for word and line for line. Zimri and Og begat Wharton and Sporus; *Mac Flecknoe* begat the *Dunciad;* the *Religio Laici* and *The Hind and the Panther* begat the *Moral Essays;* the *Cecilia* of 1687 begat the *Cecilia* of 1708; the *Virgil* begat the *Homer;* and the *Fables* begat the *Paraphrases from Chaucer.* Yet in another sense Pope derived not from Dryden at all, but from the smooth, equable tradition of Sandys and Waller. Poets who knew this, and who set Dryden's "genius" over against Pope's correctness, thought to capture the secret of that "genius." In the first place, they remarked, Dryden, for an Augustan, was bewildering in his variety. A passage of only eight lines from *Tyrannic Love,* for instance, combined three styles as far apart from one another as those of Shakespeare's *Julius Caesar*, Pope's *Pastorals*, and Beattie's *Minstrel:*

> Him have I seen (on Ister's banks he stood,
> Where last we wintered) bind the headlong flood
> In sudden ice; and, where most swift it flows,
> In crystal nets the wondering fishes close.
> Then, with a moment's thaw, the streams enlarge,
> And from the mesh the twinkling guests discharge.
> In a deep vale or near some ruined wall,
> He would the ghosts of slaughtered soldiers call.

In the second place he was impetuous and, when need was, negligent. The negligence was easy to approximate, the impetuosity not so easy. Gildon inveighed against versifiers who aped Dryden's mannerisms without reviving his spirit, John Hughes and Walter Harte being conspicuous among those who affected triplets and Alexandrines so as to become like the author of *The State of Innocence*. Harte introduced his *Vision of Death* in 1767 with a tribute which might have done for a contemporary Dryden creed:

> Who but thyself the mind and ear can please,
> With strength and softness, energy and ease;
> Various of numbers, new in every strain;
> Diffused, yet terse, poetical, though plain;
> Diversified midst unison of chime;
> Freer than air, yet manacled with rhyme,
> Thou mak'st each quarry which thou seek'st thy prize,
> The reigning eagle of Parnassian skies. . . .
> Thy thoughts and music change with every line;
> No sameness of a prattling stream is thine. . . .
> Infinite descant, sweetly wild and true.
> Still shifting, still improving, and still new! . . .
> To Spenser much, to Milton much is due;
> But in great Dryden we preserve the two.

Dryden's essential energy went by no means unobserved. Aken-side's *Epistle to Curio* of 1744 was a more powerful poem than it might have been if its author had never studied *Absalom and Achitophel*. Gray told James Beattie, according to Mason, that he had learned all he knew about versification from the long-resounding Dryden; "Remember Dryden," he wrote to Beattie in 1765, "and be blind to all his faults." "By him," concluded Dr. Johnson, "we were taught *sapere et fari,* to think naturally and express forcibly." More obstreperous disciples rushed to him because they were tired of Pope and thirsty for poetic license. Goldsmith, in the dedication of his *Traveller* in 1764, remarked without tenderness upon the "blank verse, and Pin-daric Odes, choruses, anapests and iambics, alliterative care and happy negligence" with which poets were amusing themselves though not their readers; a man like Churchill the satirist, he intimated, was receiving credit that scarcely was due him; "his turbulence is said to be force, and his frenzy fire." Churchill fled Pope for Dryden and Shakespeare. He complained in *The Apology* that contemporary verse had degenerated into

> A happy tuneful vacancy of sense.

He wished to restore "Great Dryden" to his own, and to cultivate

> The generous roughness of a nervous line.

He succeeded in striking up a fresh but not a lasting tune. Cowper reviewed his achievement in *Table Talk:*

> Churchill, himself unconscious of his powers,
> In penury consumed his idle hours,
> And, like a scattered seed at random sown,
> Was left to spring by vigour of his own. . . .
> Surly and slovenly, and bold and coarse,
> Too proud for art, and trusting in mere force,
> Spendthrift alike of money and of wit,
> Always at speed, and never drawing bit,

> He struck the lyre in such a careless mood,
> And so disdained the rules he understood,
> The laurel seemed to wait on his command,
> He snatched it rudely from the Muse's hand.

Cowper himself had not been ignorant of Dryden. The lines in *The Task*,

> There is a pleasure in poetic pains
> Which only poets know,

harked back to *The Spanish Friar:*

> There is a pleasure sure
> In being mad which none but madmen know.

And the "characters" in *Conversation* and other poems recalled Dryden as much as Pope. But now it was fairly rare that either Dryden or Pope was called upon as tutor to an English poet. Cowper, and later Crabbe, wrote for another world than either of theirs had been; Gifford's *Juvenal* only echoed, not recalled the past; the chime of Augustan verse was done, and thenceforth one who went to Dryden for aid went because he recognized an intrinsic gift, not because Dryden was the mode.

Wordsworth, inhospitable to his predecessors though he was, knew many thousand lines of Dryden and Pope by heart, and was never insensible to the effects that Dryden had gained by virtue of his "excellent ear." Tom Moore, said Leigh Hunt in the *Autobiography*, "contemplated the fine, easy-playing, muscular style of Dryden with a sort of perilous pleasure. I remember his quoting with delight a couplet of Dryden's which came with a particular grace from his lips:—

> Let honour and preferment go for gold;
> But glorious beauty is not to be sold."

Hunt himself was one of the first of the Cockney School to succumb to that "stream of sound" which Hazlitt called the *Fables*. His *Story of Rimini* derived from Dante in plot, in

style from Dryden. As he explains in the *Autobiography*, "Dryden, at that time, in spite of my sense of Milton's superiority,
and my early love of Spenser, was the most delightful name
to me in English poetry. I had found in him more vigour, and
music too, than in Pope, who had been my closest poetical
acquaintance; and I could not rest till I had played on his
instrument . . . My versification was far from being so vigorous as his. There were many weak lines in it. It succeeded best
in catching the variety of his cadences; at least so far as they
broke up the monotony of Pope." *The Story of Rimini* is liber-
ally Alexandrined after the manner of the *Fables*, but it sig-
nally fails to achieve Dryden's strong-backed vigor. It has a
Cockney limpness and pertness, but there is nothing significant
in its metrical variety.

What Hunt did not do Keats in some measure did in his
Lamia, which according to Charles Armitage Brown he wrote
"with great care after much study of Dryden's versification."
In "Sleep and Poetry," in the *Poems* of 1817, he had taken
pains to address a most unscholarly rebuke to Dryden and
Pope:

> Why were you not awake? But ye were dead
> To things ye knew not of,—were closely wed
> To musty laws lined out with wretched rule
> And compass vile; so that ye taught a school
> Of dolts to smooth, inlay, and clip, and fit,
> Till, like the certain wands of Jacob's wit,
> Their verses tallied.

The *Endymion* had shown not even the slightest acquaintance
with the secrets of Dryden's meter. But now in *Lamia*, Keats,

> Whom Dryden's force and Spenser's fays
> Have heart and soul possessed,

as Landor wrote to Joseph Ablett, not only stiffened and bright-
ened his verse, cleaned and sharpened his pen, improved and

simplified his narrative procedure, but indulged in the very tricks of Dryden: the Alexandrine, the triplet, the triplet-Alexandrine, the antithesis, the inversion, the stopped couplet; and he took to harmonizing his sentence-structure with his verse form.

> From vale to vale, from wood to wood, he flew,
> Breathing upon the flowers his passion new,
> And wound with many a river to its head,
> To find where this sweet nymph prepared her secret bed.
>
> She was a gordian shape of dazzling hue,
> Vermilion-spotted, golden, green, and blue;
> Striped like a zebra, freckled like a pard,
> Eyed like a peacock, and all crimson barred. . . .
> She seemed, at once, some penanced lady elf,
> Some demon's mistress, or the demon's self.

He even ventured into graceful cynicism; his heroine was canny in her behavior towards Lycius the lover:

> So threw the goddess off, and won his heart
> More pleasantly by playing woman's part,
> With no more awe than what her beauty gave,
> That, while it smote, still guaranteed to save.

He seldom caught the accent exactly, or caught it for long at a time, nor did his new cloak always fit him; to be caustic was hardly his role. It was as if a gardener had suddenly called for a two-handed sword to trim stray petals from his gentlest rose. But his ambition to become another man than himself is everywhere apparent. Not that Keats wished to be Dryden; he only wished to extend his metrical bounds. Just once did he help himself to an idea of Dryden's for its own sake. The third stanza of *Annus Mirabilis,*

> For them alone the Heavens had kindly heat,
> In Eastern Quarries ripening precious Dew;

> For them the Idumæan Balm did sweat,
> And in hot Ceilon spicy Forrests grew,

became the fifteenth stanza of *Isabella:*

> For them the Ceylon diver held his breath,
>   And went all naked to the hungry shark;
> For them his ears gushed blood; for them in death
>   The seal on the cold ice with piteous bark
> Lay full of darts; for them alone did seethe
>   A thousand men in troubles wide and dark;
> Half-ignorant, they turned an easy wheel
> That set sharp racks at work, to pinch and peel.

Byron's imagination seems to have been saturated with the *Fables*, particularly with *Theodore and Honoria*. Ravenna to him meant deep romantic woods and a lady pursued by hounds, as it had meant them to Gibbon before. His letters from that place were full of Dryden's story, and in the third canto of *Don Juan* he apostrophized the scene of Honoria's punishment:

> Evergreen forest! which Boccaccio's lore
> And Dryden's lay made haunted ground to me.

Later in the century poets as different from Dryden and from one another as Tennyson, Poe, and Francis Thompson drew upon him for musical effects. Tennyson studied his meters, both in the couplet-poems and in the songs, admiring, even envying, the force of both. "'What a difference,' he would add," writes Hallam Tennyson, apropos of translating Homer, "between Pope's little poisonous barbs, and Dryden's strong invective! And how much more real poetic force there is in Dryden! Look at Pope:

> He said, observant of the blue-eyed maid,
> Then in the sheath returned the shining blade,

then at Dryden:

He said; with surly faith believed her word,
And in the sheath, reluctant, plunged the sword."

It is difficult to believe that Poe did not have in mind the superb second stanza of the *Song for St. Cecilia's Day* (1687) * when he began his *Israfel* thus:

In Heaven a spirit doth dwell
    "Whose heart-strings are a lute";
None sing so wildly well
As the angel Israfel,
And the giddy stars (so legends tell)
Ceasing their hymns, attend the spell
    Of his voice, all mute.

Francis Thompson, writer of rapturous odes, was intoxicated by Dryden's verse, and proposed an essay upon it. His ambition was that he might endure as long as Dryden, Milton, and Keats. He returned to the poet who·spiritually is least like him to learn the secret of full and level music, of generous but sober ratiocinative procedure through antitheses and Alexandrines. So the story goes on. Dryden the satirist, the journalist, the celebrant, the reasoner in verse will continue to show the way to those who would deal in frost and iron; Dryden the manifold metrician will continue to reveal new melodies to those who would deal in bronze or gold.

Good poets long dead have a way of defying changes in taste and of belying reasons why they should not be read. It may be urged against Dryden that he was the too unctuous spokesman of a decaying order; that, clear though he may have seemed to a smaller, more literary world, for the purposes of modern life he is opaque; that he handles not images but facts, that by naming he destroys and by failing to suggest he fails to create, that he elaborates and disguises rather than foreshortens and intensifies experience; that he is more journalist than artist, more orator than seer. But even while this is urged,

* See page 202.

warning may issue from other quarters that foreshortening implies bad perspective and intensification a heat that withers as well as inspirits. If there was something fatuous about the opulence of the Augustans there is often something desperate about the simplicity of the moderns. If an aristocratic society fattens and sleeks the poets of its choice, democracy grinds many of its sons to powder. A man who composes verse too exclusively out of his faculties can hardly be judged by men who write too much with their nerves; the imagination, the umpire of art, might acknowledge neither. Dryden lives not as one who went out to rear great frames of thought and feeling, nor as one who waited within himself and caught fine, fugitive details of sensation, but as one who elastically paced the limits of a dry and well-packed mind. He braces those who listen to his music; he will be found refreshing if, answering his own invitation,

> When tired with following nature, you think fit,
> To seek repose in the cool shades of wit.

APPENDIX

The Authorship of *Mac Flecknoe*

R ECENT investigations * having overcast *Mac Flecknoe*
with curious uncertainties concerning the authenticity
of its first publication, the date of its composition, and
the identity of its author, it becomes necessary to summarize
both what is known and what can be reasonably conjectured
about a poem which it has not been unusual to consider Dryden's masterpiece.

There seems to be no doubt that the edition of 1682, recognized now as the first, was a pirated one. The publisher was
not Dryden's Jacob Tonson, as would be expected, but D.
Green, who not only was obscure but desired to remain so,
since he printed no address other than London adjacent to his
name on the title page. The publication of the pamphlet could
hardly have proceeded under the supervision of its author.
There was no preface, strangely enough at least for Dryden,
and the text was one of which an intelligent man would have
been permanently ashamed; as witness line 82,

---

* Babington, Percy L., "Dryden Not the Author of *Mac Flecknoe*." *Modern Language Review*, January, 1918. Thorn-Drury, G., "Dryden's *Mac
Flecknoe*: A Vindication." *Ibid.*, July, 1918. Belden, H. M., "The Authorship
of *Mac Flecknoe*." *Modern Language Notes*, December, 1918.

> Amidst this monument of *varnisht* minds,

or line 92,

> Humorists and Hypocrites *his pen* should produce,

metrically impossible, or lines 135-6,

> And from his brows damps of oblivion shed,
> Full *of* the filial dulness,

where the only conceivable point is lost, or line 167,

> But write thy best, *on th' top;* and in each line—

which means nothing.

Had the poem been brand new in 1682, as has been supposed by those who have believed it an almost *extempore* reply to Shadwell's *Medal of John Bayes,* it is difficult to see why it should have escaped so completely from the author's hands; since surely he would lose no time himself in getting it to a printer. The fate of *Mac Flecknoe* was a fate not uncommonly visited upon works for some time existent and circulating in manuscript. That *Mac Flecknoe* was such a work is far from impossible. It is possible, for instance, that it had been composed upon the occasion of Flecknoe's death (1678?), an event somewhat ambiguously referred to by Dryden in the dedication of *Limberham* in 1680. As a satire on Shadwell it would have been as timely in 1676 as it was in 1682. It alludes to no play published by Shadwell later than 1676. It makes no capital out of Shadwell's politics, which were conspicuously Whiggish after the Popish Plot and which would naturally draw Dryden's fire after *Absalom and Achitophel, The Medal,* and particularly *The Medal of John Bayes.* The epithet applied to Shadwell on the title page, "True-Blew-Protestant," may only have been D. Green's; it was not repeated in later editions. The occupation of the poem is wholly with personalities and literary principles; chastisement is administered not to a Whig, or even to a drunken treason-monger, as in the second part of *Absalom and Achitophel,* but simply to a fat dull poet who deals too much in "humours." Furthermore, there is incontrovertible evidence that the verses were in existence, either in manuscript or in pamphlet form, eight months before the date traditionally assigned to them on the strength of a note by Narcissus Luttrell and considerably before Shadwell's *Medal of John Bayes.* Luttrell's date was October 4, 1682. But the following passage has been cited from an attack on Shadwell in *The Loyal Protestant and Domestic Intelligence* for February 9, 1681-2: "he would send him his Recantation next morning, with a *Mac Flecknoe,* and a brace of Lobsters for his Breakfast."

That *Mac Flecknoe* was not the work of Dryden has been argued from evidences of varying worth. D. Green's attribution of the poem to "the author of Absalom and Achitophel" has been dismissed on the grounds that that gentleman, being a liar no less than a pirate, knew he could sell ten times more copies under such auspices than he could sell under any other. It cannot be shown that Dryden was particularly at outs with Shadwell during the later '70's. The two men had combined against Settle in 1674, in their remarks on *The Empress of Morocco,* and in 1678 Dryden had furnished Shadwell a prologue to be spoken before his *True Widow.* In Tonson's *Miscellany* of 1684, a volume more or less edited by Dryden, *Mac Flecknoe* occupied first place, being followed by *Absalom and Achitophel* and *The Medal;* but it had no title page, and it was not assigned, as *The Medal* was, to "the author of Absalom and Achitophel." A legend dating from the next year has been taken as proof that Dryden was strangely unfamiliar with the general class of mock-heroic material which the satire represents. One of Spence's anecdotes relates that Dean Lockier went when a boy to Will's Coffee-house and heard Dryden claiming a complete originality for the poem. Upon the boy's interposing that Boileau's *Lutrin* and Tassoni's *Secchia Rapita* were obvious models, Dryden, the story goes, turned and said, " 'Tis true, I had forgot them." Shadwell insinuated a doubt as to Dryden's right to the poem in 1687, in the dedication of his Tenth *Juvenal:* "It is hard to believe that the supposed author of *Mac Flecknoe* is the real one, because when I taxed him with it, he denied it with all the Execrations he could think of." Tom Brown gleefully quoted this passage in the preface to his *Reasons for Mr. Bayes Changing His Religion* in 1688. Dryden did not openly claim the poem until a year after Shadwell's death (1692), when in his *Discourse of Satire* (1693) he spoke of "my own, the poems of *Absalom* and *Mac Flecknoe.*" He had omitted it altogether from a list of his works which he appended to *Amphitryon* in 1690.

A more arresting piece of evidence against Dryden's authorship is a late seventeenth-century manuscript volume in the Bodleian Library at Oxford (Rawlinson Poetry 123) containing most of John Oldham's works transcribed by a single hand, as if for the printer, under the title *"Poems on Several Occasions."* Three items in this volume, *A Satyr upon Man, A Letter from Artemisia in the Town to Chloe in the Country,* and *Upon the Author of a Play called Sodom,* are generally believed to be the work of Rochester, "that incomparable person," according to Oldham in his *Preface* of 1681, "of whom nothing can be said, or thought, so choice and curious, which his Deserts do not surmount." They are entered without comment; but more than half of the pieces are dated and placed in this manner: "July, 1676, at Croydon;" "October 22-76, at Bedington;" "Written at Croydon Anno 167⅞;" "Writ Feb 1680 at Rygate;" "March 18th, 167⅞;" "Aug 5, 1677;" "Written in May 82;" "Wrote the last day of the year 1675." In the three cases where comparison is possible between these dates and those printed under the titles of poems in Oldham's volumes of 1681 and 1683, the agreement is perfect. On pages 232, 233, 234, 235, and 214 is found:

> *Anno 1678.*   *Mac Fleckno*
> *A Satyr.*

Four pages, or lines 49-150, are missing; the rest is written smoothly, without interlineations or erasures, but hastily, with here a word omitted and there a word varied from the accepted text. On no account may 1678 be taken as the date of transcription, since it is plain that the volume as a whole was drawn up later than 1680, either by Oldham himself during the last two years of his life or by another person after his death. Whether 1678 stands for the date of composition, and whether Oldham is the author, are questions of a more perplexing sort. The affirmative in each case is supported by certain coincidences that cannot be ignored.

Oldham, no less than Dryden, though perhaps in common with all his contemporaries, understood the name Flecknoe to be synonymous with the name of bad poet; so that the idea for the satire which, as it happens, has immortalized that name might easily have occurred to him. In his imitation of Horace's *Art of Poetry* he opposed Flecknoe as the worst of poets to Cowley as the best:

> Who'er will please, must please us to the height.
> He must a Cowley, or a Flecknoe be;
> For there's no second rate, in poetry.

The idea, furthermore, of giving bad poetry and Flecknoe a mock-heroic send-off is one he is even more likely than Dryden to have come readily by in 1678, the date, not impossibly, of Flecknoe's death. It will be remembered that Dryden had forgotten by 1685, or had pretended to forget, *Mac Flecknoe's* debt to the mock-heroic tradition in general and to Boileau's *Lutrin* in particular. Boileau was certainly no stranger to Dryden in 1678 or 1679; and it was in 1680 that he revised Soame's translation of the *Art Poétique*. But Oldham was still more significantly involved with the Frenchman. He "imitated" the eighth Satire and "translated" the fifth; and if the Bodleian Manuscript is to be believed, he translated the entire first Canto of the *Lutrin* itself, "Anno 1678." It would appear that he was trying out his mock-heroic vein that year, at first as the disciple of a foreigner and later as an independent artist with a native theme. Not only that; there are specific parallels between passages in works known to be his and passages in *Mac Flecknoe*. In his *Imitation of Horace, Book I, Satire IX*, which does not appear in the Bodleian Manuscript but which, according to the *Poems and Translations* published by him in 1683, was "written in June, 1681," occurs a line,

> St. André never moved with such a grace,

that is unmistakably akin to line 53 of *Mac Flecknoe:*

> St. André's feet ne'er kept more equal time.

A Satyr against Poetry, dated in the manuscript 1678, printed first in 1683 without remark, and reprinted as a pamphlet in 1709 in company with *Mac Flecknoe* (whether as the result of a resemblance only then observed between the two poems or on the strength of authentic evidence concerning their original relation is not known), is considerably like *Mac Flecknoe* 100-103, which runs,

> From dusty shops neglected authors come,
> Martyrs of pies and relics of the bum.
> Much *Heywood, Shirley, Ogleby* there lay,
> But loads of *Shadwell* almost choked the way,

in the following passage:

> How many poems writ in ancient time,
> Which thy Fore-Fathers had in great esteem . . .
> Have grown contemptible, and slighted since,
> As *Pordage, Fleckno,* or the *British Prince?*
> *Quarles, Chapman, Heywood, Withers* had applause,
> And *Wild,* and *Ogilby* in former days.
> But now are damned to wrapping drugs and wares,
> And curst by all their broken stationers.

And so mayst thou perchance pass up and down,
And please a while th' admiring Court, and Town,
Who after shalt in Duck-Lane shops be thrown,
To mould with *Sylvester* and *Shirley* there,
And truck for pots of ale next Sturbridge Fair.

A number of deductions can be arrived at from these parallels: (1) the coincidences are only coincidences; or (2), if a manuscript *Mac Flecknoe* was circulating in 1678, it was Dryden's, and Oldham drew upon it while writing his *Horace* and his *Satyr against Poetry*, or (3) it was Oldham's, and Dryden knew nothing of it until it was published as by him in 1682; (4) if a manuscript *Mac Flecknoe* did not exist before 1682, neither did the Bodleian text of Oldham's poems. In support of (2), it will be remembered that Oldham was borrowing from *The Rival Ladies* in 1678,* so that his interest in Dryden, no doubt always great, can be supposed to have been especially keen that year, even to the extent of his occupying himself with a Dryden manuscript. If (3) is true, it must also be true that Dryden, having Oldham's manuscript by him in 1684, several months after the young satirist's death, followed it scrupulously as he corrected the 1682 *Mac Flecknoe* for Tonson's 1684 *Miscellany*. Tonson's text contains 33 variants from D. Green's. The Bodleian text differs considerably from both, but of its 15 variants from either alone, only 3 are in favor of Green, while 12 are in favor of Tonson.† Now it is improbable that the 1684 *Mac Flecknoe* derives from the Bodleian

---

* See page 147.

† Another seventeenth-century manuscript of *Mac Flecknoe* in the Lambeth Palace Library (vol. 711, no. 8), palpably from the hand of a copyist, contains, among many variants that are uninteresting, 6 that coincide with 6 otherwise unique readings in the Bodleian manuscript.

> line 11: And pondering which of all his sons *were* fit.
> line 12: To reign, and wage immortal *wars* with wit.
> line 29: Heywood and Shirley were but types *to* thee.
> line 178: *Or* rail at arts he did not understand.
> line 185: But so *transfuse* as oils on waters flow.
> line 196: But sure *thou art* a kilderkin of wit.

manuscript or from any manuscript of Oldham's. It is more
probable that the Bodleian manuscript derives from the 1684
Mac Flecknoe, which would mean, what is more probable still,
that (4) is the safest deduction—that the whole of the volume
at Oxford was transcribed after Oldham's death by an admirer,
perhaps a literary executor, who, having both of the editions of
Mac Flecknoe at hand, transcribed that poem too because he
liked it, as Oldham before him had liked it.

Whatever the date of *Mac Flocknoe,* and 1678 deserves consideration, Dryden's right to the poem still is and must be
always, except as definite evidence to the contrary comes to light,
undeniable. It is not true that he ever seriously disclaimed
responsibility for it. The edition of 1684 was equivalent to a
full confession of authorship. The execrations with which he
reassured Shadwell could have reassured only Shadwell, who
seems to have been devoid of humor in personal and controversial relations. He omitted to list *Mac Flecknoe* with his other
works in 1690; but so did he omit to list the *Heroic Stanzas,*
The Hind and the Panther, and *Britannia Rediviva.* The
Lockier anecdote proves that Dryden carried affairs with a high
hand at Will's, and was not accustomed to interruption or
emendation by his juniors; but this has been a proverb for two
centuries. It is not difficult to believe him incapable of treating
Oldham so badly as to steal from him a poem worth five times
all his others put together; "there being nothing so base," according to his preface to *The Tempest* (1670), where he was
thinking of Davenant, "as to rob the dead of his reputation."
Oldham had ample opportunity to reclaim *Mac Flecknoe* while
he was yet alive; one wonders why, if the poem were his, he
failed to include it in the volume of *Poems and Translations*
which he published in 1683. It is not known in the first place
that he had ever had an occasion for writing a satire on Shadwell; he had had no quarrel with that indefatigable disciple of
Ben Jonson. On the other hand, it is well known of Dryden
that from the beginning of his career he was subject to irrita-

tion by Shadwell; and it is to be supposed that the differences between the two were personal as early as they were literary. His contempt no doubt was intermittent, but it must have been easy to excite; that he wrote a prologue for Shadwell early in 1678 does not mean that *Mac Flecknoe* was impossible for him the same year or the next. It has been remarked that *Mac Flecknoe* was in large part an attack on Shadwell's theory and practice of "humours" in comedy. It is significant that Dryden had for an even decade before 1678 been Shadwell's chief decrier on these points. The Restoration battle between Wit and Humor during those years had almost been fought by Dryden and Shadwell alone. Dryden's *Essay of Dramatic Poesy* and *Defence of the Essay* (1668), his preface to *An Evening's Love* (1671), his epilogue to the second part of *The Conquest of Granada* and his *Defence of the Epilogue* (1672) had been answered by Shadwell's prefaces to *The Sullen Lovers* (1668), *The Royal Shepherdess* (1669) and *The Humourists* (1671), and by the dedication of *The Virtuoso* (1676). Dryden, then, rather than Oldham or anyone else, was likely to be familiar enough with Shadwell's critical utterances to hit upon a parody, in lines 189-192 of *Mac Flecknoe,*

> This is that boasted bias of thy mind,
> By which one way to dulness 'tis inclined,
> Which makes thy writings lean on one side still,
> And in all changes, that way bends thy will,

of these four lines in the epilogue to *The Humourists:*

> A humour is the bias of the mind
> By which with violence 'tis one way inclined.
> It makes our actions lean on one side still,
> And in all changes that way bend our will.

If there are passages in Oldham's miscellaneous works that suggest an interesting affinity between their author and the author of *Mac Flecknoe*, there are passages in Dryden that are more than interesting, that in fact are convincing. There are coincidences that seem better than coincidences. No one would have been readier, for example, than Dryden, considering his close acquaintance with Davenant's *Gondibert,* to borrow from that poem the line (Canto V, stanza 36)

> And called the monument of vanished minds

for *Mac Flecknoe:*

> Amidst this monument of vanisht minds.

It has been pointed out * that *Mac Flecknoe* parodies a line in Cowley's *Davideis,*

> Where their vast courts the mother-waters keep,

a line that could not have been strange to Dryden in 1678, since he had quoted it as recently as 1677 in his *Apology for Heroic Poetry.* Nor was Flecknoe out of his mind during these years. In the dedication of *Limberham* (played 1678, printed 1680) he was writing: "You may please to take notice how natural the connection of thought is betwixt a bad poet and Flecknoe." He even was turning Flecknoe's pages and reading them, though it may have been somewhat later than this that he did so. One of the happiest images in his "character" of Doeg,

> He was too warm on picking-work to dwell,
> But fagotted his notions as they fell,
> And if they rhymed and rattled, all was well,

seems to be borrowed from Flecknoe's *Enigmatical Character* of a schoolboy: "For his learning, 'tis all capping verses, and fagoting poets' loose lines, which fall from him as disorderly as fagot-sticks, when the band is broke." The poet who made merry with Shadwell's bulk in *Mac Flecknoe* was at least very

* See page 20.

nearly related to the poet who made merry with that same bulk in the second part of *Absalom and Achitophel*. Whatever the relation, if it was not identity, the creator of Og can be said to have had *Mac Flecknoe* by heart. So had the author of *The Medal* when he sketched

>   Whole droves of blockheads choking up his way

in remembrance of the line

>   But loads of Shadwell almost choked the way;

so had the author of *The Vindication of the Duke of Guise* when he called Shadwell "the Northern Dedicator" in remembrance of the line

>   And does thy Northern Dedications fill;

so perhaps had the author of the ode on Anne Killigrew when he wrote of

>   A lambent flame which played about her breast

in remembrance of the line

>   And lambent dulness played around his face.

In addition to all this, there is the fact that no other man living and writing in 1678 or 1680 or 1682 had the genius for *Mac Flecknoe*. Every fresh reading either of Dryden or of his contemporaries proves this fact yet more a fact. Certain Persons of Honor were clever enough to have conceived the poem and to have done a line of it, or a paragraph; but in none of them was there energy enough to carry him triumphantly through it as Dryden came through. Oldham had carrying power and staying power, but he had not this much humor; his canto of the *Lutrin* approaches the *Satires upon the Jesuits* as a limit, not *The Rape of the Lock*. The verse also was well and away beyond his reach. Professor Belden has demonstrated that he never elsewhere wrote this many perfect rhymes in succession. A simple appeal to the ear will convince an experienced reader of Augustan poetry that here is meter twice happier than Oldham's happiest. The poem, in short, is almost better than Dryden himself. But that is for Dryden to explain.

INDEX

A selected list of MIDLAND BOOKS

(continued on next page)